# THE
# DILETTANTE
# BOOK OF CHOCOLATE
## AND CONFECTIONS

For
Great Uncle Julius (1886–1954)
and
Grandpa Davenport (1886–1971)
Happy 100th Birthday!

# The Dilettante Book of

## Chocolate

## and Confections

BY DANA TAYLOR DAVENPORT    WITH RUTH REED

PERENNIAL LIBRARY

HARPER & ROW, PUBLISHERS
New York, Cambridge, Philadelphia, San Francisco, Washington, Mexico City, São Paulo, Singapore, Syd

THE DILETTANTE BOOK
OF CHOCOLATE AND
CONFECTIONS.

Copyright © 1986
by Dana Taylor Davenport.

FIRST EDITION

Designer: Tim Girvin Design, Inc.

Library of Congress Cataloging-
in-Publication Data

Davenport, D. Taylor (Dana Taylor)
    The Dilettante book of chocolate
and confections.
    Includes index.
    1. Chocolate candy.   2. Dilet-
tante Chocolates (Firm) I. Reed,
Ruth.   II. Title.
TX767.C5D38   1986
641.8'53      84-48153
ISBN 0-06-091223-5 (pbk.)

86 87 88 89 RRD 9 8 7 6 5 4 3 2 1

Cover Photo: Dana Taylor
            Davenport, author,
            with
            Master formula
            notebook
            Photo by Marsha
            Burns

The Master notebook shown on the
front cover contains the candy formulas and experiments recorded
between 1927 and 1960 by my
grandfather, Earl Remington Davenport. Most of these formulas were
dictated to Grandpa by his brother-
in-law, Julius Rudolf Franzen, during the time they worked together in
the early 1920s after Julius came to
the United States. Julius's own
records begin as early as 1896.
When he was only ten years old he
began compiling recipes he learned
during his pastry and candy appren-
ticeship in Budapest. His expertise
eventually won him a prestigious
appointment as Master Pastry Chef
to Austria's Emperor Franz Josef,
and later as Master Candymaker to
Czar Nicholas II. Also represented in
the Master notebook are many original American formulas Grandpa col-
lected during the latter part of the
Depression. The Davenport-Fran-
zen collaboration produced over 400
recipes which are recorded in the
Master notebook and various
smaller journals Grandpa kept until
his death in 1971. With the addition
of our own formulas and experiments, the Davenport family tradition of candymaking is now in its
ninetieth year.

# Contents

# Acknowledgments

Fresh ideas, extraordinary recipes, good timing, luck, and a positive mental attitude are all necessary ingredients for success in the world of specialty foods, I suppose. But for me, more important still are friends and family who have been willing to help—far beyond the call. From the time our first Dilettante shop opened its doors just before Easter in 1977 right up to the present moment, we have discovered hosts of friends and helpers. Follows here a list (which admittedly can't be complete), acknowledging some of those kind hearts.

David Bamburg, my dearest and most supportive friend, marketing director without peer responsible for our first entrance into the national market.

Gary Martin, my longtime friend. He was my first partner, financial backer, and business mentor.

Ralph and Marliss Palumbo, my ever-vigilant legal counsel. A first-rate husband-and-wife team who regularly lead us back to firm footing whenever rapid growth threatens our business.

Bern Herbolsheimer and Dr. James Savage, two of my college buddies, both professional musicians and university professors. They volunteered their precious evenings to serve our first customers at the Broadway Dilettante.

Moira Wood, friend and inspired office manager.

David Rutherford, our architect, who designed the new factory kitchen.

Alma and Gill Centioli, fine partners and invaluable advisors.

Pat Hickey at first, and now Tim Girvin, who put in immeasurable amounts of time designing packaging colors, boxes, and roses, all the while allowing me to peer over their shoulders and "advise."

Phil Archibald, designer at Tim Girvin Design Inc., who is responsible for the eye-appealing makeup of this book.

Illustrator Michael J. Marshall who accomplished the difficult task of visualizing the candymaker's jargon to enhance these pages.

The long-suffering gentlefolk at Harper & Row, who have kept us on course. Thank you, Executive Editor Larry Ashmead, Editors Craig Nelson and Margaret Wimberger, and Art Director Joseph Montebello.

Sherry Robb, my agent, and partner in Andrews & Robb Agents of Hollywood. Her unflagging spirit kept this book alive.

Ruth Reed, my right hand on this project. She's a longtime journalist, free-lance writer, and good friend. I sometimes call her *Ruth the Sleuth* because she's so good at digging out the essentials in a piece of badly organized written matter and turning it into lucid prose. We have her to thank for the polished and lively style of this book.

Jerome Franzen Davenport, my father. Candymaker, administrative genius, creative thinker, rock-solid support.

Skip Davenport, my oldest brother, who can do anything, from operating a jack hammer to carpentry to plumbing.

Glenna Davenport, my sister-in-law (Skip's wife), our first pastry cook. She drove to Seattle from her home on Mount Rainier (260 miles round trip) twice a week to keep our pastry shelves stocked.

Brian Davenport, my next-older brother, possessor of both undergraduate and graduate degrees from Harvard. He came on board several years ago after picking up an MBA degree at the University of Washington. He is currently our chief financial officer.

Uncle Irving Davenport, my dad's oldest brother, who taught me how to dip chocolates and transcribed the family journals.

Aunt Gene Davenport (Irving's wife). A feimschmecker, generous heart and wonderful encouragement to me. She safeguarded all the family pictures.

And of course, there's my Uncle Bert Neff. If you don't have an Uncle Bert, don't go into the candy business. It takes the experience of a retired Boeing engineer to keep highly specialized equipment and refrigeration running.

Patricia Davenport Neff (my Aunt Pat). She's one of my father's sisters and is married to Uncle Bert. I'm beholden to her for the little anecdotal reminiscences scattered throughout the book (and attributed to Aunt Pat) on the subject of her parents (my grandparents), Earl Remington Davenport and Ottilia Franzen Davenport.

And of course, all of us owe a tremendous debt of gratitude to Julius and Grandpa Davenport, those two remarkable brothers-in-law. There are still a lot of their candy formulas left for us to explore together. Hardly a day goes by that we don't refer to the old tattered notebooks. I never knew Julius personally and my grandfather I knew not well enough. But I have come to know them much better now through their writing. They had the patience and fortitude—not to mention the foresight—to document their daily efforts.

My sincerest thanks and respect go to both of them for their devotion to the candymaker's craft.

Again, I thank you all!

Dana Taylor Davenport
Seattle, 1986

Davenport Crest

# Prelude

One day, when this century was still in its early teens, a certain family of artisans was preparing to leave its home in Hungary. All Europe had begun to hear again the distant rumblings of the juggernaut. It appeared certain that war would descend upon the land and extinguish one more time the bright hopes of families with grown sons.

In the village of Mediash, not far from Budapest, the Franzen family had held its own private council of war. The cruelly difficult decision they had reached was bold. They would leave the Old World, where their roots were deep, and seek a new life in America. Resolutely, then, the Franzens packed up their hopes and their family and set out for the United States, a land as distant from the menace of war as they could find in the western world.

From the fabled mountains of Transylvania to our own Pacific shores the family journeyed. Mother, father, two grown sons, and the sole daughter.

Assuredly, the Franzens were not seeking economic aid in their search for a new life. They were proud and self-respecting people, well prepared to earn their own way wherever they might be domiciled. In Budapest, in the European tradition, the sons had completed long and arduous apprenticeships, each in a different trade.

Habsburg Crest

One son had chosen to become a pastry chef. He apprenticed first in Budapest. Then, in his search for excellence, he studied and worked in Paris. Then on to Vienna and finally to St. Petersburg, becoming, in the end, both a master pastry chef and a master confectioner. His name? Julius. A name which was to become very significant to the generations that followed him.

But let a member of the present family tell you about him. The speaker is Jerome Davenport—whose mother was Julius Franzen's sister. "Uncle Julius made his mark while he was still in Europe. First, according to the family records, he was appointed to the palace of the Habsburgs in Vienna, as Master Candymaker to the Emperor Franz Josef, then later to the court of the Romanovs as Master Candymaker to Czar Nicholas II. Not bad for a boy from the country! And he accomplished all this while he was still in his early twenties!"

Early twenties? Yes indeed. At the time that Julius opted to leave Europe with his family, he was twenty-four years old!

The Franzens prospered in their new home. And in the fullness of time, the daughter married an American, one Earl Remington Davenport. He in his turn became a candymaker— under the tutelage of his brother-in-law, Julius.

Earl and Julius were born in the same year, 1886, two continents and an ocean apart. Now in their twenties, they became very close friends. So close were they, in fact, that bit by bit, Julius began to entrust his friend with a precious cargo, his closely guarded formulas and recipes. Having sworn Earl to secrecy, Julius allowed him to start recording these treasures brought from Europe, along with the secret techniques Julius had developed himself.

Before long, using a scientist's meticulous approach, Earl was also recording the new experiments that he and Julius undertook—the failures along with the triumphs. His notebooks reflect the hard work they did. Now and then, the cool scientist ceded something to human emotion. At one point, Earl had recorded a long and trying experiment which ended in success. As he finished his notes, he inscribed one final word. "Hooray!"

These two men working in harmony together set a happy precedent. For thus was born a family tradition. Thus began a family heritage. Their collection of formulas and recipes became a living document to cement the generations together. Each succeeding generation has added to the inheritance, changing, rearranging, experimenting, bringing something new to the recipes. Always enlarging the collection. Always rethinking, always refining. A remarkable achievement.

But back to Julius. On his arrival in this country he had found himself wholly alone for the first time in his life, with only his talent and the technical mastery of his craft to sustain him. No royal patronage, no influential friends to prepare the way for him.

What an adventure it must have been, what a challenge, to overcome the towering odds against succeeding in this new land, where everything, from the language to the business practices, was alien to him.

But in the end he did it all. He targeted in on San Francisco, a city that knows how to appreciate Old-World craftsmen. Julius founded a candy business there. But of course, he was much more than just a craftsman. Worldly, urbane, with an eye for the ladies, he fitted perfectly into the cosmopolitan life of San Francisco, having lived for periods of time in four of Europe's most alluring cities at a point in history when they

Romanov Crest

were at the peak of their ascendancy as the gastronomic capitals of the entire western world.

Obviously, Julius's business thrived. Soon other members of both the Franzen and the Davenport families were involved in the enterprise. And that set the pattern of family participation that has persisted to this day. At the present writing, there have been six master candymakers in the four generations which began with the Franzen-Davenport alliance. All along the line, brothers and sisters joined the family enterprises which developed up and down the West Coast. And a fourth-generation candymaker operates his own candy business in Canada using the recipes from the family collection, of course.

It happens, however, that there was a period of a number of years between the second and third generations when no member of the Davenport branch was actively engaged in making candy commercially. It was the third-generation Dana Taylor Davenport who was responsible for the rebirth of the whole tradition. Loath to see the family skills die away, it was Dana who studied and trained to become a master confectioner.

Then, using the handed-down formulas of his great-uncle and grandfather and father—along with the recipe books they wrote, he organized a new family business. The enterprise, which he now heads, calls Seattle its home and comprises Dilettante Chocolates, Café Dilettante, and Dilettante, Inc. Nearly all the extended family is involved in the present business—brothers, sisters, aunts, uncles, cousins. The family tradition is now whole again. And prospering.

To Dana Davenport's surprise, the fledgling enterprise took off like a rocket. It quickly became a standard for quality in an ever-expanding national market. The exalted superiority of his hand-crafted creations—in the Old World style is the most obvious reason for this runaway success. But, too, it seems clear that a certain thread of entrepreneurial talent runs down through the generations to stitch together the other inherited gifts. Successful business undertakings have dotted the family heritage as much as have the prized confections.

The Dilettante name is now displayed on four ultrachic shops, all of them in ultrachic locations in the Seattle area, serving a knowledgeable and ecstatic clientele. From opening day in 1977, Seattleites were quick to realize that they had a truly European-style chocolate and coffee house here, serving Dana's superb desserts with specially blended coffees. But they found an old-fashioned soda fountain and beverage bar as well, with a menu that sounds as American as *The Music Man*, but in reality carries out the European theme in the truffled ice cream toppings and other exalted offerings. And of course, the

Franzen Crest

whole gamut of Dilettante chocolates and other confections is available in the shops, too.

The Dilettante people have been delighted to find that they're serving customers from all social and economic levels, from students who drop in for an espresso, to the schoolgirls "shopping around" in a suburban shopping center after school, to the tax lawyer who popped into the downtown Dilettante, in the new Interstate Bank Building Plaza, on her way to the parking garage. The wife of one of her most prestigious clients had asked her and her husband to dinner, she said, and she wanted to take a superb hostess gift.

At the moment, there is another new Dilettante shop on the architect's drawing board. The wholesale and mail order business is booming, and the end is not in sight.

Now it seems the Davenports are embarking on a new venture. One of Dana's theses is that superb candy can be made at home with the help and advice of a master confectioner at one's elbow. So the Franzen-Davenport formulas are about to be disseminated to a national audience.

With the consent and cooperation of his whole family, Dana Davenport has agreed to share the family heritage with all of us. This cookbook is the result.

And what is the significance of the name Dilettante as it applies to the family's product? It was Dana's idea. And not surprisingly. He's a man who is deeply involved in the arts, especially music, a veteran of six college years majoring in music, and seven years of operatic voice training. His clear lyric tenor is audible even in his speaking voice.

Serenely ignoring the negative connotations of *dilettante*, then, and going back to the original Italian sense, he blithely tagged his creations Dilettante Chocolates—and has been defending the choice ever since. "But why not dilettante?" he says. "I consider myself a dilettante in the true sense of the word. I take delight in all the arts, and look for the best possible experience to be had from any one of them—including candymaking." Voilà!

Ruth Reed

---

**dilettante** *1a:* **An admirer or lover of the arts** *b:* **a person who has discrimination or taste especially in aesthetic matters:** CONNOISSEUR *2a:* **a person who cultivates an art or branch of knowledge as a pastime without pursuing it professionally.**
**—Webster's Third New International Dictionary**

# Foreword

To paraphrase Shakespeare, brevity is the soul of instruction. With this observation in mind, we've made our recipes as terse as we could. Each master recipe contains detailed procedural instructions for its group, of course. But the recipes that follow the master are written in a somewhat shortened form.

EXAMPLE: Nearly all candy formulas require you to cook granulated sugar, corn syrup, and a liquid to a given temperature. Obviously, the procedural steps are essentially identical for all such formulas. Hence, except in the master recipe, you'll repeatedly find the instruction: "Blend thoroughly. Boil. Wash down. Insert thermometer. Cook to xxx degrees." This is a litany you'll come to memorize, recognize, and act on—automatically. But in case of doubt, you're never stranded; the master recipe is always there as reference and guide.

In short, simply refer to the master recipe for clarification on any point of procedure.

A comment on recipe yields. Most of the recipes in this book will yield 60 to 75 medium-size pieces of candy. The candymaker's rule of thumb is: one pound of finished product will comprise about 32 medium-sized chocolates. Batch sizes in this book run two to three pounds. So calculating approximate yield becomes a matter of simple multiplication.

You'll notice we've used candymakers' terms wherever possible. If you're a purist, you'll find our spelling and usage a bit unorthodox in some specific cases. But these transgressions can be accepted as matters of style within a trade, we believe, a jargon developed over centuries of professional use.

EXAMPLES: *Candymaker* and its extended forms like *candymaking*. Surely candymakers deserve a one-word term (other than the more generalized *confectioner* or *confectionery*) to apply to themselves and to their trade.

*Creme* and its extended forms like *cremed* and *cremeing*. The candymakers pronounce this word *cream*, so we feel it's a bit precious to put a French *accent grave* on the word, causing possible confusion about its pronunciation—and even its usage.

It's our hope that the user of this book is a reader as well as a cook. The introductions to entire sections and to each recipe are often instructional in content, as are the notes, comments, and suggestions following many of the recipes. If we've done our job properly, you'll find them enlightening.

Blend thoroughly

Boil. Wash down.

Insert thermometer. Cook to xxx degrees.

*The evolution of the Dilettante rose*

1977

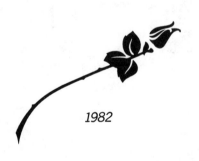

1980

1982

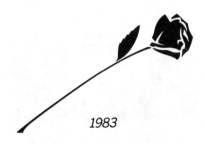

1983

For further enlightenment, we've surrounded the recipes on the page with brief tips, anecdotes, glossarial terms, observations, and so on, to brighten the moments while you wait for a batch to cool or a dipped chocolate to set.

In addition, we've given entire sections to detailed information on the complexities of such candymaking staples as chocolate, sugar and flavoring agents. This we did for the cook with an interest in the chemical nature of these substances—their reactions to heat and cold, their interrelations with each and with other ingredients. You'll learn how to make friends with all of them.

Most importantly we have designated specific pages throughout the book for you to record your own experiments. Slight variations in temperature will make big differences, and should be carefully notated. We have deliberately kept the recipes quite basic, and as the years go by, your own variations will make this book truly *yours*.

In closing, let us wish you good reading, good luck, and good eating. Above all, have a good time!

At the time I was designing our first chocolate box, Seattle Opera staged *Der Rosenkavalier*. By the end of the second act, I was resolved: a silver rose would be our company logo. Here are a few of the roses designed through the years, culminating in our favorite—and final—version.

Quote from the opera: *Der Rosenkavalier,* Act II
(The presentation of the rose)
Translation by Dana T. Davenport

Wie himmlische, nicht irdische,
wie Rosen vom hochheiligen Paradise.
Ist Ihm nicht auch?

Ist wie ein Gruss vom Himmel.
Ist bereits zu stark,
als dass man's ertragen kann.
Zieht einen nach,
als lagen Stricke um das Herz.

Translation
Like heavenly roses, not earthly,
like roses of holy paradise.
Doesn't it seem so to you?
It's like a greeting from Heaven.
Already so strong,
one can scarcely bear it.
It draws one near,
as though with reins around the heart.

# Utensils and Candymakers' Specialized Equipment

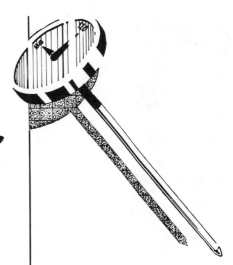

1. Double boiler. Nice to have, but if you don't, a simple pot with a bowl placed in it is an easy improvisation.
2. Flat-edged wooden spoon
3. Heavy 3-quart and 5-quart saucepans. A thick saucepan or kettle for high-heat cooking, with tall enough sides to clip a thermometer onto, heavy so that it is stable on the stove.
4. High-cook mercury candy thermometer. Should register at least from 120° Fahrenheit up to 320°, and be mounted on a metal frame with a clip for attaching to the sides of the pot.
5. Chocolate thermometer. Taylor puts out an instant-reading Bi-Therm thermometer that registers from 25° Fahrenheit to 125°F. A yogurt thermometer registers in the crucial range for chocolate as well (from 80°F. to 120°F.)
6. Thick pastry brush. Wooden handled, having bristles that stand up to heat.
7. Marble (pastry) slab (see note below). The minimum size is ¾ x 16 x 24 inches. Larger is better.
8. Scraper. A 4-inch putty knife or wall scraper is sufficient. Specialty kitchen equipment stores have various types.
9. Metal side bars (see note below)
10. Long metal spatula
11. Grater
12. Pastry bag and tips
13. Heavy kitchen shears
14. Eyedropper
15. Kitchen parchment
16. Paper or fancy foil cuplets for presenting chocolates
17. Set of dipping forks
18. Serving dishes

A flat-bottomed wooden spoon is best for home candy cooking because it scrapes all the surfaces of a flat-bottomed saucepan, moving the milk solids that could scorch and capturing all the sugar crystals from the corners, where they could be trapped and later cause a grain. (In a professional candy kitchen, we use round-bottomed kettles to avoid this problem.)

*Marble slabs*

Here is a supplementary list of things you probably already have, but if you don't, and you want to take candymaking seriously, now is the time to make the acquisitions.

19. Electric tabletop mixer
20. Blender
21. Food processor
22. Knives (various sizes)
23. Heavy canvas gloves and various hot pads
24. Rubber spatula
25. Cookie sheets and baking pans (various sizes)
26. Measuring utensils
27. Room thermometer
28. Measuring spoons and cups
29. Kitchen scale (see note below)

The quantities produced by most recipes in this book will fit on a slab ¾ x 16 x 24 inches. This size was chosen because it accommodates candy *and* is fairly easy to lift *and* fits in the refrigerator for chilling—which is handy for some types of butter-intense pastry crusts if you're making them in August. However, since few of us are in the kitchen on hot August afternoons, and most cooks are fairly strong, I heartily recommend a larger piece of marble. The slab should be ¾ inch thick to pull the heat off a batch of fudge quickly. A trip to your local marble cutter is really an eye-opening excursion, and there'll be a lot of colors to choose from. The slab needn't be marble. Any highly polished granite would be excellent. Just be sure it is absolutely smooth and has no pits.

*Metal side bars*
*(for recipes in this book)*

*Size.* They should be large enough to frame the minimum-size marble slab (16 x 24 inches) to accommodate doubling a batch of fondant or for a batch of caramels. If your slab is bigger than the minimum size, have the bars cut accordingly. (You can always set them inward to frame a smaller batch.) They should be ¾ inch thick. (You can always pour the batch shallower.)

*Material.* Iron or stainless steel is heavy (and useful for that reason). However, iron will rust and must be stored lightly oiled. Aluminum tubing is lightweight, easy to clean, and will not rust. And it is usually heavy enough to hold home-size batches.

*Scales*

Basically there are two types of scales spring action and balance. Spring action scales are not accurate. Don't try to use them for weighing candy ingredients. Balance scales that accommodate the weight of a kettle or a bowl are available and excellent.

# Your Candy Thermometer

Buying a thermometer

1. Use a mercury thermometer that reads from at least 100 to 320 degrees or more. (Your chocolate thermometer is a separate utensil.) Get a thermometer with a metal clip to attach to the side of the pot. Make sure the clip will slide upward or downward, so you can adjust it to the depth of the pot you're going to use.

2. Test it before using. Besides altitude changes, your thermometer is sensitive to daily changes in air pressure. Check it each time you start a batch, by putting it into boiling water and making any necessary adjustments in your formula. Place it in hot tap water before you put it in boiling water. When you take it out of a sugar solution, put it into hot water again. This will minimize the breakage factor.

**Check your thermometer for accuracy before beginning each batch.**

1. Make sure the bulb doesn't touch the bottom of the pot, or your temperature reading will be higher than the actual batch.
2. Make sure the bulb is entirely in the solution and not just in the foam that boils up.
3. Always read your thermometer *from eye level*.
4. When cooking batches containing butter, cream, or nuts, it is important to slide the thermometer around the sides of the saucepan occasionally in order to stir on all sides of the pot—to prevent scorching.

*Reading your thermometer from eye level while cooking a batch*

Don't store it in your utility utensil drawer where it will get knocked around. It is a valuable and delicate instrument.

*Storing your thermometer*

*Altitude adjustments in temperature readings*

The higher the altitude, the lighter the air pressure and the lower the temperature of water at the boiling point. Therefore, if you live above sea level, put your thermometer in cold water, bring the water to a rolling boil, and note the degree of heat registered. Subtract it from 212 degrees, then subtract this difference, whatever it is from the degree of cook given in each formula in this book. For example, if water boils at 204 degrees at your altitude, then, since 212 minus 204 equals 8, subtract 8 from each of the temperature readings called for in any formula you're using. For example, let's say you're going to make fudge. The final cook called for (in the fudge recipe you're using) is 236 degrees. Just subtract 8 from 236, and there you are. The final cook for that fudge recipe at your altitude is 228 degrees.

**Water boils 1 degree lower on the thermometer for every 570 feet of altitude above sea level.**

# Some Standard Measurements

## U.S. Liquid Measure

| | | |
|---|---|---|
| 3 teaspoons | = 1 tablespoon | = ½ fluidounce |
| 2 tablespoons | = 1 fluidounce | |
| 4 tablespoons | = ¼ cup | = 2 fluidounces |
| 5 tablespoons plus 1 teaspoon | = ⅓ cup | |
| 8 tablespoons | = ½ cup | = 4 fluidounces |
| 16 tablespoons | = 1 cup | = 8 fluidounces |
| 2 cups | = 16 fluidounces | = 1 pint |
| 2 pints | = 1 quart | |
| 4 quarts | = 1 gallon | |

## Some Equivalents

| CUPS | WEIGHT |
|---|---|
| *Granulated sugar* | |
| ¼ cup | = 1 ¾ ounces |
| ½ cup | = 3 ½ ounces |
| 1 cup | = 7 ( + ) ounces |
| 2 cups | = 15 ( + ) ounces (1 pound) |
| 2 rounded cups | = 1 full pound |
| *Powdered sugar (sifted)* | |
| 1 cup | = 3 ounces |
| *Brown sugar (firmly packed)* | |
| 1 cup | = 7 ounces |
| *Corn syrup/Honey/Molasses* | |
| 1 tablespoon | = ¾ ounce |
| ¼ cup | = 3 ounces |
| ½ cup | = 6 ounces |
| 1 cup | = 12 ounces |
| 2 cups | = 24 ounces |
| *Butter* | |
| 1 tablespoon | = ½ ounce |
| ¼ cup | = 2 ounces |
| ½ cup | = 4 ounces (¼ pound = 1 stick) |
| 1 cup | = 8 ounces (½ pound = 2 sticks) |

**When reducing our large batch formulas for this book, we rounded off the sugar to the nearest pound or half-pound increment. Therefore all cup measurements of sugar should be "rounded cups."**

| | |
|---|---|
| 2 cups | = 16 ounces (1 pound = 4 sticks) |

*All-purpose flour (unsifted)*

| | |
|---|---|
| ¼ cup | = 1 ¼ ounces |
| ½ cup | = 2 ½ ounces |
| 1 cup | = 5 ounces |
| 2 cups | = 10 ounces |

*Eggs*

| | |
|---|---|
| 1 whole egg | = 1 ½ ounce |
| 1 egg white (8 per cup) | = 1 ounce |
| 1 egg yolk (16 per cup) | = ½ ounce |

*Chocolate (melted)*

| | |
|---|---|
| 1 cup | = 10 ounces |

*Cocoa powder (sifted)*

| | |
|---|---|
| 1 cup | = 3 ounces |

# Metric Conversions

WEIGHT

| | |
|---|---|
| 1 ounce | = 28.35 grams (usually rounded off to 30 grams) |
| 1 pound | = 16 ounces = 454 grams |

U.S. LIQUID MEASURE

| | |
|---|---|
| 1 teaspoon | = 5 milliliters |
| 2 teaspoons | = 1 centiliter |
| 1 Tablespoon | = 1 ½ centiliters |
| 3 Tablespoons | = ½ decaliter |
| 6 ½ Tablespoons | = 1 decaliter |
| 1 cup | = ¼ liter |
| 4 cups | = 1 liter |

FAHRENHEIT AND CELSIUS

To convert *Fahrenheit to Celsius*: Subtract 32, multiply by 5, divide by 9.

Example: End of cook for fudge is at 236 degrees Fahrenheit.
236 minus 32 equals 204.
204 multiplied by 5 equals 1020.
1020 divided by 9 equals 113 degrees for fudge at Celsius.

To convert *Celsius to Fahrenheit*: Multiply by 9, divide by 5, add 32.

Example: End of cook for fudge is at 113 degrees Celsius.
113 multiplied by 9 equals 1017.
1017 divided by 5 equals 203.
203 plus 32 equals 235 degrees for fudge at Fahrenheit.

*Glucose.* Another name for corn syrup, usually in a thicker form. It has 20 percent less moisture than corn syrup. If you find a recipe calling for glucose, simply use light corn syrup, and add one quarter more than the amount of glucose called for to compensate for the lack of concentration.

# The Witchery of Sugar

Even if it weren't so appealing to our taste, sugar holds a fascination in its chemistry. It can be grainy or smooth, tender or chewy, pull like taffy or shatter like glass. The sugar maker's problem is to bring about a crystallization of the juices of the beet and the cane. The candymaker's challenge is to control these crystals.

Essential to sugar cookery is the confectioner's understanding that two opposing elements *combine* to create an infinite variety of pleasing tastes and textures: Sugars that *REPEL* moisture vs. sugars that *ATTRACT* moisture.

The confectioner always finds himself the referee in the constant battle between these two adversaries. He must find ways to force them into peaceful coexistence—until the next battle flares. Then he has it all to do over again. Still there are some laws that both camps obey. Enunciated below, these are the laws the confectioner relies on to control his unruly charges.

*Sugar (sucrose).* The refined product of the sugar cane or sugar beet. Chemically it is a complex sugar composed of two simple sugars: dextrose (glucose) and levulose (fructose). It is crystalline, repels moisture, and is water soluble.

*Corn syrup.* Also known as glucose, it is noncrystalline, attracts moisture, and is used to retard crystallization in fondant-type candies. By candymakers it is grouped among the inverted sugars, although it is less tender than inverted sugars made from sucrose.

*Invert sugar.* A sugar that has been treated with acid and/or heat so that its structure is changed from crystalline to liquid. It has the power to invert other sugar. It is used like corn syrup to retard crystallization. But it is more tender than corn syrup and also sweeter than the equivalent amount of corn syrup.

Crystalline candies such as fondants, fudges, and creme centers dry out when left uncovered. (They *repel* moisture.) Brittles and other higher-cooked candies are entirely inverted and will therefore become sticky when left uncovered. (They *attract* moisture.)

# SUGAR CRYSTALLIZATION

*"Doctoring" or "cutting":* The candymaker's terms for adding glucose or inverted sugar to a sugar syrup.

*"Greasing"* the batch: Adding colloids, such as butter, cream, coconut oil or cocoa butter, to a crystalline solution to lubricate the sugar molecules. This helps to keep them from clumping up.

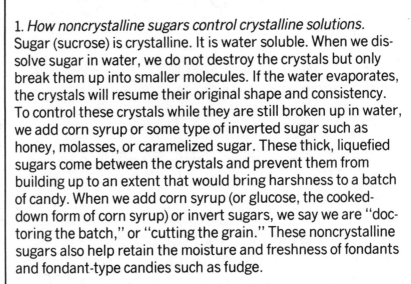

1. *How noncrystalline sugars control crystalline solutions.* Sugar (sucrose) is crystalline. It is water soluble. When we dissolve sugar in water, we do not destroy the crystals but only break them up into smaller molecules. If the water evaporates, the crystals will resume their original shape and consistency. To control these crystals while they are still broken up in water, we add corn syrup or some type of inverted sugar such as honey, molasses, or caramelized sugar. These thick, liquefied sugars come between the crystals and prevent them from building up to an extent that would bring harshness to a batch of candy. When we add corn syrup (or glucose, the cooked-down form of corn syrup) or invert sugars, we say we are "doctoring the batch," or "cutting the grain." These noncrystalline sugars also help retain the moisture and freshness of fondants and fondant-type candies such as fudge.

2. *Forming a "smooth grain" or "cremeing" the batch.* A batch of sugar, with 20 percent glucose added and enough water to dissolve the sugar, cooked to 240 degrees, when allowed to cool undisturbed, becomes a thick syrup. If we apply steady, constant friction to this syrup when it is cool and thick, we get a smooth fondant. We call this "cremeing the batch" or "graining off" the batch. If we work the batch while it is still hot, we get a coarse-grained substance like the sugar before it was dissolved. This is because the corn syrup in the batch, when it is hot and thin, offers very little resistance to the buildup of crystals. (The formation of crystals is caused by friction.) When a sugar syrup is still hot, there is already much internal molecular violence present, without our adding to it. So we tread softly, exercising the utmost care to cool fudge and fondant syrups quickly and with as little agitation as possible.

3. *How much corn syrup should be used.* The amount of corn syrup to be used in a batch is determined largely by the temperature at which the batch is to be cremed. Another factor that affects the amount of non-crystalline substance we use is whether other colloids, such as butter, cream, or chocolate, have been added to the batch. When we add any of these, we say we are "greasing" the batch.

Examples: If you cook a batch of fudge to 236 degrees and then cool it to 120 degrees before cremeing it, 2 ounces (weight) of corn syrup to 32 ounces (weight) of sugar will be sufficient to achieve a smooth consistency, because the butter and cream are also part of the fudge formula. They lubricate the molecules, which helps to keep them separated. But in fondant, we use corn syrup *alone* as grain control, so we need 6 ounces of corn syrup to 32 ounces of sugar, to achieve the same degree of smoothness as in the fudge (where corn syrup has the help of the colloids to control crystallization). In addition, if you intended to creme this same batch of fudge as soon as it comes off the heat, you would then need 16 ounces of corn syrup to produce a smooth grain. But such a batch would not be tender. It would be more like a caramel than a fudge, and as such would be more suitable for use in Log Rolls, for instance.

4. *"Seeding a batch."* Another way to grain off a batch of fondant or fudge is to add some superfine sugar or previously prepared fondant. The introduction of crystallized sugar creates a chain reaction of crystallization. We call this method "seeding" the batch. We only use precremed fondant, as in Genesee fudges (or superfine sugar), because the crystals thus formed will be the same size as the crystals added to the batch. This explains why the candymaker must be very cautious not to inadvertently allow granulated sugar crystals to get into any batch of candy *prematurely*. This, of course, is the reason for the constant exhortations to "wash down the sides of the pan."

**"Seeding" a batch: Adding a crystallized sugar or cremed fondant to a sugar syrup to start a grain when that is desirable.**

# SUGAR INVERSION

1. *Inverting crystalline solutions with acid.* Another method of grain control (doctoring) is the use of acids, such as cream of tartar, acetic acid (vinegar), or lemon juice. These have a direct chemical effect on the sugar crystals, progressively changing them from *crystalline* sugar to *inverted* sugar as long as heat is applied. For this reason, chemical doctors cannot be depended upon to give the same results in each individual case. So many things are involved, such as intensity of heat, amount of water to be cooked out of the batch, and strength of acid to be used. It is hard to line up all these things so that the proper amount of glucose is manufactured in the batch by the time it has reached the desired cook. For this reason, most candymakers prefer to use a predetermined amount of corn syrup to achieve more uniform results.

**Acid-inverted sugars can produce *remarkably* tender cremes of the highest quality. In fact, acids were used as doctors exclusively in turn-of-the-century formulations.**

# THERMOMETER READINGS AND DENSITY OF CANDY

| STAGE | THERMOMETER READING (°F.) | DESCRIPTION Drop a large spoonful into some very cold water and gather it into a ball between your fingers. It should: |
|---|---|---|
| Crystal syrup | 220-226 | disperse |
| Thread | 223-234 | form a thin, fine thread |
| Very soft ball | 234-236 | form a flat ball, be very sticky, and eventually dissipate |
| Soft ball | 238-240 | form a flat ball, be very sticky, and eventually disperse |
| Medium ball | 240-242 | form a slightly firmer flat ball, and be very sticky |
| Firm ball | 244-248 | form a firm ball, still be sticky, and lose its shape after a few seconds |
| Hard ball | 250-266 | form a firm ball, still stick a little, and hold its shape |
| Force crack | 264-268 | form a ball that's a little firmer than hard ball |
| Soft crack | 270-285 | stretch between the fingers to form a soft stick, be slightly sticky to the fingers, and be very sticky to the teeth when chewed |
| Hard crack | 290-300 | break easily, not stick to the fingers, and stick only a little to the teeth |
| Very hard crack | 310-315 | break quickly and not stick to the teeth at all |
| Light caramel | 320-340 | behave as above, but be a light golden honey color |
| Dark caramel | 340-365 | behave as above, but be darker |
| Carbon | 370 and up | Throw it away! |

2. *Heat alone can invert crystalline solutions*. Prolonged cooking at lower temperatures will also eventually break down sucrose, splitting it into its two simpler forms: glucose and fructose. If the necessary amount of inverted syrup has already been added to doctor the batch, additional unexpected inversion may cause your fondants and fudges to become chewy and tough. Therefore, it is important to cook candy batches as quickly as your ingredients will allow. (The milk and cream used in caramels usually require lower temperatures to avoid scorching.) Sucrose begins predictable active inversion at 265 degrees and is completely inverted at caramelization (320 degrees).

# SUGAR DENSITY

1. *Measuring density with a thermometer*. Cold water holds in solution one and a half times its weight in sugar. If more sugar is added, it only suspends itself in the water and can be seen floating in it. Boiling water holds four times its weight in sugar. This is what we call a hot supersaturated solution. As the solution boils, the water begins to evaporate rapidly. When enough moisture has left the batch, the sugar itself takes the heat. Sugar will hold 320 degrees—and more—of heat before turning to carbon completely. If the thermometer reading is less than 320 degrees, we know there is still water in the batch, retarding the maximum buildup of heat. In other words, as the water boils away, the boiling point rises until the sugar burns. Therefore, thermometer readings are our indication of the percentage of moisture left in a sugar solution.

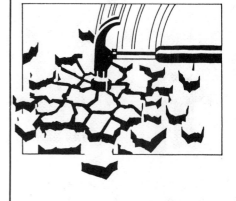

   The amount of moisture in the batch determines the final hardness or softness of a batch. For example, when the thermometer reads 235 degrees, it means there is about 15 percent moisture in the batch—which is what we want for fudge. At 270 degrees, there is only 10 percent water left in the batch—which is ideal for taffy. For the brittle, glasslike quality of praline (brittles) or lemon drops, we want no percentage—or to be more exact, an infinitesimal percentage—of water remaining. So we cook the batch until it registers 320 degrees on our thermometer. (If the water were totally cooked away, we'd have the sugar burned to carbon.)

**Cold water holds in solution one and a half times its weight in sugar and is called a cold saturated solution. Boiling water holds four times its weight in sugar and is referred to as a supersaturated solution. When it is cooled it is called a cold supersaturated solution.**

2. *Measuring syrup density in cold water by hand.* Because the temperature reading of your thermometer can be inaccurate, we include instructions for testing without a thermometer. It was always done this way by old-time candy makers, and it is very reliable. Drop a spoonful of syrup solution into a wide glass of very cold water. Very quickly gather the solution into your fingers and lift it out. Form it into a ball or as the case may be, stretch it apart between your fingers. You will see to what consistency the sugar has cooked. (Each time you test, use fresh cold water.)

3. *Slacking back the batch.* If you have overcooked the syrup, you may add a little more water to the batch. We call this "slacking back" the batch. Often we deliberately cook more moisture out of the batch in the initial cook than our texture would dictate—in anticipation of "slacking back" the batch after it is removed from heat. This is usually done with water-based flavorings. In this way, we can get the proper density along with the concentration of flavor we're seeking.

Be careful not to overcook too much, however. In a batch containing only 1 pound of sugar, the difference between 245 degrees (softball) and 270 degrees (soft crack) is only 2 table-spoons (1 ounce) of liquid. You can use these proportions as a guide when you're adding flavorings—unless they're extracts. These contain such a large percentage of alcohol that they make no appreciable difference in the degree of cook. (The alcohol evaporates away, and besides, you'll be measuring extracts by teaspoonfuls, not by tablespoonfuls.)

**"Slacking back" the batch: Putting some water into it, to lower the cook. Increasing the percentage of water makes the final consistency less dense.**

**If you find you have *slacked back* too much, you can simply cook away the unwanted moisture until the batch has come back up to the temperature you want.**

# Chocolate the Inimitable

## The Cocoa Bean

Cocoa beans are really seeds about 1 inch long and are taken from pods that are about half the size of a football. There are thirty or so seeds in each pod. Oddly enough, they grow on the trunks as well as on the lower branches of an evergreen tree called *Theobroma cacao*. There are literally hundreds of varieties of the cacao tree, which grows only to a maximum height of 20 feet and is harvested all year but most heavily between June and January. These trees grow well only 20 degrees north and south of the Equator. (The only known cacao tree growing on the North American continent is in the reception lobby of the Guittard Chocolate Factory in Burlingame, California. It seems the roots are heated by the hot water pipes that run under the building.) The largest portion of the world's supply (approximately 80 percent) comes from West Africa. Brazil is a large producer as well.

Like coffee beans, or any tree fruit, the cocoa bean does not ripen uniformly. They are very temperamental and respond unfavorably to even the slightest fluctuations in climate. Consequently, during roasting, not all the beans will arrive at the same degree of doneness, a fact that contributes significantly to the final flavor of the chocolate. The beans are also processed inconsistently in the countries in which they grow. I've seen pressed cakes of cocoa in markets in the Carribean and in Mexico, and they all taste differently. They travel through a highly competitive and complex network of marketing and are a volatile commodity on the world's stock exchanges.

**Cocoa trees require up to seven years to mature and bear fruit. Razor-sharp machetes are used by harvesters to sever the seed pods (cocoa beans) from the trunk and lower branches of the tree. If a blade penetrates ever so slightly too deep, the fragile trees bleed and die, wasting years of careful and costly nurturing.**

## Manufacturing

In most cases, the chocolate manufacturers, like the great Champagne makers, manage year after year to develop the same flavor consistently, the flavor that has become the trademark of that individual house.

It's clear that there has to be great artistry all along the entire manufacturing chain, and control as well. When my grand-

It is said that the artistry of chocolate making is in the roasting. This is because cocoa beans do not ripen uniformly, and the different species vary in the degree of temperature they will tolerate. Therefore, the roaster must gain much experience in order to blend a variety of beans and maximize the roast without damaging the batch.

Roasted cocoa beans are very tender and crumble easily into small bits and chunks we call nibs.

*Some countries that produce cocoa beans:*

| | |
|---|---|
| Ghana | Ecuador |
| Guinea | Mexico |
| Ivory Coast | Peru |
| Nigeria | Venezuela |
| Togo | Dominican |
| Brazil | Republic |
| Bolivia | Trinidad |
| Philippines | New Guinea |

The invention of the steam engine allowed mass production of pulverized cocoa beans. Heretofore crushed by hand, chocolate had been reserved for consumption by the very rich—those wealthy enough to maintain a large, muscular kitchen staff (late 1700's).

father was in business, there were a dozen U.S. companies producing high quality couvertures. Today we can safely say there are only four: Guittard, Merckens, Nestlé and Van Leer: They deserve recognition, since they have withstood the test of time. Guittard, for example, has been a family-owned-and-operated business since 1866. My grandfather used their chocolate, and so do we.

I should mention in passing a common misconception many of our customers have expressed. They have supposed that small confectioners who make chocolate-coated candies and molded novelties also make their own coating chocolate as well. But chocolate manufacturing is very complex, and the machinery very costly. Today's economy of scale debars small chocolate manufacturers. In addition, the process falls under government regulation to standardize the definition of the product. So all in all, it is a highly specialized manufacturing process.

But don't be misled. Notwithstanding the scale, couverture manufacture epitomizes the highest culinary artistry. Personal judgment is necessary all along the line.

# Steps in Chocolate Manufacturing

1. Cocoa beans are harvested by hand. More than 80 percent of the world's supply is provided by small farmers.

2. Pods are split open and left to ferment for several days, usually in the sun.

3. Beans are cleaned and sent to the manufacturer.

4. They are cleaned again and spend some time in quarantine until all possibility of plant disease is removed.

5. Beans are roasted.

6. They are cracked, then fanned (a process called winnowing). At this point they win the distinction of being referred to as *nibs*.

7. The nibs are then separated, either to be left natural or to be "Dutched." Dutching is an alkalization process designed to neutralize the acids developed during the fermenting period. This Dutch process makes the chocolate milder in flavor and darker in color.

8. The beans are now ground to make "liquor." (See page 31.) Then, depending on whether bar (solid) chocolate or cocoa is being made, the procedure goes like this:

*Cocoa Manufacture*
9. Pressing (dividing into cocoa cake and cocoa butter)
10. Pulverizing
11. Sifting
12. Barreling up for sale

*Bar Chocolate Manufacture*
9. Ingredients mixed (sugar, liquor, and extra cocoa butter)
10. Refining
11. Conching
12. Molding in 10-pound slabs for sale

• Even the best chocolate manufacturers make a wide variety of qualities of both chocolate and couverture to accommodate a broad market. It's our responsibility to taste and determine the quality of each product a company manufactures in order to decide which chocolate is best for our purposes.

• Quality as it relates to taste is purely a matter of consumer discrimination. Some cocoa beans are very bland and others highly coveted for their strength of character. The manufacturer can manipulate each step in the formulation to create an infinite variety of flavors and textures. If the fermentation step were eliminated, for example, you'd hardly recognize the bean as chocolate.

• The roasting levels vary dramatically from very dark, used for baking and bittersweet chocolate, to very light, for milk chocolate.

• Sugar is the least expensive element in chocolate. Sophisticated palates desire less sugar. This requires a larger ratio of cocoa solids and cocoa butter in the product making it more expensive, naturally.

• The amount of cocoa butter creates a big difference in the "eating" quality of the final product.

• Last of all, amalgamating all the ingredients is called "conching". During this procedure, the cocoa and sugar particles are further refined. The duration of this process can have significant effect on the final perception of smoothness. And, of course, as shop time grows, so does the price.

Conching takes place when the ground, roasted cocoa beans, additional cocoa butter, sugar, and milk solids (in the case of milk chocolate) are all combined under gradual heat and slowly agitated in a large vat. This process releases any acidic harshness that may remain in a batch of chocolate after the roasting process is completed. The motion of conching gives further smoothness to the sugar crystals that are suspended, not dissolved, in chocolate.

Couverture (the highest grade of coating chocolate) is distinguished from lower grades of chocolate not only by the blend of beans, but also by the degree of smoothness it has as a result of prolonged conching.

While cocoa butter is very hard at room temperature, it seems to literally disappear at body temperature. One moment it is hard; the next moment it has melted in your mouth. For this reason, we say cocoa butter has a "sharp" melting point.

Even when other vegetable fats, such as palm kernel oil or coconut oil, are treated to melt at the same temperature as cocoa butter, they melt more slowly. We call them plastic butters.

29

The chocolate industry is relatively new in culinary terms. The use of chocolate as enrobement is a late 1800's phenomenon. The technique peaked by the turn of the century, and formulations have not improved much since that time although the technology has advanced tremendously.

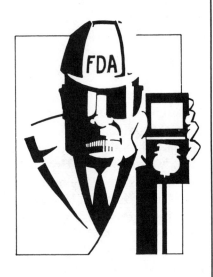

• When all these variables are raised to the highest quality, the chocolate is categorized as *couverture.* This is what high-grade bars are molded from, and what we use to coat our chocolate cremes and truffles. In relation to couverture, you'll hear a lot about longer conching from European manufacturers. But don't be fooled. The quality producers in this country generally achieve a particle size as small as the European. Many Europeans do conch the chocolate longer. At best, this can affect the sugar crystals, but generally it is a matter of eliminating some of the acidic quality of the chocolate, and some of the positive flavor elements are sacrificed. This is why European chocolate is blander than its American counterpart.

• European manufacturers put a slightly higher percentage of cocoa butter in their bar chocolate, because most of their chocolate confections are formed in molds, and the higher cocoa butter content allows the chocolates to pop out of the molds easily. This higher cocoa butter content gives the illusion of smoother chocolate. American couvertures are made for a viscosity that will accommodate hand-dipping. For this reason, American couvertures have a little less cocoa butter but proportionately more chocolate flavor.

# Government Standards

If it says *chocolate*, it's got to be "real." This means that the U.S. Government guarantees that there is nothing in the chocolate besides the allowed ingredients: cocoa solids, cocoa butter, sugar, milk solids, lecithin, vanilla, vanillin, and salt. This does not guarantee that the chocolate will taste good. However, in almost every case, "real" chocolate, no matter how indifferent it may be, tastes better than those products that look and feel like chocolate but are not 100% chocolate. The latter are called *compound coatings*, and they may have a lot of chocolate in them with a little something else, or they may have just a little chocolate in them with a lot of something else. To glamorize them they're sometimes called *confectioner's coatings.* This term is ridiculous, because no serious confectioner would ever consider coating those beloved centers with anything less than chocolate.

But compounds are much easier to handle, so pastry chefs sometimes use them when they want to make their cakes and petit fours look like confections. Ice cream vendors use them to cover frozen novelties. (And, of course, there are no doubt confectioners who use the stuff, too.)

We mention the compounds here because we don't want you to use them. Read the label. Watch for hydrogenated vegetable fats that may be replacing cocoa butter. Very good chocolate is seldom prepackaged but is displayed in bulk. And if it's designated *chocolate*, then the rules for "real" chocolate apply. Your retailer is responsible that what he's selling as chocolate is not compound coating. I've found only a few vendors who have tried to sell compounds as chocolate, and that could come from ignorance rather than misrepresentation. But do discuss the matter when you're buying.

I've explained all this because the way we handle chocolate for dipping or molding is largely determined by the physical properties of its various base ingredients. When we melt, cool, and agitate chocolate before dipping or molding, we say we are *tempering* the chocolate. If it contains something other than what should be found in chocolate, the rules of tempering change, not to mention the price, which should be substantially lower.

Because chocolate flavor is so intense, it is possible to mask adulterants. This is why chocolate is a government-regulated substance.

# What is Chocolate?

What's in the chocolate we find on the market today? Here are the components.

1. *Chocolate "liquor."* Chocolate liquor is made from cocoa beans that have been harvested when ripe, then fermented, roasted, shelled, and milled to as fine a particle size as is dictated by the final use (as small as 5 to 6 ten-thousandths of an inch, as measured by micrometer). This liquor is actually a semi-fluid paste. When it is hardened and sold at retail, it is referred to as *baking chocolate*. But manufacturers and confectioners call it liquor. It is bitter to the taste and contains about 53 percent cocoa butter and 47 percent cocoa solids, the same as the bean in its natural state.

2. *Added cocoa butter.* Cocoa butter is added to couverture to give the chocolate its characteristic smooth, melt-in-the-mouth quality. When extracted from the rest of the cocoa bean it is a pale yellow, has no flavor, and only the faintest aroma of cocoa. There is poor and good-quality cocoa butter, depending from which part of the bean it is extracted and how carefully it is refined. It has an incomparable and totally unduplicatable texture. It conducts the flavor of chocolate better than any other fat. It is very expensive—and wonderful stuff. I love it.

**Old-time candymakers used to use malt to mask the flavor of bad chocolate when the high grade was unavailable.**

**However inconsequential it appears, without the relatively short fermentation process, chocolate would not taste like chocolate to us.**

**Three ounces of chocolate contains twice the daily recommended requirement of magnesium.**

**In the mid-nineteenth century, it was discovered that by adding a little *extra* cocoa butter in the conching process, one could create a solid, smooth bar chocolate—very much like our couverture today. This discovery opened new vistas to the confectioner and pastry chef and led to new heights of chocolate consumption from which we have never turned back.**

The invention of sweetened condensed milk was very important to chocolate production. Its formulation made milk chocolate possible. Sweetened condensed milk was actually invented by an American just prior to 1860 and introduced into Switzerland by Charles Page in the same year. Nestlé took over the process and eventually Peters made the first solid milk chocolate using sweetened condensed milk. So the Swiss got all the credit. Dried milk is most generally used today.

Caffeine is present in chocolate liquor at percentages ranging Seven one-hundredths of one percent to seven tenths of one percent. The percentage of liquor (baking chocolate) found in regular table chocolate varies from 12 percent (milk chocolate) to 35 percent (bittersweet). This reduces the caffeine content to infinitessimal amounts. (In a 2-ounce solid chocolate candy bar, that signifies very, very low levels of caffeine.)

*Lecithin* is a natural oil derived from soybeans. In the old days it was made of egg yolks and had an off flavor. Today it is highly refined, having no flavor. It is used to improve the suspension of sugar, cocoa solids and milk solids in cocoa butter.

3. *Sugar (sucrose).* Granulated white sugar.

4. *Dried milk solids.* (In the case of milk chocolate only.)

5. *Lecithin* (usually less than three-tenths of one percent). An emulsifying agent, this is a 100-percent natural ingredient derived from soybeans. It is used in such small proportions that it has absolutely no effect on flavor or perceived eating quality, but is highly effective in amalgamating the ingredients.

6. *Vanilla, or vanillin.*

7. *Clarified butterfat.* Used by manufacturers in small quantities for making what is called "bloom-resistant chocolate."

# Percentage of Base Ingredients for Various Forms of Chocolate

I'm often asked how much of any one ingredient is in a particular type of chocolate. It is very interesting to see. What follows are just approximations, each chocolate is different.

Chocolate generally falls into only three categories: "liquor," milk chocolate, and semisweet. Bittersweet is becoming a fourth classification as more and more people ask for it, but it is simply a dark, semisweet eating chocolate with less sugar and proportionately more liquor. Here's the way the different types of chocolate compare in their base ingredients:

| Type of Chocolate | Liquor | Sugar | Added Cocoa Butter | Milk | Total Cocoa Butter |
|---|---|---|---|---|---|
| Milk | 12–14% | 45–52% | 21–22% | 11–20% | 31–35% |
| Semisweet | 35–42% | 45–50% | 12–14% | none | 33–34% |
| Bittersweet | 65–70% | 30–35% | none | none | 30–35% |

Lecithin .2–.3%
Vanilla or vanillin .6–1.5%
Clarified butterfat (for bloom-resistant chocolate) 3–6%, replacing some of the cocoa butter

# Cocoa: Dutch Processing Vs. Natural Processing

Until the middle of the eighteen hundreds, the world thought of chocolate principally as a beverage, and a medicinal one at that. They consumed a good deal more chocolate as beverage than we do today.

Chocolate has a natural acid content that gives it a certain lively complexity. It very much resembles wine in that respect. This acidic quality in large quantities of daily chocolate intake is considered by some to be undesirable because it can be hard to digest. A Dutchman named Van Houten, using a potash solution, found a way to neutralize the acid, a process we refer to as *Dutch processing*.

Today the alkaline solution used to neutralize the acid is potassium carbonate. It raises the pH level of cocoa from 5.5 to 7 or sometimes 8. The chocolate is a darker color afterward. People associate this with a stronger, "richer" flavor, but it is simply not the case. The flavor is actually more bland. But since Van Houten's time (the early 1800's), Europeans have been accustomed to this bland dark cocoa powder. The methods for making bar chocolate were developed a little later in the same century, and the taste for dutched chocolate carried over, into them, as well.

Americans are more accustomed to natural-process cocoas, because the industry developed along different lines here. In the small quantities of chocolate we consume, acid is scarcely an issue. To my taste, European chocolate is too bland. I should add to this, however, that this differentiation applies only to high-quality couvertures. Most commercial plain chocolate candy bars made in this country are not representative of good eating chocolate, be they dutched or natural. Many of the European imported chocolate bars are superior to American bars, not by virtue of being dutched but by virtue of the use of good-quality beans and good mixing of ingredients. But couvertures sold to small confectioners in this country are as good as if not better than many European couvertures.

The ability to extract the cocoa butter from the crushed beans came early in the 19th century. This led to powdered cocoa—and development of much more palatable beverage cocoa than the fat-heavy drink which was made earlier on. The Dutchman, Van Houten, refined the powdered cocoa still further with his patented alkalization process to remove much of the acid in the cocoa. This was thought to make it more digestible. So, suddenly cocoa became the favorite beverage of the general populace.

# The "Eating" Quality of Chocolate—
# Homage to Cocoa Butter

Have you ever gone to the movies and found that the oil from the popcorn seemed to coat the roof of your mouth? This is vegetable oil that has been treated with hydrogen to raise its melting point. Hydrogenated vegetable fat is used because it has a high melting point. The popcorn won't scorch—and hydrogenated oils are cheap. Many candymakers use them and call them plastic butters or hard butters. (Incidentally, nothing melts in the mouth quite as quickly and cleanly as cocoa butter. It's perfect for popcorn.)

Cocoa butter is a saturated fat but contains no cholesterol.

Texture as it relates to candy of any type is a very important consideration. When I was growing up, the question in our family was not only how does it taste but how does it "eat"? The textural distinctions are sometimes extreme, as with a marshmallow versus a peanut brittle. But at other times, the distinction is very subtle, as with a truffle made with cream versus butter. The texture of chocolate greatly contributes to the complex "eating" quality of confections, largely because of the nature of cocoa butter.

Cocoa butter is very hard at room temperature. It has a "snap" that needs a firm bite to penetrate. But it melts almost like butter in the mouth, quickly and immediately. Because it's hard one moment and melted the next, we say it has a "sharp" melting point. What olive oil is to Italian cuisine, what butter is to French cuisine, cocoa butter is to chocolate cuisine. It conducts the flavor of chocolate to our taste buds and gives great pleasure in its melting quality in a way no other hard vegetable fat can.

It is very expensive. Tremendous amounts of money are spent in search of suitable substitutes. This has resulted in many other oils and hard fats being used as substitutes for cocoa butter. So far, nothing has been found that truly duplicates the melting quality of cocoa butter or the easy way the body absorbs and digests it. The irony is that refined cocoa butter has virtually no flavor itself. It is its melting quality that is unique. And of course, it shares with other fats the ability to enhance, for the benefit of the taste buds, all the flavors of its accompanying ingredients.

# Quality as a Question of Intended Use

Before I close this discussion about the nature of chocolate, I feel I would be remiss not to address a question that I'm often asked: What is the best chocolate on the market today? After a lifetime of chocolate tasting, I am extremely reluctant to pronounce a "best." There is too little specificity in a simple answer. And as a matter of fact, a more meaningful question would be, which chocolate is best for a given occasion?

First, let me reiterate that there is no one who can do your tasting for you. You already have all the sensory equipment necessary to develop an informed palate. Comparison tasting will lead to palatal memory. Your own tastes—as to texture, richness of flavor, and aroma—will sharpen as you learn to discriminate between brands and national origins, and to separate the complexities of each chocolate you taste. You'll develop marked preferences—and don't be surprised if they change as you go along.

But you'll still have to choose the chocolate that's right for the use you have in mind. You have the guidelines in the types we have talked about in this section, you may have to experiment a little before you hit on the right solution. Let me give you a personal example. Most people wouldn't argue that when eaten alone, some of the European chocolate bars are superior to a simple chocolate chip. But I've repeatedly tried exotic milk chocolate, and bittersweet couvertures in chocolate chip cookies for our shops, only to return by popular request to sweet, dark vanilla chocolate with a rather sharp taste. If it doesn't have the proper amount of sweetness, it doesn't balance the cookie dough. And it needs the slight sharpness that American processing gives it. Is that an answer you can live with?

Cocoa powders range from low fat in the area of 10 percent to high fat of 35 percent. They range from natural cocoas that are quite red to the darkest and most highly Dutch-processed cocoas. The danger here is assuming that because the cocoa is dark, it has a stronger flavor (quite often the reason for the admonition to use Dutch process cocoas in baking). The absolute opposite is true. Natural process cocoas are more flavorful. You must try out many cocoas until you find what you like the best—taking into consideration what its final use will be.

Chocolate cookie wafers that are almost black are made from what is called "black cocoa." It was designed for consumers who shop with their eyes. The chocolate flavor is literally leached out because so much alkaline solution is used to achieve the dark color.

# Flavoring Agents

"More flavor than sweetness" is the guiding philosophy in creating Dilettante confections. The formulas that Julius brought from Europe catered to the aristocracy. The centers were richer; that is, more of them were butter and nutmeat centers than sugar-based candies. Julius continued this style in San Francisco, even through the Depression. The white Russian community was strong there. In the Northwest, Grandpa guided the craft through the Depression and developed many fudges, brittles, and candy bars that became popular. The renaissance of good cooking in this country is leading to a rebirth in quality and an awakening to what the planet has to offer in real flavorings.

We believe that there is a market out there for products made with natural flavors and subtle blends of flavors along with interesting contrasts in textures. And many a discriminating palate will no longer be satisfied with sweets for sweets' sake. For instance, the predominant chocolate sold in this country today is milk chocolate. But 80 percent of what we sell is dark to semisweet. It is less sweet and has greater flavor complexity. When we say more flavor than sweetness, we mean more richness than sweetness. We achieve this by adding more butter or nuts to a formula than are usually called for. This takes experimentation. As for flavoring and extracts, the temptation is to overflavor. Flavorings should be subtle and give the feeling that another bite is appropriate in order to satisfy the taste. Balance is the key, and this is the beauty of home candymaking: You are in control. For those of you interested in flavors, confectionery is the great frontier.

Finding good flavorings is the confectioner's greatest challenge, especially in the United States where synthetic flavorings reign supreme. Taste buds of the world unite and make your wants known! Only the fervor of the masses will call out the "real" competitors.

*Essential oils and extracts*

Excellent sources of real flavors. They are extracted by pressure or distillation. Oils and extracts differ in their effect. Oils tend to linger longer and leave some afterflavor. Extracts dissipate more quickly. Depending on the desired effect, both are superlative.

*Liqueurs*

A very good source of flavorings. Their alcoholic content is low, 30 to 40 percent, as opposed to vanilla which is 80 percent. The fruit-flavored distillates are nearly the only source of fruit flavors we have, although the Hains company is marketing some wonderful fruit syrup concentrates. We have also found some imported from Yugoslavia, France, and Italy.

Learning about flavorings is very important to candymaking. Measure and record your flavoring experiments very carefully. It will be your greatest source of satisfaction in candy cookery. We leave some space for note-making in this book. That's one of the things that candymaking's all about: experimentation and documentation.

*Floral attars*

Extracts obtained by distillation which are very expensive. It takes 20,000 pounds of rose petals to produce 1 pound of rose attar. The main source of rose attar is Bulgaria. The petals of the damask rose are steam-distilled to get the extract.

*Mint*

Grown extensively in eastern Washington state. Mentha piperita is a native of the Mediterranean region. Japanese peppermint is derived from the herb Mentha arvensis. Mints are usually steam-distilled. Spearmint (Mentha viridis) is grown principally in the United States.

*Licorice or sweet root*

Comes from a plant that is a member of the legume family. The extract is made by boiling the root of the plant in water. After evaporation, the essential oil is left behind, along with glyceric acid which is very, very sweet. England is famous for its licorice confections. The English began making licorice candies in the late eighteenth century. The plant was first cultivated in Asia, where the confections originated.

*Musk*

A popular flavor of some European lozenges and perfumes, is derived from glands of the male musk deer of Tibet.

*Vanilla*

Taken from the pod of a plant which belongs to the orchid family. It is grown mostly in Central America and the east coast of Mexico. The pods are processed when green. They are left in the sun fifteen days or so and dried for several months. Vanilla is usually suspended in water or alcohol for flavoring purposes. But the whole pods have also been available for years to the serious home cook.

*Vanillin*

Vanillin is the predominant flavor constituent of the vanilla bean. Because it is such a strong flavor, chocolate manufacturers find it a superior alternative to vanilla, which contains a variety of more subtle aromatics which are overpowered by the chocolate. Vanillin is crystalline and found naturally in clove and some species of oak (French winemakers use oak with vanillin in it to cure their wines).

# Brittles to Crunchy Toffee

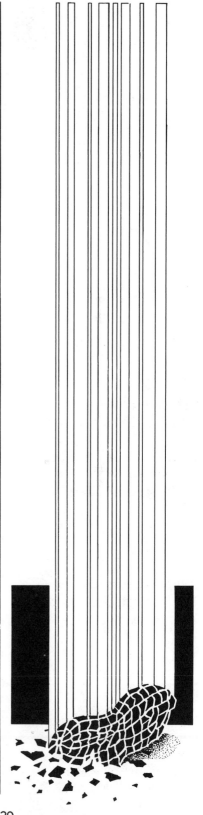

The French Comte de Plessis-Praslin is credited with giving his name to the confection which has become one of the most useful elements in the confectioner's bag of tricks, the praline. Dating from the seventeenth century, then, this original almond brittle which the French call *pralin*—or sometimes *praline* just to confuse matters—was the precursor of all the nut brittles, the butter crisps, the toffees, and all the pralined confections, too, that fertile minds could fabricate.

Pounded in a mortar, or ground in some fashion, it becomes the chief flavoring ingredient in countless desserts. And cream fillings for dipped chocolates would suffer a serious loss without it.

We regularly use the French term *praliné*—or *pralinée*—making three syllables of it in either case, to indicate, as the French would, anything flavored with, or topped with, or even rolled in powdered praline. The French have simply made a verb form out of a noun. So we think we should feel free to do the same thing, and coin an English word, as we did above, and speak of *pralined* dainties.

Now, not everyone can have a whole category of confections named for him—or her—of course, but after a little experimenting with the brittles group that we've presented here, perhaps you'll stumble on a variation that's very personal. And delicious. Name it for yourself. Or for someone you want to honor. It's a longtime culinary tradition!

# Master Recipe
# PEANUT BRITTLE

The recipe we present here is the result of much experimentation on the part of my grandfather Davenport. He worked with the European formulas for nut brittles, which had been brought from Europe by his brother-in-law, Julius. But none of those recipes included peanuts, an American favorite. Some of his discoveries? Less baking soda in the batch made it easier to pull thin. Also, the higher the "cook," the more brittle and easier to eat the confection became.

Grandpa and Great Uncle Fay had a long-running argument about the "high cook." Great Uncle Fay preferred a more delicate caramel flavor, so he cooked his peanut brittle to only 290 degrees, added the butter, and finished the cook at 300 degrees—instead of 320.

If this gives you ideas, do your own experimenting!

**½ teaspoon salt**
**1 teaspoon baking soda**
**1 teaspoon vanilla extract**

1. Mix together and reserve.

**3 cups raw Spanish peanuts**
   **(See note below)**
**2 tablespoons butter**

2. Measure each and reserve.

3. Warm the marble slab under running hot water. Dry *thoroughly*. Wipe with mineral oil. (Slab dimensions should be ¾ x 16 x 24 inches. See page 16.)

**3 cups granulated sugar**
**1¼ cups light corn syrup**
**1 cup water**

4. Measure into a heavy 3-quart saucepan. Blend thoroughly before placing on the burner.

5. Bring to a boil. Then wash down the sides of the pan with a pastry brush dipped in water. Put the thermometer in the batch. Cook to **240** degrees.

6. Add the peanuts. As soon as the batch starts to boil again, stir it in a figure-8 pattern to keep the peanuts from burning. Do not let the spoon touch the sides of the pan above the surface of the batch. (see note) Cook to **320** degrees.

Did you remember to test your thermometer before starting batch? (See "Your Candy Thermometer" page 17).

*WASH-DOWN:* Use wet pastry brush. Start at top and be thorough. Wash down sides of pan. Dip brush in water as often as necessary, and don't worry about excess water in batch. It will cook away. Every granule of sugar must be brushed down into the batch. If any escape, they could cause crystallization of entire batch.

7. Stir in the butter. Immediately remove from the heat. The batch will be a light golden brown.

8. Off heat, add the salt/soda/vanilla mixture. Stir well and allow to bubble up.

9. Pour out onto the middle of the slab. Do not scrape the pan. Spread the peanuts with a metal spatula to the outside edges of the batch. Then slide another clean, oiled spatula underneath the batch, running it along beneath all four edges, to let a little air enter between the slab and the candy. This is to prevent sticking.

For brittles, it's essential to dry the slab *thoroughly* after warming it under running water. If you leave damp areas on the surface, the oil won't cling to those spots, and as a result the batch will stick to the slab.

10. As soon as the mixture is cool enough to hold together, pull upward the far edge of batch, just enough to get hold of it with your fingertips. Then, carefully easing it toward you, turn the whole thing over in one smooth motion. This allows the liquid brittle to run evenly back down over the peanuts. If your skin is too tender to handle the hot brittle, put on clean canvas gloves, dip the fingertips in mineral oil, and proceed in comfort.

11. When it gets cooler (but long before it gets completely cold), stretch the batch in all directions. The thinner the brittle, the better for eating.

NOTE: We always use raw peanuts because (1) They do their roasting in the batch, thus adding their flavor to the syrup. (2) If you add *pre-roasted* peanuts to a batch of syrup, the husks come off the nuts and give the brittle a muddy appearance. But if you use *raw* peanuts, the husks stick to the nuts and the brittle is clear. (3) Pre-roasted peanuts have already expelled 7 percent of their weight in lost water, and consequently draw moisture back into them. This turns the peanuts first stale and then rancid.

12. Cool thoroughly. Break into pieces and store in an airtight container.

**NOTE:**

If spoon scrapes sides of pan above the boiling batch, friction can form crystals. These can no longer dissolve in thickened syrup, so the whole batch could crystallize. The confectioner's term for crystallize is "grain." (Using a wooden spoon helps cut down friction-caused crystallization.)

# BLACK-WALNUT BRITTLE

Unless you're a black-walnut freak, you'll probably want to dilute their flavor a little. We prefer to use a bland nut like cashews to accomplish this—so you could call this recipe Half-and-Half Nut Brittle if it makes you feel better.

Also, if you're a purist, you could make it up entirely with *raw* cashews, using whole nuts and putting them in at 240 degrees, then proceeding exactly as you would for peanut brittle, using our master recipe for this section.

Black walnuts, and English walnuts as well, can't take very much roasting, so they go into the batch at the end of the "cook."

½ teaspoon salt
1 teaspoon baking soda
1 teaspoon vanilla extract

1. Mix together and reserve.

¾ cup black walnut pieces
¾ cup *roasted* cashew pieces
2 tablespoons butter

2. Measure each and reserve.

3. Warm the slab. Apply mineral oil.

3 cups granulated sugar
1 ¼ cups light corn syrup
1 cup water

4. Measure into a 3-quart saucepan. Mix thoroughly before starting to cook.

5. Boil. Wash down. Insert thermometer. Cook to **290** degrees.

6. Stir in the butter. Cook to **310** degrees.

7. Add the *roasted* cashews. Stir until incorporated. Remove from the heat.

8. Let the batch cool 2 minutes (see note below). Add the black walnuts. Then immediately add the salt/soda/vanilla solution and stir well—until the batch becomes foamy.

9. Pour onto the warm, oiled slab, spreading the nuts evenly out to the edges of the batch. Slide a greased spatula underneath and run it around the edges to prevent sticking. When cool enough to hold together, turn the batch over. When a little cooler, stretch it in all directions.

NOTE: If the batch is too hot when the walnuts are added, the oil from the nuts will disperse throughout and prevent the brittle from foaming up and taking in air when the soda/salt/ vanilla solution is added. Without incorporated air, brittle is hard to eat.

10. Cool thoroughly. Break into pieces and store in an airtight container.

# ASSORTED-NUT BRITTLE

This recipe is included here to illustrate the way in which the chemical properties of different kinds of nuts legislate their use in brittle. You'll note that the almonds are added to the batch at one temperature, and the other nuts at other times, each according to how much roasting it requires.

Following these examples, you can now sucessfully mix and match your own varieties. Have fun!

1. Mix together and reserve.

2. Measure each and reserve.

3. Warm the slab. Apply mineral oil.

4. Measure into a 3-quart saucepan. Mix thoroughly before starting to cook.

5. Boil. Wash down. Insert thermometer. Cook to **240** degrees.

6. Add the almonds. Cook, stirring, to **290** degrees.

7. Stir in the butter. Cook, continuing stirring, to **310** degrees.

8. Add the English walnuts and the roasted cashews. Stir until incorporated. Remove from the heat.

9. Let cool 2 minutes. Add the black walnuts. Then immediately add the salt/soda/vanilla solution, and stir well—until the batch becomes foamy.

10. Pour onto the warm, oiled slab, spreading the nuts evenly out to the edges of the batch. Slide a greased spatula underneath and run it around the edges to prevent sticking. When cool enough to hold together, turn the batch over. When a little cooler, stretch it in all directions.

11. Cool thoroughly. Break into pieces and store in an airtight container.

**Did you remember to test your thermometer before starting batch? (See "Your Thermometer" section for procedure.)**

**½ teaspoon salt**
**1 teaspoon baking soda**
**1 teaspoon vanilla extract**

**½ cup almonds (small)**
**¾ cup English walnut pieces**
**¾ cup *roasted* cashew pieces**
**½ cup black walnut pieces**
**2 tablespoons butter**

**3 cups granulated sugar**
**1¼ cups light corn syrup**
**1 cup water**

# ALMOND BRITTLE

Almonds are very dense. They hold their moisture longer than peanuts, so this batch will take a little longer than peanut brittle to reach its ultimate temperature. Just watch the thermometer—and keep stirring!

NOTE: The procedural instructions below are somewhat abbreviated. For more detail, see master recipe this section.

½ teaspoon salt
1 teaspoon baking soda
1 teaspoon vanilla extract

1. Mix together and reserve.

2¾ cups raw whole or half
    almonds
2 tablespoons butter

2. Measure each and reserve.

3. Warm the slab. Apply mineral oil.

3 cups granulated sugar
1¼ cups light corn syrup
1 cup water

4. Measure into a 3-quart saucepan. Mix thoroughly before starting to cook.

5. Boil. Wash down. Insert thermometer. Cook to **240** degrees.

6. Add the almonds. Cook, stirring, to **300** degrees—or until golden brown.

7. Stir in the butter. Immediately remove the batch from the heat.

8. Off heat, add the salt/soda/vanilla mixture. Stir well and allow to bubble up.

9. Pour onto the warm, oiled slab, spreading the nuts evenly out to the edges of the batch. Slide a greased spatula underneath and run it around the edges to prevent sticking. When cool enough to hold together, turn the batch over. When a little cooler, stretch it in all directions.

10. Cool thoroughly. Break into pieces and store in an airtight container.

# COCONUT BRITTLE

Coconut! A touch of the tropics to give your morale a boost on a drizzly winter day.

1. Mix together and reserve.

½ teaspoon salt
1 teaspoon baking soda
1 teaspoon vanilla extract

2. Measure and reserve.

1 cup coconut, shredded, desiccated
More coconut for coating the slab and finishing the top of the cooked batch

3. Warm the slab. Apply mineral oil. Sprinkle the slab with a layer of coconut.

4. Measure into a 3-quart saucepan. Mix thoroughly before starting to cook.

3 cups granulated sugar
1¼ cups light corn syrup
1 cup water

5. Boil. Wash down. Insert thermometer. Cook to *290* degrees.

6. Add the coconut. When the batch is boiling again, stir steadily until the coconut starts to turn brown. Immediately remove the batch from the heat. The temperature should be between *300* and *305* degrees. Don't overcook. Let the batch cool 2 minutes off heat.

7. Then add the salt/soda/vanilla solution and stir well—until the batch becomes foamy.

8. Pour carefully onto the warmed, oiled, coconut-coated slab. Spread the batch out as evenly as possible (to a thickness of ⅜ inch). Slide a greased spatula underneath and run it around the edges to prevent sticking. Sprinkle more coconut over the batch and roll with a rolling pin to press the coconut in.

9. Let cool somewhat, then score the batch with a knife.

10. When nearly cold, turn over the batch and break it into pieces along the scored lines. When completely cold, store in an airtight container.

# GRANDPA DAVENPORT'S TOFFEE

The toffees fall into two major categories—the crunchy versions and the chewy ones. Properly, the chewy toffees are an extension of the caramel formulas (see page 98), and the crunchy ones belong to the brittles. The recipe we present here comes directly from Grandpa Davenport. He called it, very simply, Toffee. We don't think it needs any other appellation.

1. Prepare the marble slab. It should be *cold*, and wiped with mineral oil. Oil the perimeter bars for the slab, as well. (See Utensils section for discussion of slabs and bars.)

**½ cup raw almonds,
    unblanched, ground**

2. Measure and grind. Reserve.

**1 pound butter
1 teaspoon salt
1 teaspoon vanilla extract**

3. Measure and reserve.

**4 cups granulated sugar
⅓ cup light corn syrup
1 cup water**

4. Measure into a 3-quart saucepan.
Mix thoroughly before starting to cook.

5. Bring to a boil. Wash down the sides of the pan. Insert the thermometer. Cook, stirring, to *280* degrees.

6. Stir in the butter. Cook, continuing stirring, to *315* degrees.

7. Stir in the salt and the ground almonds. Cook, stirring constantly, to *320* degrees. Immediately remove from heat.

8. Off heat, stir in the vanilla. Then pour the batch onto the cold, oiled slab to a depth of ¼ inch. (Use oiled bars to contain the batch.)

9. While the batch is still warm, use a dull knife to score it in squares or small rectangles.

These tender, crunchy nuggets are wonderful to eat just as they are, but Grandpa dipped his in milk chocolate and rolled them in finely chopped walnuts. This is the traditional treatment.

10. When the batch is cold, turn it over and break it into pieces. Store it in an airtight container, and allow it to mellow for 24 hours before serving—or dipping in chocolate.

# WALNUT BUTTER CRISP

What could be more exciting to your taste buds than this buttery, walnutty, caramel perfume wafting through your kitchen. Hey, let the batch cool for a while or you'll burn your tongue!

1. Measure each and reserve.

**10 tablespoons (5 ounces) butter**
**2¼ cups English walnut pieces**

2. Warm the slab. Apply mineral oil.

3. Measure into a 3-quart saucepan. Mix thoroughly before starting to cook.

**2 cups granulated sugar**
**¾ cup light corn syrup**
**½ cup water**

4. Boil. Wash down. Insert thermometer. Cook to *300* degrees.

5. Stir in the butter. The temperature will drop. Cook until the thermometer comes back up to *300* degrees.

6. Add the walnuts and stir until well incorporated in the batch. Remove from heat.

7. Pour onto the warm, oiled slab. Spread as thin as possible, making sure the nuts are evenly distributed out to the edges of the batch. Slide a greased spatula underneath and run it around the edges to prevent sticking.

8. Let cool somewhat, then using a knife, score the batch in squares. When the batch is fairly cool, turn it over and break it into pieces along the scored lines. When completely cold, store in an airtight container.

If you want to square up a batch of butter crisp—or toffee—for scoring, use perimeter bars on your slab. See "Utensils" section (page 15) for information on buying, cutting and use of such bars.

# BUTTER-NUT BRITTLE

When is a brittle not a brittle? Or anyway, *almost* not a brittle? When it's *almost* a toffee. With the addition of a lot more butter to any basic brittle formula, you can *almost* create a toffee.

½ teaspoon salt
1 teaspoon baking soda
1 teaspoon vanilla extract

1. Mix together and reserve.

½ cup coconut, fine, desiccated
2 cups raw almonds,
    unblanched, small
½ cup black walnut pieces
½ cup English walnut pieces
6 tablespoons butter
⅓ cup light molasses

2. Measure each and reserve.

3. Warm the slab. Apply mineral oil. Cover evenly with the coconut. Keep the slab warm.

3 cups granulated sugar
1¼ cups light corn syrup
1 cup water

4. Measure into a 3-quart saucepan. Mix thoroughly before starting to cook.

5. Boil. Wash down. Insert thermometer. Cook to *240* degrees.

6. Add the almonds. Cook, stirring, to *290* degrees.

7. Add the butter and the molasses. When boiling again, cook, stirring, to *310* degrees—or to 320 if the almonds are not getting too brown.

8. Add both the black walnuts and the English walnuts. Stir until incorporated. Remove the pan from the heat.

9. Add the salt/soda/vanilla solution. Stir well. The batch will puff up. Stir again.

10. Pour onto the warm, oiled, coconut-covered slab. Spread the nuts out to the edges of the batch. Slide a greased spatula underneath and run it around the edges to prevent sticking.

Brittles, crisps, and toffees are very good to eat just as they are. But they're even better dipped in chocolate—or half-dipped.

11. Let cool somewhat, then using a knife, score the batch in squares. When the batch is fairly cool, turn it over and break it into pieces along the scored lines. When completely cold, store in an airtight container.

*Creme for fruit centers*

40# of 75/25 – 242
15# " pure sugar 240
Slack back with
water – Test (dip a
cherry & see how it
sets – cast 2 rows
at a time and fill
with fruit.

Conscientious experimenting deserves conscientious notes. I've seen many successful candy experiments wasted because someone neglected to keep careful notes.

# Popcorn Crisps

## *Master Recipe*

## POPCORN CRISP WITH MOLASSES

First a word about corn popping. Hydrogenated vegetable fats and solid vegetable shortenings are widely used commercially for popping corn because these fats don't scorch as easily as other fats at the high temperatures they are subjected to. But unless the popped corn is eaten immediately, the fats solidify again, giving a pasty quality to the corn. If you must use a fat that will resist scorching at high heat in your home popper, use a high quality vegetable oil, unflavored. The flavored ones are apt to taste artificial.

We feel that the home air pumps—which use no fat at all—make the popped corn a little tough.

So, after much experimenting, we've found our own method. We use cocoa butter in a heavy-bottomed saucepan, and shake the pan by hand directly over a burner. With this method we can use less heat. The result is a popped corn of unbelievable lightness, fluffiness and tenderness. It is so dry that you cannot detect that there was any fat used in its production. By the way, cocoa butter has virtually no flavor. And of course, it's not sweet.

1. Measure, mix, and reserve.

1 teaspoon vanilla extract
1 teaspoon baking soda
1 teaspoon salt

2. Measure and reserve.

1 cup raw Spanish peanuts
    with husks left on
½ cup light molasses
4 tablespoons butter

3. Pop and empty into a large bowl. Keep hot in the oven at 200 degrees. When the syrup is added, both the corn and the bowl must be hot. Cold corn will not mix well. A cold bowl will make the syrup stick to it.

½ pound popcorn, unpopped

4. Measure into a 3-quart saucepan. Blend thoroughly. Bring to a boil. Wash down the sides of the pan with a pastry brush dipped in water. Insert the thermometer. Cook, without stirring, to **240** degrees.

2 cups granulated sugar
½ cup light corn syrup
½ cup water

5. Stir in the peanuts. Cook, stirring, to **290** degrees.

6. Stir in the molasses. Cook, continuing to stir, to **300** degrees.

7. Stir in the butter and mix well. Remove from heat.

8. Stir in the vanilla/soda/salt solution. The batch will foam up. Stir again.

9. Now take the popped corn out of the oven. Pour the syrup over it, and mix together well.

10. Tip out onto a cold dry slab or cookie sheet—which need not be oiled.

11. Spread out while hot. Or shape into balls, if you prefer.

12. Store in an airtight container.

# POPCORN CRISP
# WITH BROWN SUGAR

This is a first variation on the master recipe—for those who prefer brown sugar to molasses.

1 teaspoon vanilla extract
1 teaspoon baking soda
1 teaspoon salt

1. Measure, mix, and reserve.

1 cup *roasted* Spanish peanuts,
    with or without husks
4 tablespoons butter

2. Measure and reserve.

½ pound popcorn, unpopped

3. Pop and empty into a large bowl. Hold in the oven at **200** degrees.

1 ½ cups granulated sugar
1 cup dark brown sugar
⅝ cup light corn syrup
¾ cup water

4. Measure into a 3-quart saucepan. Blend. Boil. Wash down. Insert thermometer. Cook, stirring, to **300** degrees.

5. Stir in the peanuts and butter. Mix well. Remove from heat.

6. Stir in the vanilla/soda/salt solution. The batch will foam up. Stir again.

7. Now take the popped corn out of the oven. Pour the syrup over it, and mix together well.

8. Finish as in the master recipe.

*Brown sugar* for flavor, primarily. Brown sugar is white granulated sugar with molasses reapplied to the crystals. (It must be kept in mind that molasses is inverted sugar and, as such, will partially doctor any batch to which brown sugar is added.)

# CARAMEL POPCORN CRISP

This is a second variation on the master recipe—for those who take their caramel neat.

1. Measure, mix, and reserve.

1 teaspoon vanilla extract
1 teaspoon baking soda
1 teaspoon salt

2. Measure and reserve.

1 cup *raw* Spanish peanuts, with husks
4 tablespoons butter

3. Pop and empty into a large bowl. Keep hot in the oven at **200** degrees.

½ pound popcorn, unpopped

4. Measure into a 3-quart saucepan. Blend. Boil. Wash down. Insert thermometer. Cook, without stirring, to **240** degrees.

2 ½ cups granulated sugar
⅝ cup light corn syrup
¾ cup water

5. Stir in the peanuts. Cook, stirring, to **320** degrees.

6. Stir in the butter. Mix well. Remove from heat.

7. Stir in the vanilla/soda/salt solution. The batch will foam up. Stir again.

8. Now take the popped corn out of the oven. Pour the syrup over it, and mix together well.

9. Finish as in the master recipe.

# Hard Candies

## *Master Recipe*
## PLAIN MIX

In this recipe, we give you the general procedure for all the hard candy formulas which follow it.

This formula calls for oil of peppermint, a flavoring so concentrated that it must be measured in drops for a recipe of this size. So buy an eyedropper and count the drops with care.

1. Prepare the marble slab. It should be cold. Make sure it is entirely moisture-free, then wipe it with mineral oil.

**5 cups granulated sugar**
**⅔ cup light corn syrup**
**1 ¼ cups water**

2. Measure into a 5-quart saucepan. Blend thoroughly. Bring to a boil. Wash down the sides of the pan with a pastry brush dipped in water. Insert the thermometer. Cook without stirring at high heat to **265** degrees. Lower the heat and continue the cook to **325** degrees. Remove from heat.

3. Pour out on the prepared slab. As the batch cools, fold the slightly hardened edges in toward the middle, so the cooling will be even.

**WORK THE BATCH**

4. When it is cool enough to pile up, WORK THE BATCH. Run a large knife underneath it. Slide the knife to the center and lift. Let the batch fold over the knife so that the under part of the batch comes together. Lay the folded batch on its side. Remove the knife and repeat the process until the candy is firm enough to be handled with canvas gloves. If it is too hot it will stick to the gloves.

**PULL THE BATCH**

5. PULL THE BATCH. Handle it as if it were taffy. Use gloves. Hard candy is hotter than taffy.

**10 drops peppermint oil**
**OPTIONAL: paste color**

6. Add to the batch while you're pulling it. If you want to color the batch, do that while you're pulling, as well. Use paste color rather than liquid. It's available at specialty shops.

7. In working hard candy, pull the batch out deliberately and evenly. As you fold it back on itself and pull again, keep in mind that you want the flavoring and coloring evenly distributed. Continue pulling until the candy is firm enough to hold its shape when it is stretched out on the slab.

8. Now, pull it out into uniform half-inch strips. Dispose these on a flat work surface. Using scissors, cut into half-inch lengths.

9. When the pieces are cold, put them in a sieve, shake them over a steaming kettle until they are sticky and pour them into a dish of granulated sugar.

10. Sieve the sugar off them and put them in an airtight container. This is called "sanding" them, and will keep them from sticking together.

# LEMON DROPS

We Davenports are a surprisingly close family, considering how many of us see each other every day at work. We're forever gathering at one or another's house for dinner and the evening. Or in the case of my oldest brother, Skip, overnight. Incidentally, Skip is the oldest of six brothers—and I'm fourth in the pecking order.

Skip's involvement in the family business these days allows him to live at some remove from the city. We're all envious, of course. He's found the spot most Seattleites dream about. He actually lives, year-round, on Mount Rainier. His house is up on the far flank of the mountain, barely outside the national park boundary. It's about three hours away from town—unless you're a real cowboy behind the steering wheel. Then maybe two hours. But not when winter's made the higher roads slick. Or you insist on traveling at rush hour.

A couple of us were up there last weekend and stayed over Saturday night. What did we do to entertain ourselves during the evening? What do we do three times out of five when we get together? We experimented on a batch of candy. Just happened to be lemon drops. We felt that it might be a good idea to give them a little higher cook than we habitually did. And Skip said he had never had lemon drops tart enough. So we raised the cook to 320 degrees instead of our usual 310.

Chocolate Suckers.

10/20/- 280°- 1pt molasses- Salt & Lemon flavor- pull- Kiss cutter-stick eurober or dip in dark choc.-

Hore-Hound Lumps

6 oz. herbs- 1gallon H₂O- Steep- Strain into- 42/8- 315°- drop machine

Hard-Candies

42/6- 325°- Hot to 260°-then slow

Lemon Drops

40/8- 310°- 4 oz tartaric acid- 1 oz lemon- Drop machine- Sand

Lars Peanut Squares

8/6- 18" Blanched Peanuts Salt - Soda - Van- cook lower than brittle - cut as nut cuts -

And put in more flavoring than usual. We volunteered Skip to do the tasting for tartness. When he finally quit putting in lemon emulsion and nodded his head, saying, "Now that's more like it!" he was speaking through pursed lips. Judicious. Wise. That's my big brother. Or had he just determined to get enough pucker power into the lemon drops for once?

When the batch was finally finished and cooled, we all tried it, of course. All except me, that is. I suddenly had to leave the room for a minute. I had decided we needed another log on the fire. When I came back in, everyone was coughing and sputtering, their eyes running tears. They were gulping down glasses of milk. Talk about pucker power!

Well of course, poor Skip got blamed for the whole thing. No judgment. No sense of taste.

No one knows until this appears in print that some rotten little brother slipped more lemon emulsion into the batch—after Skip had pronounced it perfect.

Honest, guys, I didn't mean to add so much lemon. It just spilled. Oh well, I was planning to take a few days off anyway...

REMARKS: A teaspoonful or so of citric acid added to any batch of fruit candy is always permissible—to achieve a little extra tartness. But always add it after the batch has cooled slightly. Too high heat will turn it bitter.

1. Prepare the slab. Cold. Dried. Then oiled.

2. Mix together. Reserve.

**2 teaspoons powdered citric acid (available at pharmacies)**
**¼ teaspoon lemon emulsion**

**1 cup light corn syrup**

3. Measure into a small saucepan. Bring to the boil. Remove from heat and keep hot until you're ready for it.

**2 cups granulated sugar**
**½ teaspoon cream of tartar**
**½ cup water**

4. Measure into a 3-quart saucepan. Blend thoroughly. Boil. Wash down. Insert thermometer. Cook to *320* degrees.

5. Add the hot corn syrup. Be careful. The batch will splash and sputter.

6. Bring the temperature back up to only *300* degrees this time. Remove from heat.

7. Pour out on the prepared slab and work as in Plain Mix just preceding this recipe, steps 4 through 10.

**WORK THE BATCH**

**Add the mixed flavorings**

56

# HOREHOUND LUMPS

These old-time throat lozenges were very popular a generation or two ago. You could prepare this basic formula with any herbal tea of your choice. We also give you a menthol version as a variation.

1. Prepare the marble slab. Cold. Dried. Then oiled.

2. Steep the tea in 1 cup of water. Strain and reserve.

¼ ounce dried horehound tea leaves
1 cup boiling water

3. Measure into a 3-quart saucepan. Blend thoroughly. Boil. Wash down. Insert thermometer. Cook at high heat to *265* degrees. Lower heat and continue the cook to *315* degrees. Remove from heat.

4 cups sugar
⅝ cup light corn syrup
The hot tea

4. Pour out on the prepared slab. As the batch cools, fold the slightly hardened edges in toward the middle, so the cooling will be even.

5. When it is cool enough to pile up, WORK THE BATCH. Run a large knife underneath it. Slide the knife to the center and lift. Let the batch fold over the knife so that the under part of the batch comes together. Lay the folded batch on its side. Remove the knife and repeat the process until the candy is firm enough to be handled with canvas gloves. If it is too hot it will stick to the gloves.

**WORK THE BATCH**

6. PULL THE BATCH. Handle it as if it were taffy. Use gloves. Hard candy is hotter than taffy.

**PULL THE BATCH**

7. In working hard candy, pull the batch out deliberately and evenly, repeatedly folding it back on itself and pulling again. Continue pulling until the candy is firm enough to hold its shape when it is stretched out on the slab.

8. When the batch is firm enough, cut off a piece and pull it out like taffy. Make it the size of your thumb. Cut it into lumps with kitchen shears.

9. Repeat this process until the entire batch is cut up. (The uncut part of the batch should be kept on the warm part of the slab so it will not get too cold to cut.)

10. When the lumps are cold, put them in a sieve, shake them over a steaming kettle until they are sticky and pour them into a dish of granulated sugar.

11. Sieve the sugar off them and put them in an airtight jar. (Called "sanding" to keep them from sticking together.)

**VARIATION**

HOREHOUND MENTHOL LUMPS
1. Make a batch of horehound lumps, steps 1–5.
2. When it is cool enough to handle with the gloves, put it on the warm part of the slab and punch a hole in it with one finger to a depth of ½ inch.
3. Empty ⅛ teaspoon menthol crystals into the depression. Fold the batch over them and work them in well.
4. Finish as in the plain horehound formula.

We had some friends who had a big beautiful dog named Pal. He looked like Lassie. When we would visit, Papa would take off his coat and hang it over the back of a chair. That was the signal for Pal to start looking for the candy Papa had brought for him. He would nose into every pocket until he found the one with the candy.
—*Aunt Pat*

# MOLASSES LOLLIPOPS

This time we offer you the option of coating your all-day sucker with dipping-grade chocolate. But be warned, you'll probably have to make a rule that the kids have to stay out-of-doors until they've consumed the whole thing!

1. Prepare the marble slab. Cold. Dried. Then oiled.

**3 cups granulated sugar**
**⅝ cup light corn syrup**
**¾ cup water**

2. Measure into a 3-quart saucepan. Blend thoroughly. Boil. Wash down. Insert thermometer. Cook to **280** degrees.

**¼ cup molasses**

3. Stir in and bring the cook to **280** degrees again, stirring constantly. Remove from heat.

**WORK THE BATCH**
**PULL THE BATCH**

4. Pour out on the prepared slab and work as in Horehound Lumps, steps 4 through 8.

**lollipop sticks**

5. Insert a lollipop stick in the side of the lump and press the lump flat against the slab with the heel of the other hand.

6. Lay the lollipops on the slab until they are thoroughly cold. Store in an airtight container. Or dip in chocolate if you wish.

**OPTIONAL:**
**1 pound dipping chocolate,**
    **dark or light—your choice**
**2 ounces (weight) cocoa butter**

7. Melt together. Cool until the mixture feels cold to the lips. (See "Dipping" section, page 138, for more detail.)

8. Stir the chocolate before dipping. Dip the lollipops into the chocolate until the candy is covered. Raise above the surface and twirl the stick to let excess chocolate drip off. Lay on a flat surface on waxed paper and allow to set.

# CLEAR LOLLIPOPS

Choose your own flavorings and colors for these. We form them with the help of special steel rings which are made for this use. You can also use small piston rings in such way that the spring of the steel holds the sticks in place. But if neither of these is available, you can handle the lollipops exactly as we do in the Molasses Lollipops recipe just preceding this one.

NOTE: Good flavorings for lollipops are lemon, orange, anise, among the extracts, and peppermint or cassia among the oils.

1. Prepare the marble slab. Cold. Dried. Then oiled.

2. Place the rings, if you're using them, on the slab.

**steel rings or lollipop sticks**

3. Measure into a 3-quart saucepan. Blend thoroughly. Boil. Wash down. Insert thermometer. Cook at high heat to *265* degrees. Lower heat and continue to cook to *310* degrees. If you have no rings, remove from heat. Proceed directly to step 6, ignoring steps 4 and 5.

**4 cups granulated sugar**
**⅝ cup light corn syrup**
**1 cup water**

4. If you're using rings, immediately stir in the flavoring at *310* degrees, then remove the batch at once from the heat and pour the hot syrup into the rings on the slab.

**1 teaspoon flavoring extract**
***Or* 10 drops flavoring oil**

5. When completely cool, remove the candy from the rings and store in an airtight container.

6. If you're not using rings, then at the end of the cook (*310* degrees), pour the syrup out on the prepared slab and work as in Horehound Lumps, steps 4 through 8, adding the flavoring (and the optional color paste) while you're PULLING the batch.

**WORK THE BATCH**
**1 teaspoon flavoring extract**
***Or* 10 drops flavoring oil**
**OPTIONAL: Color paste**
**PULL THE BATCH**

7. Insert a lollipop stick in the side of the lump and press the lump flat against the slab with the heel of the other hand.

8. Lay the lollipops on the slab until they are thoroughly cold. Store in an airtight container.

# Fudges

What does *fudge* mean to you?

There are many sorts of recipes for fudge—the marshmallow–chocolate chip type, the old-fashioned one-pan beaten type, *or* the professional approach which we begin with here. Call together a few good cooking buddies, and learn the principles that these fudge recipes offer you. It'll turn into a party in spite of your serious intent! You can use a few extra hands in the kitchen, taking turns with the scraper when you get down to the cremeing process, and a few extra eyes watching for the white "creme" to begin to show up.

*Creme* as we use it here is a confectioner's term. It's probably an anglicization of the French word *crème* that has gotten a little out of hand, and now serves as a verb—as well as a noun—in the candymaker's lexicon. Since the French don't use it in the way American confectioners do, nor even pronounce it in the same way (confectioners pronounce it *cream*; the French say *krem*), we've decided not to use the accent mark—and in fact to think of it as an American word pronounced *cream*.

The process of cremeing is aimed at controlling the "grain." All through the cooking and cooling stages, we've taken great care to *prevent* "graining"—*premature* graining, that is. If *premature* graining occurs, it's because we've broken one of the rules governing graining (crystallization) in the batch. Some calamity has caused the sugar molecules to clump together in big, coarse crystals. We candymakers don't like that. We want the crystals to be very fine, and undetectable to the tongue.

Now we know that in the end, in the case of fudges and some other candies, the batch has to

*"Cremeing"* the batch or *"graining off"* the batch. Terms we use to describe the application of friction to induce crystallization in a crystalline solution.

"grain" in order to become firm, to "set" as we say. So we've developed this process of cremeing. It allows us to recrystallize the batch, but on our own terms. We've found that after the batch has cooled down to lukewarm, we can create our own crystals—tiny ones—by friction. How do we produce this friction? Well, we can scrape a marble slab with a metal scraper—or in the case of pan fudges, we can use a spoon, scraping it against the sides of a metal saucepan. Same result. We obtain a "grain" all right, but it's so fine that the creamy fudge melts in the mouth. It is satiny to the eye and invitingly smooth to the tongue.

But you don't really have to know all of the above. Just follow the recipe. It touches all the bases. And when the fudge is finished and ready, you'll find that your proof is in the eating.

# Master Recipe
# CREMED FUDGE

We've offered you a vanilla fudge here because in our family it's a favorite. In fact my father prefers it above all others. Both texture and flavor are exceptional.

If you'd like to make a cremed *chocolate* fudge, simply use this recipe exactly as it is—but with the addition of the optional baking chocolate. The broken-up chocolate should be measured into the saucepan along with the other ingredients that are to be blended together before starting to cook.

1. Prepare the marble slab: it should be cold and slightly damp. (If you pour hot fudge on a dry slab, the friction might cause the batch to "grain" before you've even started the cremeing process.) Slab dimensions should be ¾ × 16 × 24 inches. (See "Utensils" section, page 16, for a discussion of slabs.)

**4 tablespoons butter**
**4 cups granulated sugar**
**¼ cup light corn syrup**
**1 cup whipping cream**
**¼ cup water**
**½ teaspoon salt**
**(Optional: 4 one-ounce squares baking chocolate, unsweetened)**

To avoid crystallizing a batch (confectioner's term is "graining"):
1. Always wash down sugar from sides of pan.
2. Never let spoon touch sides of saucepan above surface of boiling batch.
3. Always use a wooden spoon for stirring batch.

2. Measure into a 3-quart saucepan. Blend thoroughly before placing on the burner. Bring to a boil. Wash down the sides of the pan. Put the thermometer in the batch. Do not stir again until the fudge is boiling. Then cook, stirring constantly, to **236** degrees. Do not let the spoon touch the sides of the pan above the surface of the batch.

3. Pour out carefully on the cold, damp slab. Do not scrape the pan.

4. Allow the batch to cool down to lukewarm (neither warm nor cold). Then **CREME**:

**CREME THE BATCH**

Use a 3½- to 4-inch candy scraper or wall scraper. Work the batch in parallel lines from one end of the slab to the other. Starting at one end, run about half the scraper's width under the edge of the batch. Scrape through to the other end. Then turn the scraper over and bring it back across the top of the batch. Repeat this over and over, working back and forth, up and down the slab from one edge to the other, scraping the surface well whenever the metal is in contact with the slab. (Remember, it's the friction of the scraper against the slab that causes the fudge to creme.) Continue this motion, in easy rhythmical strokes, taking your time. But once started, do not stop until a white "creme" begins to form clearly on the back edge of the scraper. This is the indication that the batch is starting to creme. Normal time for this process is about 10 minutes.

If you want a softer-textured fudge, you may knead the batch after it is fully cold. It will then soften up and stay soft. (There is no point in kneading it while it is still warm. It will soften up at first, but left until it cools, it will harden again.)

The colder the batch when you start cremeing, the longer it takes to creme it, but the smoother the fudge. If you would like it to creme up a little fster, next time start the cremeing a little sooner, before the batch is quite so cool.

5. Now add the walnuts and vanilla to the batch, and continue cremeing until the fudge begins to lose its tanslucent quality and starts to hold its shape. It will become increasingly opaque.

**1 cup English walnuts, chopped**
**1 teaspoon vanilla extract**

6. Before the batch "sets" (it won't take long at this stage), remove it to a lightly oiled platter or a sheet of waxed paper. Use the scraper for this, along with a metal spatula in the other hand to scrape the fudge off the scraper. Work quickly to clean all the candy off the slab. Then immediately smooth out the batch, shaping it with a swirling motion of the spatula.

If the batch gets too thick before it is removed from the slab, it will look rough and dull instead of smooth and glossy. But it still tastes good and is of fine quality.

7. When the batch is completely cool, it should be cut in pieces of desired size and stored in an airtight container. It will dry out and get hard if air gets to it.

A little time is needed for fudge to ripen so that it may be sliced without crumbling. While there is still heat in the batch the crystals grip together. But when the heat is all out of the batch, the crystals begin to relax. This is called "mellowing," as well as "ripening."

# DOUBLE CHOCOLATE FUDGE

NOTE: See Notes for the master recipe, Cremed Fudge, page 62.

This is another version of cremed fudge, but with some very important differences in ingredients and techniques. These require a little explanation. First, there is much more corn syrup in proportion to sugar than in most fudge recipes. You see, in confectioner's parlance, corn syrup is a "doctor" used to help keep the batch from "graining" prematurely. This is the role of corn syrup in any candy recipe. Not having any crystals itself, it helps inhibit crystallization of granulated sugars.

Now in this recipe, we have need for more "doctor" than usual because we're ignoring one of the prime rules for preventing premature graining, "Cool to lukewarm before cremeing." This time, we're starting the cremeing almost immediately after the cooking is finished! Not to worry, though, the recipe has foreseen all the pitfalls, and works very well. Trust us!

If you love the dark, sensually rich flavor of unadulterated chocolate, this one's for you.

1. Prepare the slab. It should be cold and slightly damp.

**9 ounces unsweetened chocolate**

2. Melt and reserve.

**2 tablespoons butter**
**4 cups granulated sugar**
**6 tablespoons powdered cocoa**
**Pinch of salt**
**1¼ cups light corn syrup**
**3 cups whipping cream**

3. Measure into a 5-quart saucepan. Blend. Boil. Wash down. Insert thermometer. Cook, stirring, to *238* degrees. That's right, *238*.

4. Stir in the melted chocolate and cook until the thermometer again registers *238*. (Turn down the heat a little and stir constantly to prevent the chocolate from scorching.)

5. Pour out carefully on the cold, damp slab. Do not scrape pan.

**CREME THE BATCH**

6. Cool only slightly—2 to 3 minutes. CREME. (For detailed instructions, see master recipe, Cremed Fudge, steps 4, 5, 6)

**1 teaspoon vanilla extract**
**2 cups English walnut pieces**

7. Add the vanilla and walnuts to the batch. Continue cremeing until the batch is almost ready to "set."

8. Remove to a lightly oiled platter or a sheet of waxed paper.

9. Cool thoroughly. Cut in squares. Store in an airtight container.

x x x
Ice cream Fudge
5# fondant (109/10 - 24%
2½ 96 butter
2½ Marietta
flavor & nuts

The classes Papa held became very popular. In one class I remember my Aunt Marie (Papa's sister) stood up when he was making fudge and said, "This is very good fudge, Earl, but I still like the gritty kind we made when we were children." Papa was always alert to the opportunity to make a point, so he said, "If you like that kind, just creme it immediately after you remove it from the fire. Remember, the hotter the candy when it is cremed the coarser the grain. The cooler it is, the finer (or smoother) the grain."

—*Aunt Pat*

*Colloid*. For the candymaker, colloids are substances that retard crystallization, such as butter, cream, cocoa butter, invert sugar, or corn syrup. They are also substances that bind other substances together, such as gelatin, pectin, or starch.

When colloids such as cream or butter are added to any sugar solution such as in fudges or caramels or at the end of a batch of brittles or crisps, we must continuously stir the batch to prevent the butter solids from scorching. This is an important distinction between hard candy, brittles before the nuts are added, and simple fondants.

# SOUR CREAM CHOCOLATE FUDGE
## *Master Recipe— Pan Fudges*

We Davenports couldn't give you only *professional* fudge formulas—not when we have so many time-honored family recipes for old-fashioned beaten fudges or pan fudges. We'd like to share some of our favorites with you. This first one's a flavor combination few of us can resist.

1. Butter a 9x9-inch cake pan and reserve.

**1 cup nuts of your choice**

2. Measure, chop, and reserve.

**5 ounces unsweetened chocolate**

3. Chop and reserve.

**4 cups light brown sugar**
**The unsweetened chocolate that you have just chopped and reserved**
**1 ¾ cups sour cream**

4. Measure into a 3-quart saucepan. Blend thoroughly before starting to cook.

*"Washing down."* Done to prevent crystals from invading a sugar solution, causing unwanted grain. After a batch has come to the boil, the candymaker always washes down the utensils and the sides of the pan with a pastry brushed dipped in water, to dissolve any stray sugar crystals. Any water thus added to the batch will be boiled away during the cooking.

5. Bring to a boil. Wash down the sides of the pan with a pastry brush dipped in water. Put the thermometer in the batch. Cook, stirring constantly, to **236** degrees. (Do not let the spoon touch the sides of the pan above the surface of the boiling fudge. You don't want to start a premature "grain," do you! You'll get to scrape the sides of the pan plenty when you're beating the batch—after it has cooled.)

6. At *236* degrees, remove from heat, and cool down, undisturbed, to *120* degrees. (To hasten cooling, place the saucepan in a larger container of very cold water.)

7. When the batch has cooled to *120* degrees, place the saucepan in a container of warm water just long enough to release the candy from the sides of the pan. Then CREME the batch with a metal spoon.

**CREME THE BATCH**
   **NOTE: The sides of the pan *should* be scraped with the spoon during cremeing, because now we want the batch to grain in a controlled fashion (see page 61).**

**1 teaspoon vanilla extract**

8. Just before the batch "sets," it will start to stiffen and become opaque. Immediately stir in the vanilla and the nuts. As soon as they are incorporated, scrape the batch into the buttered cake pan. Then, using a clean spatula, smooth the surface in a swirling motion.

9. Cool thoroughly. Cut in squares. Store in an airtight container.

**1 cup fresh coconut, grated**
**3 cups pure maple syrup**
**⅔ cup whipping cream**

# MAPLE CREAM FUDGE

This glorious collaboration of maple and rich cream and fresh coconut cannot be described. It must be tasted!

1. Butter a 9x9-inch cake pan. Reserve.

2. Grate the coconut, and measure it into a 2-quart saucepan. Then measure and add the maple syrup and the whipping cream. Blend thoroughly before starting to cook.

3. Boil. Wash down. Insert thermometer. Cook, *stirring constantly,* to **236** degrees.

4. Remove from heat, and cool down, undisturbed, to **120** degrees. (To hasten cooling, place the saucepan in a larger container of very cold water.)

5. Now while the batch is cooling is a good time to read the introduction to this section (page 61).

6. When the batch is cooled to **120** degrees, place the saucepan in a container of warm water just long enough to release the candy from the sides of the pan. CREME.

7. Just before the batch sets, scrape it into the buttered cake pan. Smooth the surface.

8. Cool. Cut. Store in an airtight container.

**CREME THE BATCH**

# COCONUT FILLING OR FROSTING FOR CAKE

What's this recipe doing in a candy cookbook? Well, if you look closely, you'll see that it's essentially a pan fudge. A homemade cooked frosting of substance and flavor is sometimes hard to find, so we offer you this one, a long-time favorite in our family. It's wonderful on chocolate cake. And it will make a handsome two-layer white cake if you concoct a double batch of frosting, divide it in two, color one half pink, and leave the other half white. Spread the pink frosting on the bottom layer.

If you want to frost the sides of the cake, either chocolate or white, use either a standard seven-minute frosting or a butter-cream type. Go as fanciful as you like in compatible flavors and colors, either contrasting or similar, for these.

1. Have your cake baked, cooled and ready to frost.

2. Weigh and reserve.

**¾ pound fresh coconut, shredded**
**OR ½ pound medium dessicated coconut, unsweetened**

3. Measure into a 3-quart saucepan. Blend thoroughly. Bring to a boil. (If using fresh coconut, add it at this time.) Wash down the sides of the pan with a pastry brush dipped in water. Insert the thermometer. Cook, stirring constantly, to *250* degrees. Remove from heat.

**2 cups granulated sugar**
**⅝ cup light corn syrup**
**⅔ cup water**

4. Stir in the cocoa butter and the vanilla. (If using dessicated coconut, add it at this time.)

**4 ounces (weight) cocoa butter**
**1 teaspoon vanilla extract**

5. CREME the batch, without waiting for it to cool. Stir, right in the pan, until it grains. Mash out any lumps that develop.

**CREME THE BATCH**

6. When the batch has thickened and is nearly ready to set, scrape it out onto the cake and spread it in swirls with a spatula.

7. Do not cut the cake until the frosting is thoroughly cold.

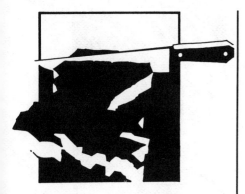

# LOUISIANA FUDGE

No one in the present family knows where this name came from. Perhaps from the ingredient that gives it its informing flavor, peanut butter. But we all love this fudge with the Southern accent. Bet you will, too.

1. Butter a 9x9-inch cake pan. Reserve.

¼ cup peanut butter (of a very dry consistency, not at all oily)

2. Measure and reserve.

4 tablespoons butter
3 cups light brown sugar
½ cup granulated sugar
1 cup evaporated milk

3. Measure into a 3-quart saucepan. Blend thoroughly before starting to cook.

4. Boil. Wash down. Insert thermometer. Cook, stirring constantly, to **236** degrees.

5. Remove from heat. Cool down, undisturbed, to **120** degrees. (To hasten cooling, place the saucepan in a larger container of very cold water.)

6. Right now, while the batch is cooling, is a good time to read the master recipe, Sour Cream Chocolate Fudge, page 66. You'll find detailed instructions there which apply to nearly all beaten fudges—certainly to this one.

## CREME THE BATCH

7. When the batch is cooled to 120 degrees, place the saucepan in a container of warm water just long enough to release the candy from the sides of the pan. CREME.

8. Just before the batch sets, add the peanut butter. The minute it's incorporated, scrape the batch into the buttered cake pan. Smooth the surface.

9. Cool. Cut. Store.

If a recipe includes butter, you can grease the sides of the saucepan with part of the butter before putting the batch in the pan. This makes washdown easier.

# GRANDPA DAVENPORT'S PENUCHE

Grandpa found that Penuche was apt to be a little on the grainy side. This apparently didn't suit his preference, so he tried cutting down the proportion of brown sugar to white. Still not satisfied, he added a much greater proportion of corn syrup to the formula. This resulted in a more chewy fudge, smooth and delicious. Happy with his experiment, Grandpa handed down the recipe we offer you here, a master's variaton on the Penuche theme.

   Because of the large quantity of corn syrup in the batch, it is necessary to creme it while it is still hot. If it is allowed to cool, the batch becomes very thick and impossible to manipulate.

   Attention! Because it's hot, this batch "sets up" a lot faster than the fudges that are cooled before cremeing.

1. Butter an 8x8-inch cake pan and reserve.

2. Measure and reserve.

**½ teaspoon salt**
**1 teaspoon vanilla extract**
**1 cup English walnut pieces**

3. Measure into a 2-quart saucepan. Blend thoroughly before starting to cook.

**2 cups granulated sugar**
**1 cup dark brown sugar**
**¾ cup light corn syrup**
**1 cup whipping cream**

4. Bring to a boil. Wash down the sides of the pan. Insert thermometer. As soon as the mixture is boiling again, cook, stirring constantly, to *236* degrees.

5. Remove from heat. Begin to stir the batch at once. It will soon start to show signs of graining, because it is hot. Immediately add salt, vanilla and walnuts.

**CREME THE BATCH**

6. Continue beating until the mixture starts to "set." Scrape the batch into the buttered cake pan. Then, using a clean spatula, smooth the surface in a swirling motion.

7. Cool thoroughly. Cut in squares. Store in an airtight container.

See notes for the master recipe, Cremed Fudge, page 62.

1 pound Cremed Fondant (See recipe page 84.)

1 cup English walnuts, chopped
½ pound dried apricots, chopped

2 cups granulated sugar
3 tablespoons light corn syrup
1 cup whipping cream
The reserved apricots

**CREME THE BATCH**

2 teaspoons vanilla extract

When adding fruit to fudge it's best for it to be dried or glazed.

# APRICOT GENESEE FUDGE

We've decided to offer you a pair of Genesee fudges to broaden your grasp of candymaking variations. These employ a commercial technique that is, in fact, a very useful "trick of the trade." It involves using already-cremed fondant for half the batch. In my grandfather's notes it was referred to as "adding bon bon creme." The fondant is added to the batch before the start of cremeing and cuts the cremeing time in just about half.

Oh, incidentally, you're going to need a reasonably accurate kitchen scale for these recipes. (See "Utensils" page 15.)

1. Prepare the slab. It should be cold and slightly damp. Break up the fondant into small pieces and scatter them evenly over the surface of the slab.

2. Chop and reserve.

3. Measure into a 3-quart saucepan. Blend thoroughly. Bring to a boil. Wash down the sides of the pan with a pastry brush dipped in water. Insert the thermometer. Cook, stirring constantly, to *236* degrees. Remove from heat.

4. Pour the hot syrup over the fondant on the prepared slab. Cool the batch to lukewarm. (It won't take as long as usual because of the cooling effect of the already cremed fondant.)

5. Press out any lumps of fondant still remaining in the batch. CREME. (For detailed instructions, see master recipe, Cremed Fudge, steps 4, 5, and 6.)

The reason for using fondant is to make cremeing go faster, so watch for graining in half the usual time— or even less.

6. As soon as graining starts, add vanilla and reserved walnuts. Continue cremeing until the batch is almost ready to "set."

7. Remove to a lightly oiled platter or sheet of waxed paper. Spread and smooth with a spatula.

8. Cool thoroughly. Cut. Store in an airtight container.

# PENUCHE GENESEE FUDGE

Here we offer still another variation on our old friend Penuche, also sometimes called Panocha, the Mexican-Spanish word for raw sugar, or even Panoche, which appears to be a hybrid combination of the first two.

     Whatever it's called, it's always greeted with gladsome cries from all of us brown-sugar lovers.

**NOTE: See Notes for the master recipe, Cremed Fudge, page 62.**

1. Prepare the slab. It should be cold and slightly damp. Break up the fondant into small pieces and scatter them evenly over the surface of the slab.

**1 pound Cremed Fondant (see recipe page 84)**

2. Chop and reserve.

**1 cup English walnuts**

3. Measure into a 3-quart saucepan. Blend thoroughly. Boil. Wash down. Insert the thermometer. Cook, stirring constantly, to *236* degrees. Remove from heat.

**¼ pound butter**
**2 cups dark brown sugar**
**¼ cup light corn syrup**
**2 cups whipping cream**

4. Pour the hot syrup over the fondant on the prepared slab. Cool the batch to lukewarm. (It won't take as long as usual because of the cooling effect of the already cremed fondant.)

5. Press out any lumps of fondant still remaining in the batch. CREME. (For detailed instructions, see master recipe, Cremed Fudge, steps 4, 5, and 6.)

     Remember that the reason for using fondant is to make cremeing go faster. Watch for graining in half the usual time— or even less.

**CREME THE BATCH**

6. Add the vanilla and reserved walnuts. Continue cremeing until the batch is almost ready to "set."

**3 teaspoons vanilla extract**

7. Remove to a lightly oiled platter or sheet of waxed paper.

8. Cool thoroughly. Cut. Store in an airtight container.

# FRENCH FUDGE

Fudge is almost a misnomer for this rich and satiny confection. Because of its high chocolate content, it's more like a truffle. Included in the formula are ingredients not found in very many fudges: Mazetta, already-prepared fondant, sweetened condensed milk.

And we're using terms and techniques here that may need explanation. Couverture, for example, is dipping-grade chocolate—which implies chocolate of the highest quality. As to Mazetta and Cremed Fondant, you'll find recipes, and explanations regarding their use, in the section we call The Support Group.

"How to melt chocolate" gets a special note at the end of this recipe because we find it's one of the most mismanaged procedures in candymaking.

Now that we've put you to sleep with all the introductory matter you're being asked to read, wake up and roll up your sleeves. You're about to start cooking. It's not our fault that the next few recipes are very professional and complex. It's you who asked for them. We've just tried to oblige!

**12 ounces Cremed Fondant (page 84)**

1. Prepare 12 ounces of fondant, break into small pieces, and reserve.

**2 batches Mazetta (page 86)**

2. Prepare a double batch of Mazetta and reserve.

**1¾ cups nuts of your choice, chopped (Filberts would be most French. And you can use them whole, if they're small. They should be blanched in any case.)**

3. Chop and reserve.

4. Prepare the marble slab. It should be cold and equipped with perimeter bars to allow you the depth of batch you want. You needn't oil or dampen the slab and bars. If instead of slab and bars, you prefer to use a baking sheet with sides to mold the batch, it should be lined with waxed paper.

**1 pound semi-sweet chocolate (couverture)**
**1 pound milk chocolate (couverture)**

5. Chop into chunks and put them into the top pot of a double boiler.

6. Add to the chocolate, and melt together over hot water. Make sure that the surface of the water underneath is well below the top pot—about an inch. Make certain, also, that no moisture gets into the mixture. Melt to *110* degrees.

7. Pour the melted mixture into a 5-quart saucepan. Add the Mazetta, Cremed Fondant, and condensed milk. Warm over low heat, mashing and blending with a wooden spoon, until the entire mass is melted, *120* to *130* degrees. Remove from heat.

8. Continue stirring until batch starts to thicken. Add salt and vanilla. (At first the oils may separate, but they will emulsify again.) When all is blended and smooth, stir in the chopped nuts. The mixture will be like a paste, with a texture unlike that of other fudges.

9. Scrape the batch onto the prepared slab or into the prepared baking pan.

10. In order for the chocolate to set up, the temperature of the room should not be above 70 degrees. If necessary, use the refrigerator until it sets. It won't take long.

11. When the batch is thoroughly cool, cut into pieces (after turning it out onto a flat work surface if you've had it in a baking pan). Otherwise cut it on the slab. Store in an airtight container.

**6 tablespoons butter**

**8 ounces sweetened condensed milk**

**⅛ teaspoon salt**
**1 teaspoon vanilla extract**

**MELTING CHOCOLATE:** Chop chocolate small. Pour water into the bottom pot of a double boiler to within 1 inch of the top pot. Bring barely to a simmer and no more. Then put the chocolate in the top part of the double boiler and place it over the warm water. Stirring constantly, slowly melt the chocolate.

CAUTION: Melted chocolate, by itself (not buffered by other ingredients), must never be allowed to reach a temperature higher than *120* degrees. This rule will allow you to melt—and remelt—chocolate without harming it. A rapid-rise thermometer is helpful for monitoring chocolate temperatures.

ALSO: Make very sure that no steam or condensation from the spoon comes in contact with the chocolate—at any point. If the natural starch in chocolate combines with water, the mass will thicken, making it lumpy and unusable.

# ICE CREAM FUDGE

No one in the present family knows how this extraordinary fudge got its name. The speculation is that because it has such an unusual stand-up quality (all that cocoa butter), it would be a particularly good fudge to use for a ripple effect in ice cream—the dark chocolate type, for instance. But even if mysteries don't intrigue you, the fudge will. It's wonderful.

**½ batch Cremed Fondant (page 84)**

1. Make half a batch of Cremed Fondant, preferably the day before you want to use it. The only change in the master recipe is that you will cook the present batch to *242* degrees instead of 240 degrees.

**1 batch Mazetta (page 86)**

2. Make a full batch of Mazetta. Reserve.

3. After the fondant is finished and cooled, preferably overnight, melt it in the top pot of a double boiler to the consistency of thin melted chocolate.

**½ pound cocoa butter**

4. While the fondant is melting, gently heat the cocoa butter in a small saucepan just until it is melted, then cool thoroughly. It will still be liquid.

5. When both are ready, stir the cocoa butter into the fondant alternately with the Mazetta, a little at a time, just until the additions are incorporated into the fondant.

6. At this point, the batch may be divided, colored and flavored in numerous ways.

**1 teaspoon vanilla**
**1 cup chopped English walnuts**

7. Our favorite style (undivided) requires simply 1 teaspoon of vanilla extract and 1 cup of chopped walnuts, stirred in as soon as the cocoa butter and Mazetta are in.

8. Scrape the batch out onto waxed paper between ¾-inch bars. Or into a waxed-paper-lined baking pan about 8x8-inch depending on how thick you want your finished candy to be.

9. When the batch is thoroughly cooled, cut into squares.

10. Store in an airtight container. Or dip in chocolate.

**VARIATIONS:**

1. To the above formula, step 7, add ½ pound macaroon coconut or fresh grated coconut and ½ teaspoon vanilla extract. For a little special touch, add, at the same time as the vanilla and coconut, ½ teaspoon pineapple flavoring with a little yellow coloring. And further, if you want a more positive fruit flavor, add also ¼ teaspoon fruit acid (equal parts powdered citric acid and water, combined).

2. In step 7, instead of the walnuts, use 1 cup chopped pistachio nuts, ½ teaspoon pistachio flavor (or a few drops of almond extract), ½ teaspoon vanilla extract. And color the batch a pastel green.

# CARAMEL FUDGE IN THREE LAYERS

This thrice-blest fudge has little surprises in each of its layers. Doesn't that make it three times as good as ordinary fudge?

## RECIPE FOR TOP AND BOTTOM LAYERS

This first batch will be divided to form the top and bottom layers. The recipe for the middle layer directly follows this one.

1. Line two cookie sheets with waxed paper. Dimensions should be roughly 1x10x15 inches.

2. Prepare the slab. It should be cold and slightly damp. Break up the fondant into small pieces and scatter them evenly over the surface of the slab.

3. Prepare and reserve.

4. Measure and reserve.

For true caramel flavor in fudge, you can substitute an equal amount of caramelized sugar for the corn syrup in a recipe. Either syrup will serve equally well as a "doctor." This is because when sugar alone (not in a batch with other ingredients) is cooked past 265 degrees, it begins to invert. When it reaches 290 degrees, it is entirely inverted. This means that it cannot be reconstituted in a crystalline form. Hence, once inverted, it has the same capacity as corn syrup to inhibit premature graining in a batch.

**NOTE: See Notes for the master recipe, Cremed Fudge, page 62.**

½ **pound Cremed Fondant (page 84)**

1 **batch Mazetta (page 86)**

2 **cups Spanish peanuts, dry roasted, without husks**

77

**2 cups granulated sugar**
**⅓ cup water**

5. Caramelize the sugar: Measure the sugar and water into a 5-quart saucepan. Blend thoroughly before starting to cook. (This mixture will not be deep enough for a thermometer to register, so you won't use one. Your eye—and good judgment—will have to serve instead.) Place pan on burner. Bring the mixture to a boil. Wash down the sides of the saucepan with a pastry brush dipped in water. Cook, without stirring, until the syrup is a pleasing golden brown. This will be at approximately *320* degrees (in case you have a thermometer that will register in this situation). Remove from heat. Cool slightly to prevent spattering when other ingredients are added.

**6 tablespoons butter**
**3¼ cups granulated sugar**
**½ cup whipping cream**
**⅛ teaspoon salt**
**¼ cup water**

6. Add to the caramelized sugar— off heat. Blend thoroughly. Caramel will harden. Not to worry! It will dissolve again. Bring the batch to a boil, stirring all the while, to help dissolve the caramel. Wash down again. Insert the thermometer this time. Cook, stirring constantly, to *242* degrees. Remove from heat.

7. Pour the hot syrup over the fondant on the prepared slab. Cool the batch to lukewarm. (It won't take as long as usual due to the cooling effect of the already cold prepared fondant.)

8. Press out any lumps of fondant still remaining in the batch. CREME. (For detailed instructions, see master recipe, Cremed Fudge, steps 4, 5, and 6.)

Remember that the reason for using fondant is to make cremeing go faster. Watch for graining in half the usual time— or even less.

## CREME THE BATCH

**1 teaspoon vanilla extract**

9. When graining starts, blend in half the Mazetta. As soon as that's incorporated, blend in the other half. Then add the reserved peanuts and the vanilla. Continue cremeing until the batch is almost ready to "set." It won't take long.

10. Divide the batch between the two prepared cookie sheets and spread it out evenly to a thickness of about ¼ inch. Allow it to become quite firm before combining it with the middle layer.

# RECIPE FOR MIDDLE LAYER

1. Weigh and reserve.

**1 pound Cremed Fondant**

2. Prepare the slab.

3. Prepare and reserve.

**½ batch Mazetta**

4. Weigh and reserve.

**4 ounces shredded coconut**

5. Measure into a 3-quart saucepan. Blend thoroughly. Boil. Wash down. Insert thermometer. Cook, stirring constantly, to *245* degrees. Remove from heat.

**4 tablespoons butter**
**1½ cups granulated sugar**
**¾ cup light corn syrup**
**⅛ teaspoon salt**
**½ cup water**

6. Pour the hot syrup over the fondant on the prepared slab. Cool to lukewarm.

7. Press out any lumps of fondant remaining in the batch. CREME.

**CREME THE BATCH**

8. When graining starts, blend in the Mazetta. When it is fully incorporated, add the reserved coconut and the vanilla. Continue cremeing until the batch is almost set. It won't take long.

**1 teaspoon vanilla extract**

# FINAL ASSEMBLY

1. Scrape the middle layer batch onto the top of one of the cooled layers already residing in a cookie sheet. Spread it smooth with your trusty spatula.

2. When this middle layer has become fairly firm, turn over the remaining cookie-sheet layer on top of all. Press down firmly. Cool. Cut. Store in an airtight container.

3. Before serving, allow the finished fudge a full day to set up and fully grain off.

# PLUM PUDDING FUDGE IN TWO LAYERS

NOTE: See notes for the master recipe, Cremed Fudge, page 62.

This extraordinary fudge makes a delicious dessert.

## RECIPE FOR BOTTOM LAYER

**12 ounces Cremed Fondant (page 84)**

1. Line a cookie sheet, about 10x15x1 inches, with waxed paper.

2. Prepare the slab. It should be cold and slightly damp. Break up the fondant into small pieces and scatter them evenly over the surface of the slab.

**1 batch Mazetta (page 86)**

3. Prepare and reserve.

**6 ounces dried figs**
**5 ounces pitted dried prunes**

4. Weigh, chop and reserve.

**3 ounces white chocolate**

5. Weigh. Chop. Reserve.

**4⅔ cups granulated sugar**
**1⅓ cups light corn syrup**
**1¼ cups whipping cream**
**The reserved white chocolate**
**⅛ teaspoon salt**
**1½ cups water**

6. Measure into a 5-quart saucepan. Blend thoroughly. Bring to a boil. Wash down the sides of the pan with a pastry brush dipped in water. Insert the thermometer. Cook, stirring constantly, to **246** degrees. Remove from heat.

7. Pour the hot syrup over the fondant on the prepared slab. Cool to lukewarm.

**CREME THE BATCH**

8. Press out any lumps of fondant still remaining in the batch. CREME. (See master recipe, Cremed Fudge, steps 4, 5, and 6.)
   The reason for using fondant is to make cremeing go faster. Watch for graining in half the usual time—or even less.

**1 teaspoon orange extract**

9. As soon as graining starts, blend in half the Mazetta. When that's incorporated, blend in the other half. Then add the orange extract and the reserved figs and prunes. Continue cremeing until the batch is almost ready to "set."

10. Remove to the prepared cookie sheet and smooth the surface with a spatula.

11. Allow to set up firm before adding the top layer.

# RECIPE FOR TOP LAYER

1. Prepare the slab.

2. Weigh. Break into small pieces and scatter them evenly over the cold damp slab.

3. Prepare and reserve.

4. Weigh. Chop. Reserve.

5. Weigh and reserve.

6. Weigh. Chop. Reserve.

7. Measure into a 3-quart saucepan. Blend thoroughly. Boil. Wash down. Insert thermometer. Cook, stirring constantly, to *246* degrees. Remove from heat.

8. Pour the hot syrup over the fondant on the prepared slab. Cool to lukewarm.

9. Press out any lumps of fondant remaining in the batch. CREME.

10. When graining starts, blend in the Mazetta, half at a time. As soon as both halves have been incorporated, add the reserved coconut, fruits, and vanilla. Continue cremeing until the batch is almost set.

1½ pounds Cremed Fondant (page 84)

1 batch Mazetta (page 86)

4 ounces white chocolate

5 ounces coconut, desiccated, medium grade

5 ounces glazed cherries
5 ounces glazed pineapple

4 cups granulated sugar
1 cup light corn syrup
The reserved white chocolate
⅛ teaspoon salt
¼ cup water

**CREME THE BATCH**

1 teaspoon vanilla extract

# FINAL ASSEMBLY

1. Scrape this second batch onto the top of the first layer. Spread it smooth. Let it rest until firm, but not fully cold.

2. While it still retains a little heat, cut through both layers into serving pieces, using a wet knife.

3. When the batch is cold and fully set, turn it out onto a flat surface and remove the paper. Separate pieces. Let all surfaces dry. Then store in an airtight container.

A batch containing just sugar, corn syrup, and water—like fondant, for instance—may be cooked without stirring after it comes to a boil. It will not burn under 265 degrees. This is not true of candies containing milk or chocolate. They scorch very readily.

# The Support Group

This group comprises those confections which are basic to many other, more complex candies. They're the good little missionaries given to anonymity and good works, whose hands are busy everywhere helping others—and improving the character of all about them.

The chief of this group is the fondants. Also very useful is the mazetta. And a whole phalanx of marshmallows. Not to mention the sugar syrups of obliging disposition. There are others, but let us talk of the fondants first. In the following recipes we've presented several basic formulas for fondants, along with a discussion of the major use of each in other confections. You'll need to use these as just one ingredient in many of the other recipes in this book. Fondants are "cremed" like fudges, and in fact one could argue with logic that fudges are flavored fondants. Fondants are deliberately left unflavored so that they will blend into the background. They are never eaten just by themselves.

As to mazetta, it is a sort of meringue that is used to lighten the texture of cremes and other candies.

And the syrups? They're used in several applications—as you'll see.

But marshmallows. Ah, marshmallows! Any kid who grew up loving S'mores—or hot chocolate made sumptuous by a floating island of marshmallow cream—would be astonished to find out how simple it is to make creamy, fresh, melt-in-the mouth marshmallow, right in his own kitchen. And

what's more, he would never again consent to buy the fluffy little nuggets that are going to glorify *his* Rocky Road, or going to be dipped in *his* milk chocolate. Or if it's his wife who's the cook, vice versa. And if they're both cooks, then they've already discovered, and agree, that *fresh is better*, whether you're talking about marshmallows or, say, egg noodles, or Almond Butter Crisp, or ...

But discover your own additions to the list. It's long and wide open. Jump in any time with your own candidates. But be warned: A trained palate is a formidable taskmaster. You'll have to be prepared to curse it as a mixed blessing as often as you feel grateful for it!

# Master Recipe
# CREMED FONDANT

Simple fondants and plain hard candies should not be stirred after they come to a boil. In fact, any sugar solution that does not contain some form of colloid such as butter or cream (as do the fudges, caramels, and brittles) should not be stirred after the initial mixing, bringing to a boil and washing down. To do so may start a grain.

4 cups granulated sugar
⅝ cup light corn syrup
1 cup water

## CREME THE BATCH

NOTE: For explanation of the confectioner's term, "creme," see page 61. Also read the notes on Cremed Fudge, page 63, which apply equally to fondant.

This is a very creamy fondant. It's the basic cream for most of the cream centers that go into dipped chocolates. In Grandpa's notes, it was often referred to as bonbon creme.
Following this recipe are other fondants just as basic to other applications, such as a fondant which is used for a dipping medium—as an alternative to chocolate.

Slight differences in formula make these fondants highly specialized in the confectioner's world, but the procedural steps are essentially the same for all.

1. Prepare the marble slab: it should be cold and slightly damp. Dimensions ought to be at least 16x24 inches. (See "Utensils" section, page 16, for discussion of slabs.)

2. Measure into a 3-quart saucepan. Blend thoroughly before placing on the burner. Bring to a boil. Wash down the sides of the pan with a pastry brush dipped in water. Put the thermometer in the batch. Then cook, *without stirring*, to **240** degrees.

3. Pour out carefully onto the cool, damp slab. Do not scrape the pan. Allow the batch to cool down to lukewarm. Then CREME. (We've described this procedure in step 4 of CREMED FUDGE, but feel it bears repeating here.)
Use a 3½- to 4-inch candy scraper or wall scraper. Work the batch in parallel lines from one end of the slab to the other. Starting at one end, run about half the scraper's width under the edge of the batch. Scrape through to the other end. Then turn the scraper over and bring it back across the top of the batch. Repeat this over and over, working back and forth up and down the slab from one edge to the other, scraping the surface well whenever the metal is in contact with the slab. (Remember, it's the friction of the scraper against the slab that causes the fondant to creme.) Continue this motion, in easy rhythmical strokes, taking your time. But once started, do not stop until a white "creme" begins to form clearly on the back edge of the scraper. This is the indication that the batch is starting to creme. Normal time for this process is about 10 minutes.

4. Continue cremeing until the fondant begins to lose its translucent quality and starts to hold its shape. It will become increasingly opaque.

5. Just before the batch "sets" (it won't take long at this stage), remove it to a lightly oiled platter or pack it into a loaf pan lined with waxed paper. Use the scraper for this, along with a metal spatula in the other hand to scrape the fondant off the scraper. Smooth out and let cool.

6. Generally speaking, fondant should be allowed to ripen for 24 hours. You can keep fondant for a long time if you wrap it in heavy plastic wrap and store it in the refrigerator in a tightly covered plastic bowl, to keep it from drying out. And it will dry out even more slowly if you leave the batch in a block, uncut.

**We always cook a batch of candy as quickly as possible, because prolonged cooking starts inversion in sucrose, and too much inversion can toughen fondants and fudges and make them hard to creme—and chewy. In candies with a higher cook, excessive inversion causes stickiness.**

FONDANT FOR CHERRY CORDIALS
This is made exactly like Cremed Fondant except:

1. Use ⅓ cup corn syrup instead of ⅝ cup (step 2).

2. Just after the batch starts to creme (end of step 3), add 2 teaspoons lemon juice if you think the cherries are too sweet. Or add ½ teaspoon citric acid powder which has been made into a paste with an equal quantity of water. You may also add at this time ⅛ teaspoon of commercial invertase (trade name Convertit, available in cake-baking supply houses).

3. Continue cremeing the batch, blending in the optional flavoring and the optional invertase as you go, until the batch starts to set (step 4). Proceed as in Cremed Fondant.

4. Store for 24 hours before using as part of the Cherry Cordials recipe on page 169.

**VARIATION**

REMARKS: Invertase is a preparation involving yeast, which helps convert sugar into invert sugar. Invert sugar is sugar which has lost the ability to crystallize.

In other words, when we add invertase to the fondant which is going to coat the cherry, and then in turn will itself be coated with chocolate, the sugar in that fondant will become increasingly liquid over time.

The juice remaining in the cherries will accomplish the same thing, but possibly not as completely. There are many variables, so using invertase is one way of making more certain of dissolving the fondant completely, if that is desired.

And that's how the liquid cordial gets into the inside of Cherry Cordials.

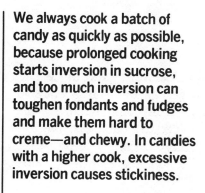

# CREAM OF TARTAR FONDANT

4 cups granulated sugar
2 cups water
¼ teaspoon cream of tartar

**CREME THE BATCH**

This fondant uses cream of tartar, an acid, to "doctor" the batch. Hence no need for corn syrup to impede premature graining. The finished fondant sets up rather more firm than the others, although it is also more tender. It has what confectioners call a "short" texture. (When you tear a chunk off a block, it breaks clean. The others pull, leaving a thin thread of confection behind.) But even so, it still has very soft, smooth sugar crystals.

One of the greatest advantages of this formula is that you can roll it out and cut it—and it will hold its shape vertically. The sides of the cut won't bulge. And still it is so tender that it dissolves more quickly and completely in the mouth than any of the others.

Cream of tartar is seldom used anymore in commercial fondant. We use it because, for us, it's the only acceptable way to get the texture we want for certain applications.

1. Prepare the slab. It should be cold and slightly damp.

2. Measure the sugar and water into a 3-quart saucepan. Blend. Bring to a boil. Add the cream of tartar. Wash down the sides of the pan. Insert the thermometer.

3. Cook, *without stirring*, to **236** degrees. Or if you want a softer fondant, cook to **234** degrees. Remove from heat.

4. Pour out carefully on the cold damp slab. Do not scrape the pan.

5. Cool to lukewarm. CREME as in the master recipe, Cremed Fondant. Then follow the rest of the steps in the master.

# MAZETTA

This is a meringue made with corn syrup or glucose instead of granulated sugar. We confectioners turn to it when we want to lighten the texture of a fudge or perhaps a cream center that is going to be dipped. It aerates the batch a bit. And it lends a useful quantity of extra corn syrup. This attracts a little moisture to soften the batch—when desired. A very obliging little helper. Mazetta, frappe, egg frappe, egg cream, nougat cream. We call it by many names—and we call *on* it often.

1. Beat with a rotary beater until soft peaks form. Reserve.

2. Boil in a small saucepan, without stirring, to **226** degrees.

3. Add the syrup slowly, in a thin stream, to the beaten egg white, beating all the while. Continue beating until stiff.

4. If you don't intend to use the Mazetta immediately, scrape it into a plastic bowl with a tight-fitting lid and refrigerate. It will keep for several weeks.

**1 medium egg white**

**⅝ cup light corn syrup**

**NOTE: One batch of Mazetta (calling for 1 egg white) is used for approximately 2½ pounds of creme center or fondant.**

# COATING FONDANT

We sometimes use this fondant for coating other centers—instead of chocolate or white chocolate. We just melt it over hot water as if it were chocolate, and dip away. (See recipes in the section on dipping.) This formula won't harden like Cream of Tartar Fondant, and it has a nice gloss.

1. Prepare the slab. It should be cold and slightly damp.

2. Measure into a 3-quart saucepan. Blend thoroughly. Boil. Wash down. Insert thermometer.

**4 cups granulated sugar**
**1½ cups water**

3. Cook, without stirring, to **236** degrees. Remove from heat.

4. Pour out carefully on the cold damp slab. Do not scrape the pan.

5. Cool to lukewarm. CREME as in the master recipe for Cremed Fondant.

**CREME THE BATCH**

6. As soon as the batch starts to grain, add the glycerin—as if it were vanilla, for example.

**2 teaspoons glycerin (available at your pharmacy).**

7. Just before the batch sets, remove it to an oiled platter or pack it into a loaf pan lined with waxed paper. Smooth out with a spatula. Cool thoroughly. See master recipe, Cremed Fondant, for advice about ripening and storing.

# CRYSTAL SYRUP

This is a syrup for coating bonbons and chocolates in a special way, to make them sparkle!

**6 cups granulated sugar**
**2 cups water**

1. Measure into a 5-quart saucepan. Blend thoroughly. Bring to a boil. Wash down the sides of the pan with a pastry brush dipped in water. Insert thermometer. Cook to **224** degrees.

2. Place the pan immediately into cold water to cool the syrup quickly.

3. Sprinkle the top of the solution with a small amount of cold water. Don't use too much water. It will slack back the batch. If crystals should appear on top, sprinkle with sufficient water to redissolve them.

**Candies to be crystallized**

4. Put the candies into a wire basket with a wire cover.

5. When the syrup has cooled to **85** degrees, submerge the basket in the syrup, and leave it undisturbed for two hours. The colder the syrup, the longer the crystals take to form.

6. Raise the basket after two hours and let the syrup drain off the candy back into the kettle. Then spread the candy out on waxed paper and allow it to dry. Behold the transformation wrought by crystal!

# SIMPLE SYRUP

We keep this on hand all the time for thinning fondants and for making flavored syrups. The corn syrup can be omitted and one teaspoon glycerin (available at pharmacies) stirred in at the end of the boil instead.

**4 cups granulated sugar**
**2 cups water**
**2 tablespoons light corn syrup**

1. Measure into a 3-quart saucepan. Blend thoroughly. Boil. Wash down. Insert thermometer. Cook to **222** degrees, without stirring. Remove from heat.

2. After syrup is thoroughly cool, store in an airtight bottle.

# CLARIFIED BUTTER

Why clarify butter that will go into chocolate? Because all the moisture in butter lies in the milk solids. And you know about chocolate and moisture. So clarify the butter. Milk solids removed. Nutty, sweet butterfat marries well with chocolate. Everybody's happy.

1. In a heavy saucepan, completely melt the butter over very low heat. Remove from heat.

2. Let stand 3 to 5 minutes. When the froth has separated, completely skim it off the top.

3. Carefully pour off the clear oil, leaving the solids to other uses, flavoring cooked vegetables, for example.

4. Pour the oil through cheesecloth several times, if necessary, to make perfectly clear.

5. Store in a tightly sealed jar in the refrigerator. It will keep almost indefinitely. Yields about ¼ less than the original volume.

**Most butter contains 15 percent moisture. (A tip: Clarify the butter before putting it on your popcorn and it won't make the popcorn soggy.)**

**½ pound butter, unsalted**

# TO PREPARE FRESH COCONUT FOR SHREDDING

1. With a screwdriver, pierce through the three eyes.

2. Drain off the liquid.

3. Turn the coconut on its side and tap sharply with a hammer until the coconut fractures.

4. With a sharp knife, remove the brown skin from the coconut meat. (We use a carpenter's tool called a "spoke shave," but a knife will do.)

5. Grate the coconut the hard way. Or use a food processor.

**Fresh coconut candies are almost impossible to find. You'll probably have to make your own, if you want to experience them. When coconut is pre-prepared it is desiccated, meaning that the moisture is taken away. It comes in a variety of shred sizes. To choose a size, determine whether you want the "feel" of coconut as well as the taste. Health food stores usually carry some nice larger-sized coconut shreds.**

# PRALINE POWDER AND PRALINE PASTE

Praline is the French designation for what we call burnt almonds (toasted almonds with a coating of caramelized sugar). By extension, our nut brittles (as in peanut brittle) are also pralines. Anywhere in Europe, praline is usually made with almonds or hazelnuts, or a combination of the two, so when we think of pralined confections, we're thinking of something that will give the flavor of filberts or almonds to the finished candy.

The easiest way to use praline in a recipe is to make a powder or paste of it. So for a base, use one of the formulas in the "Brittles" section, and make it with filberts or almonds. Or make a batch of Burnt Peanuts, page 124, substituting almonds (or filberts) for the peanuts. Obviously, the nut brittle will give you more caramel flavor, and the burnt almonds more nut flavor. Your choice.

After the batch you've chosen is cool, break it into small pieces and grind it very fine. A food processor is excellent for this, but process in short bursts until you have the texture you want. Store in a jar with a tight seal—to keep your powder dry.

If you want praline paste, simply process past the powder stage. The batch will turn into a paste something like peanut butter. Store this also in an airtight container.

All of the above can be accomplished with a blender, food grinder, or grunt-and-groan style with a mortar and pestle.

**NOTE: For dark nut brittle, cook the batch to a full 320 degrees and leave the husks on the nuts. For a light batch of praline, use blanched nuts, and cook just to light golden brown, 310 degrees or so.**

# GANACHE OR TRUFFLE PASTE

In the Truffles section, you will find the Royal Chocolate Truffle formula. We call it basic because it uses the standard ratio of cream (plus other liquids) to chocolate couverture. The result is a strong chocolate flavor and a firm enough texture for ease of handling. This is especially important when combining truffle paste with other types of candy center. This truffle paste is often referred to as Ganache. The basic formula for Ganache, then, is 2 parts chocolate couverture to 1 part cream. You may steep coffee or tea with the cream. Then filter it before using.

1. Measure the cream into a saucepan and bring just to the boil. Remove from heat at once and cool to *120* degrees.

2. Chop the chocolate fine and melt it in a double boiler to *120* degrees.

3. Add the chocolate to the cooled cream (not the cream to the chocolate) and stir until the mixture is smooth.

4. Scrape the batch onto a cookie sheet, spreading it evenly.

5. Refrigerate for half an hour or so, or until firm.

6. The Ganache is now ready to combine with other recipes— or to use as a truffle base just as it is.

**1 batch of Ganache, for our purposes, is:**

**1 cup whipping cream**

**1 pound chocolate (couverture), semisweet or milk chocolate**

# GIANDUJA

This is a very useful helper. And easy to do—in a food processor. Great-Uncle Julius called it Figaro paste. Standard proportions are 2 parts by weight of nuts and 1 part by weight of sugar. Cocoa butter is added in the proportion of 1 ounce (weight), melted, for each 2 pounds of finished paste.

1. Lightly roast the nuts. If you're using hazelnuts remove the skins after roasting.

2. Melt the cocoa butter. Reserve.

3. Grate the nuts in your food processor with the powdered sugar until the mixture starts to bind together.

4. Now, with blade running, add the melted cocoa butter.

5. Scrape the batch out onto a work surface and knead it to a paste.

6. Keep the Gianduja stored in an airtight container.

**1 batch of Gianduja, for our needs in this book is:**

**2¾ cups almonds or hazelnuts, or a combination of both**

**2 cups powdered sugar**

**2 ounces (weight) cocoa butter**

# MARSHMALLOW

Marshmallow. That most delicate, that lightest, that fluffiest of confections! Do you know what category confectioners relegate marshmallows to? Whipped goods! Fie on all of us who are guilty of such prosy insensitivity!

In atonement, allow us to offer you a variety of whipped g...uh...marshmallows. These will lend themselves to any number of delightful applications.

But first, a thumbnail sketch. Marshmallows are either coated or uncoated, cast or slab cut, grained or ungrained, made with gelatin or egg white (or a combination of both).

The oldest recipes my grandfather left are combinations of sugar, corn syrup, egg white and gum arabic. Gum arabic is not easy to find nowadays, although it is an excellent product. Today, the professionals use cornstarch as a substitute. And gelatin is most commonly used instead of egg white for the whipping agent.

Cast marshmallows are very difficult to make. They require special equipment and control of room temperatures. They will remain a factory product. Cast marshmallow is the most widely produced commercial type at present.

As for cut marshmallows, the only kind we make at home, they're more interesting anyway. If you make them yourself, you can completely control their texture and flavor, their moistness and tenderness. *Andiamo*!

There is a plant called "marsh mallow" which is closely related to the hollyhock. This plant secretes a gumlike juice. At one time the juice was used as a binding agent for a foamy egg-white confection—the forerunner of our present-day marshmallows.

*Gum arabic* (acacia) is used as a colloid or binding agent—or for glazes. It is not as common as it once was, because it has been replaced by many synthetic types of gums. We use gum arabic to make a glaze for our chocolate dragees (panned goods). The chief source of gum arabic is the Sudan.

# MARSHMALLOW I

This is perhaps the most stable of all the marshmallows. We can thank the cornstarch for that. And your Rocky Road will be grateful, too! This marshmallow will keep its cool and not weep into the chocolate.

1. Line a baking dish with plain wrapping paper. Dimensions should be about 1x10x15 inches. Or if you prefer, arrange 1-inch bars on a marble slab covered with paper. (You can stack two half-inch bars to arrive at the one-inch height required. Or you can use ½-inch bars and make miniature marshmallows. We're not dictators.) See "Utensils" for discussion of bars (page 16).

2. Stir together in the large bowl of an electric mixer—to allow the gelatin to soften before use.

**6 packets granulated gelatin (¼-ounce packets)**
**¾ cup cold water**

3. Measure and reserve.

**3⅓ cups light corn syrup**

4. Measure into a 3-quart saucepan. Blend thoroughly. Cook, stirring, over low heat until mixture thickens.

**⅓ cup cornstarch**
**⅔ cup cold water**

5. Add to the cornstarch mixture and bring again to the boil, stirring constantly. Remove from heat.

**2 cups granulated sugar**

6. Immediately add the corn syrup and stir the mixture well. Pour it over the softened gelatin and stir with a spoon until the gelatin is completely dissolved.

7. Whip with a rotary beater until the mixture will hold a peak and not flow. At the last, dribble in the vanilla while still beating.

**2 teaspoons vanilla extract**

8. Scrape out into the prepared pan or onto the prepared slab. Using a damp spatula, spread the batch evenly to achieve a flat, smooth surface and uniform thickness.

9. Sprinkle the top with toasted coconut, confectioner's sugar, or rice flour (Why *rice* flour? Because it has no raw taste—unlike some other flours and starches.)

**Coconut (toasted or plain), confectioner's sugar, or rice flour for coating the cut marshmallows**

10. When cold and set, run a knife along the edges and turn out onto a flat work surface. Dampen the paper with cold water. As soon as the water has soaked through the paper, you will be able to peel it off the batch.

11. Sprinkle this side with the chosen coating—to absorb the moisture left by the damp paper. Cut into cubes with a damp butcher knife, using about 2 inches of the tip of the cutting edge and drawing it smoothly through the batch.

12. Roll each piece in coating and allow to dry for several hours or overnight, before storing in an airtight container. If marshmallows are to be dipped—or used in another recipe—brush off excess coating before such use.

**VARIATION:** Make a batch of marshmallow as directed, but cut the corn syrup to 2½ cups, and add ¾ cup strawberry jam. Use the jam as if it were corn syrup, adding it to the batch before the start of cooking. Or you can use other jams instead of strawberry.

# MARSHMALLOW II

This recipe is very different from Marshmallow I. There is no cornstarch in it. And it adds egg white to the formula—which allows us to use less corn syrup. The egg white not only lightens the batch but imparts a subtle flavor as well. This is a delicious, delicate marshmallow to eat fresh.

**8 packets granulated gelatin**
  **(¼-ounce packets)**
**¾ cup water**

1. Prepare baking dish or slab as recommended in Marshmallow I.

2. Stir together in a small saucepan. Allow the gelatin to soften. Then heat gently until it is entirely dissolved.

**2 large egg whites**

3. Separate the egg whites into the large bowl of an electric mixer. Whip with rotary beater until stiff but not dry.

**2 cups granulated sugar**
**2 tablespoons light corn syrup**
**¾ cup water**

4. Measure into a 2-quart saucepan. Blend thoroughly. Bring to a boil. Wash down the sides of the pan with a pastry brush dipped in water. Put thermometer in batch. Cook, without stirring, to *260* degrees. Remove from heat.

5. Stir the dissolved gelatin into the sugar solution. Then gently fold the mixture into the beaten egg whites. At the very last, fold in your chosen flavoring and taste for intensity. You may want to add a little more.

**2 tablespoons rosewater**
*or* **2 tablespoons orange-**
  **flower water**
*or* **1 teaspoon vanilla extract**
*or* **1 teaspoon any extract of**
  **choice—go creative!**

6. Scrape out into the prepared pan or onto the prepared slab. Using a damp spatula, spread the batch evenly to achieve a flat, smooth surface and uniform thickness. Then follow the rest of the steps as detailed in Marshmallow I.

# MARSHMALLOW III

This formula has neither cornstarch nor egg whites. What it has is a very moist and tender texture. Wonderful for eating out of hand. Even the gelatin content is low. So this batch will take a little longer to set up than Numbers I and II.

1. Prepare the baking dish or slab as recommended in Marshmallow I.

2. Soften the gelatin in the cold water. Heat gently to dissolve completely.

**6 packets granulated gelatin (¼-ounce packets)**
**½ cup water**

3. Measure into a 3-quart saucepan. Blend thoroughly. Bring to a boil. Wash down. Insert thermometer. Cook without stirring to *236* degrees.

**2 cups granulated sugar**
**⅔ cup light corn syrup**
**½ cup water**

4. Pour the mixture into the large bowl of an electric mixer.

5. Add the dissolved gelatin and stir well.

6. Stir into the batch and whip with a rotary beater for 15 to 20 minutes, or until the batch is fluffy. It will not form stiff peaks. At the last, dribble in the vanilla while still beating.

**2⅓ cups light corn syrup**

**1 teaspoon vanilla extract**

7. Scrape out into the prepared pan or onto the prepared slab. Using a damp spatula, spread the batch evenly to achieve a flat, smooth surface and uniform thickness. Then follow the rest of the steps as detailed in Marshmallow I.

*Gum tragacanth* **is obtained from the leguminous plant known as Astragalus gummifer by exudation following incision. It is used to make jellies. It absorbs 50 times its weight in water.**

# MARSHMALLOW IV

This is an excellent marshmallow for dipping in chocolate or for making rocky road. It uses egg white for a whipping agent, with an accompanying gain in flavor. And relies on cornstarch for added stability. It is tender. And the texture is short—which means it holds its shape after it's cut.

1. Line a baking dish with plain wrapping paper. Dimensions should be about 1x10x15 inches. Or, if you prefer, arrange 1-inch bars on a marble slab covered with paper. (You can stack two ½-inch bars to arrive at the 1-inch height required.)

**6 medium egg whites, unbeaten**

2. Separate the egg whites into a small bowl and reserve.

**6 packets granulated gelatin (¼-ounce packets)**
**½ cup cold water**

3. Soften the gelatin in the cold water. Dissolve completely over hot water. It will require about 120 degrees to do the job.

**1⅓ cups light corn syrup**

4. Measure into the large bowl of an electric mixer. Reserve.

**¼ cup cornstarch**
**⅓ cup water**

5. Mix together in a small bowl. Reserve.

**2 cups granulated sugar**
**⅔ cup light corn syrup**
**⅔ cup water**

6. Measure into a 3-quart saucepan. Bring to a boil. Wash down the sides of the pan. Insert the thermometer. Stir in the cornstarch solution. Cook, stirring constantly, to *238* degrees.

7. Stir immediately into the large bowl containing the reserved corn syrup. Whip with rotary beater until cooled to *160* degrees.

8. Add the egg whites and beat until batch is light and fluffy.

**2 teaspoons vanilla extract**
**_or_ 2 teaspoons other extract of choice**
**_or_ 1 teaspoon peppermint extract together with 1 teaspoon vanilla extract**

9. Turn down the speed and add the dissolved gelatin in a thin stream until it is completely incorporated. At the last, dribble in the vanilla. *Or* other extract of your choice. You might like to try 1 teaspoon of peppermint extract. But in that case, use 1 teaspoon of vanilla as well.

NOTE: This batch should have four hours, minimum, to set. Overnight is better.

10. Scrape out into the prepared pan or onto the prepared slab. Using a damp spatula, spread the batch evenly to achieve a flat, smooth surface and uniform thickness. Then follow the rest of the steps as detailed in Marshmallow I.

# MARSHMALLOW V

This is a cold prepared marshmallow especially formulated to be piped through a pastry bag. It sets up firm, so it's wonderful to use in cake decorating. And it serves very well as a filling between cake layers. You creative cooks out there will think of half a dozen chores for such a willing assistant.

Obviously, you'll want to have your cake ready to decorate—or to layer—before you start making the marshmallow. Because you can't pipe or spread the batch once it has set.

1. Mix together. Wait until the gelatin is softened, then heat over hot water to dissolve completely. Pour into the large bowl of an electric mixer.

**3 packets granulated gelatin (¼-ounce packets)**
**⅔ cup water**

2. With the rotary beater on slow, add the powdered sugar and corn syrup, then beat until the marshmallow is light and will hold its peak. Dribble in the vanilla at the very last. Do not overbeat. If the mixture becomes too stiff, it may be thinned with a tablespoonful at a time of hot water.

**1 pound powdered sugar**
**⅔ cup light corn syrup**

**1 teaspoon vanilla extract**

3. The marshmallow is now ready for duty. Use immediately.

4. If you have some of the batch left over, you can always pipe it in teardrop shapes onto waxed paper sprinkled with finely chopped nuts or toasted coconut. Sprinkle more of the same over the top, and garnish with a whole nut or glazed cherry.

*Agar agar* **is a very valuable gelling agent. It is refined from seaweed. It is processed primarily in Japan and Australia. Because of its relatively high cost it has fallen out of fashion in the confectionery industry. It produces remarkably tender jellies. It is commonly found in health food stores today along with some recipes for candy. If you like jellies try it.**

# Caramels to Chewy Toffee

## Master Recipe
## GRANDPA'S CREAM CARAMELS

To our family, this is the definitive caramel. We've offered you an option that Grandpa noted, just as it was written down in his own hand. Some of us prefer the taste and texture of the cream/evaporated milk version, some the one that uses only cream. To you the decision. But you'll probably find, as most of the family does, that you'll like them both—and alternate from time to time. Same situation for the optional chocolate.

A number of the caramel formulas which follow ask for cocoa butter. If we've stipulated it, we think it's essential to the texture. So find yourself a source for this commodity and try not to substitute. If absolutely necessary, you can use coconut butter, but it's nearly as hard to find as cocoa butter. As for dairy butter, you can use it, and it will give you good flavor, but it has a low melting point that does not contribute to the "stand up" quality that we're seeking here.

1. Prepare the marble slab and ½-inch bars. Dimensions of the slab should be about ¾x16x24 inches. Wipe both slab and bars with mineral oil. They should be cold.

**Optional: 1 cup English walnuts, chopped**

2. Chop and reserve.

**Optional: 2 ounces baking chocolate (unsweetened), chopped**

3. Chop and reserve.

**1⅔ cups light corn syrup**

4. Measure into a small saucepan and heat to boiling. Remove from heat, but keep hot.

5. Measure sugar and *1 pint* cream into a 3-quart saucepan. Blend thoroughly. On heat, bring to a boil, stirring constantly. Continuing to stir, wash down the sides of the pan with a pastry brush dipped in water. Insert the thermometer. After a moment or two, with the batch boiling freely, slowly stir in the rest of the cream—or the evaporated milk. Don't stop the boil (cream or milk may curdle). And don't stop stirring.

**2 cups granulated sugar**
**1 quart whipping cream, divided**
***Or* 1 pint whipping cream and 1 pint evaporated milk**

6. After all of the cream, or cream-and-milk, are safely in the batch, and the boil looks normal again, stir in the cocoa butter and salt. After a minute or two, slowly add the hot corn syrup. Make these additions without stopping the boil. Cook, still stirring constantly, to **243** degrees.

**2 ounces cocoa butter**
**½ teaspoon salt**

7. Off heat, gently stir in the vanilla. (If you're going to add the optional chocolate or the optional nuts or both, this is the time to do it. Fold them in carefully along with the vanilla. Too much stirring could start a grain!)

**1 teaspoon vanilla extract**

8. Pour the batch out onto the prepared slab, between the ½-inch bars, to a depth of ½ inch.

9. When thoroughly cold, cut into ½-inch cubes, using a sharp knife. If you move the knife back and forth quickly, the caramel will hold its shape and will not stick to the blade.

10. To store: After pieces are cut, arrange them on a tray, not touching each other. When a light crust has formed on all surfaces, they can be stored in a bag without danger of sticking.

NOTE: 1. If you sieve nuts after chopping them, you'll get rid of all the debris, primarily bits of husk. So the candy will be clearer.

  2. Use only bitter chocolate to flavor this caramel. The sugar in sweetened chocolate could cause the candy to grain.

**While stirring, we never scrape the sides of the saucepan above the level of the boiling batch, because the friction of the spoon on the sides of the pan may create crystals and begin a grain when there is insufficient liquid to dissolve the sugar crystals.**

**A wooden spoon is best for stirring a batch of boiling candy, because it causes less friction than metal.**

# CREAM CARAMELS SOUTHERN STYLE

These are excellent caramels for wrapping in clear plastic. They are a little softer than Grandpa's, which are a stand-up caramel. It's the dairy butter, used here instead of cocoa butter, that makes the difference in texture. While brown sugar lends a faint molasses perfume to the batch.

**4 tablespoons butter**
**½ teaspoon salt**

**1 cup light corn syrup**

**1 cup granulated sugar**
**1 cup light brown sugar**
**2½ cups whipping cream, divided**

**1 teaspoon vanilla extract**

1. Prepare the slab and bars as outlined in the master recipe, Grandpa's Cream Caramels.

2. Measure and reserve.

3. Measure into a small saucepan and heat to boiling. Remove from heat, but keep hot.

4. Measure the sugars and half the cream into a 3-quart saucepan. Blend thoroughly. On heat, bring to a boil, stirring. Continuing to stir, wash down the sides of the pan. After a moment or two, with the batch boiling freely, slowly stir in the rest of the cream. Don't stop the boil. Don't stop stirring.

5. After all the cream is in the batch and the boil looks normal again, stir in the butter and salt. After a minute or two, slowly stir in the hot corn syrup. Make these additions without stopping the boil. Cook, stirring constantly, to **243** degrees. Remove from heat.

6. Off heat, gently stir in the vanilla.

7. Pour the batch out onto the prepared slab, between the ½-inch bars, to a depth of ½ inch.

8. Let rest overnight. Then cut and store as described in the master recipe.

# FRENCH EGG CARAMELS

Great-Uncle Julius brought this recipe from France. The egg gives it a wonderful rich flavor and tender texture. To attain the best of both, this caramel should be allowed to mature for at least a week.

1. Prepare the slab and bars as outlined in the master recipe, Grandpa's Cream Caramels.

2. Using a wire whip, gently break up the egg. Then slowly add the cream to it and blend well, without making the mixture foamy. Reserve.

**1 large egg**
**1 quart whipping cream**

3. Grease the sides of a 3-quart saucepan with a little butter.

4. Measure the sugar, the corn syrup, and *half* the egg-cream mixture into the buttered saucepan. Blend thoroughly. On heat, bring to a boil, stirring constantly. Continuing to stir, wash down the sides of the pan, then put the thermometer in the batch. When the batch has cooked for a few minutes and has begun to thicken, add the rest of the egg-cream very slowly. Don't stop the boil. Don't stop stirring. Cook to **243** degrees. Remove from heat.

**2 cups granulated sugar**
**1 cup light corn syrup**
**The egg-cream mixture, divided**

5. Off heat, gently stir in the vanilla. Pour the batch onto the prepared slab, between the ½-inch bars, to a depth of ½ inch.

**1 teaspoon vanilla**

6. Let rest overnight. Then cut and store as described in the master recipe.

*"Washing down."* Done to prevent crystals from invading a sugar solution, causing unwanted grain. After a batch has come to the boil, the candymaker always washes down the utensils and the sides of the pan with a pastry brushed dipped in water, to dissolve any stray sugar crystals. Any water thus added to the batch will be boiled away during the cooking.

# PEANUT CHEWS

These are wonderful dipped in chocolate. Oh, and if you're not a peanut nut, you can very well use cashews in this formula—or other nuts of your choice. But be prepared for a cheery gesundheit from the neighborhood wit if you offer him a Cashew Chew.

2¾ cups roasted Spanish peanuts, blanched

10 tablespoons butter (one stick plus 2 tablespoons)

1⅓ cups light corn syrup

2 cups granulated sugar
1 cup evaporated milk (unsweetened)
½ cup sweetened condensed milk

1 teaspoon vanilla extract

1. Prepare the slab and bars as outlined in the master recipe, Grandpa's Cream Caramels. Note that you will need one-inch bars for this recipe.

2. Measure and reserve.

3. Measure into a small saucepan and heat to boiling. Remove from heat, but keep hot.

4. Measure the sugar and the evaporated milk into a 3-quart saucepan. Blend thoroughly. On heat, bring to a boil, stirring. Continuing to stir, wash down the sides of the pan. After a moment or two, with the batch boiling freely, slowly stir in the sweetened condensed milk. Don't stop the boil or the stirring.

5. After all the milk is in the batch and the boil looks normal again, stir in the butter. After a minute or two, slowly stir in the hot corn syrup. Make these additions without stopping the boil. Cook, stirring constantly, to **242** degrees.

6. Immediately stir in the peanuts.

7. As soon as the nuts are well incorporated, remove the batch from the heat and gently stir in the vanilla.

8. Pour out on the prepared slab between the 1-inch bars to a depth of about ⅞ inch.

9. Let rest overnight. Then cut into strips ½ x 3 inches.

10. In cutting caramels, move the knife back and forth quickly so the pieces will hold their shape and not stick to the blade.

11. To store: After pieces are cut, arrange them on a tray, not touching each other. When a light crust has formed on all surfaces, they can be stored in a bag without danger of sticking together. But we recommend heartily that they be dipped in milk chocolate at this point, instead. Yum! (See section on dipping, page 138.)

# HONEY TOFFEE

A chewy toffee with a honeyed tone.

(See section on dipping, page 138.)

*Honey* is a natural invert sugar. But since it is easily scorched, it is usually added just for flavor when the cook is nearly completed.

1. Prepare the slab and ½-inch bars as recommended in the master recipe, Grandpa's Cream Caramels.

2. Measure and reserve.

**1⅔ cups light corn syrup**

3. Measure into a 3-quart saucepan and melt.

**½ pound butter**

4. Off heat, stir in the sugar and honey. Blend well. Then bring to a boil. Wash down the sides of the pan. Insert thermometer. Cook, stirring, to *290* degrees.

**2 cups granulated sugar**
**¼ cup honey**

5. Immediately stir in the corn syrup and cook, stirring, until the temperature returns to *280* degrees. Remove from heat.

6. Gently stir in the salt, the vanilla, and the optional orange extract, if desired.

**1 teaspoon salt**
**1 teaspoon vanilla extract**
**OPTIONAL: ½ teaspoon orange extract (in addition to the vanilla)**

7. Pour out on the oiled slab between prepared ½-inch bars.

8. Score in squares with a dull knife while batch is still warm.

9. When completely cool, cut through, and wrap in waxed paper.

10. Store in an airtight container. Given a little time, this toffee will mellow and soften.

# Taffies

## *Master Recipe*
# GRANDPA'S TAFFY

In this recipe, my grandfather Davenport offers us an option. We can have a chewy taffy or a brittle taffy. The degree of cook, alone, decides which. For chewy: **256** degrees. For brittle (also referred to as "dry"), **262** degrees.

**4 tablespoons butter**

**3 cups granulated sugar**
**1 ⅔ cups**
**1 cup water**

In making taffy, we add the butter to the batch just before it is taken off the fire, because the emulsification that occurs results in a dryer taffy. This makes the batch easier to handle.

If you want a professional taffy, add two ounces (weight) of coconut butter or cocoa butter to the batch just before the dairy butter is added.

1. Prepare the marble slab. It should be cold and wiped with mineral oil.

2. Measure and reserve.

3. Measure into a 3-quart saucepan. Blend thoroughly. Bring to a boil. Wash down the sides of the pan with a pastry brush dipped in water. Insert the thermometer. Cook, without stirring, to **256** degrees for chewy taffy, *or* to **262** degrees for dry. Immediately stir in the reserved butter. Remove from heat.

4. Pour the batch out onto the prepared slab.

5. As the batch spreads out over the cold slab, the edges will quickly become too hard to pull. So, wearing oiled canvas gloves if necessary, fold the edges inward, making a compact mass. Move this to a cool part of the slab.

6. After a moment or two, pick up the batch and turn it over. Fold the cooled side (which has been next to the slab) to the

inside. Repeat this process steadily until the batch is cool enough to pull.

7. PULL the batch. You'll need two persons for this job—or a taffy hook on the wall to drape the pulled-out taffy over as you work.

8. Add the vanilla to the batch while you're pulling it.

9. In pulling taffy, use the ends of the fingers and pull the candy out deliberately and evenly. As you fold it back on itself, work carefully so that the air in the batch is maintained. Do not squeeze. Continue to pull, without stopping, until it is firm enough to hold its shape when it is stretched out on the slab.

10. Now, pull it out into uniform narrow strips. Dispose these on a flat work surface. Using either a sharp knife or scissors, cut into desired lengths. Wrap the pieces in waxed paper, twisting the ends.

11. After the candy is thoroughly cool, store it in an airtight container.

## VARIATIONS:

1. Add ¼ cup of light molasses just before the the end of the cook. Allow the batch to come back up to temperature, stirring. Then stir in the butter and remove from heat.

2. Melt 2 ounces (weight) of unsweetened baking chocolate. Cool. Add to the batch while pulling the taffy.

3. Other flavorings to add to the batch while pulling:

| | |
|---|---|
| Peppermint | Anise |
| Maple | Orange |
| Root beer | Etc. |

Go browsing in a specialty spice shop for inspiration.

Flavorings and extracts should be added a teaspoonful at a time. Taste carefully before adding more.

The aromatic oils should be added by drops. Be careful. They're very concentrated.

Vegetable coloring may be added in the same way as the flavorings.

## PULL THE BATCH

**1 teaspoon vanilla extract**

The object in pulling taffy is to get as much air into it as possible. This lightens the texture and makes for better eating.

To prevent any graining at all from occurring in taffies, the formulas require two-thirds as much corn syrup as sugar in the batch. This is a very large proportion of corn syrup to sugar, but it is needed to keep the sugar crystals from building up again after they have once been dissolved during the cooking process.

# MOLASSES TAFFY

**Molasses.** Made from the juice of sugar cane. Depending on the grade, molasses is either a by-product of sugar refinement or, when of high quality, first run. It is often added near the end of the cook simply for flavor. But if it is of the best quality, molasses will tolerate cooking temperatures up to 315 degrees.

If you love molasses, this one's for you. Choose a good molasses with a strong, clear flavor, because you're going to use a lot of it in this formula. And the resultant taffy will taste only as good as the molasses you've used.

Be sure to stir the batch constantly. Molasses is full of solids that scorch easily.

1. Prepare the marble slab. It should be cold and wiped with mineral oil.

**4 tablespoons butter**

2. Measure and reserve.

**3 cups granulated sugar**
**⅔ cup light corn syrup**
**¼ cup water**

3. Measure into a 3-quart saucepan. Blend. Boil. Wash down. Insert thermometer.

**1 cup molasses**

4. When the batch is boiling freely again, slowly stir in the molasses. Don't stop the boil. Don't stop stirring. Cook, stirring constantly, to *260* degrees.

**⅛ teaspoon salt**

5. Immediately stir in the reserved butter, then the salt. Remove from heat.

6. Pour the batch out onto the prepared slab.

7. Proceed as in the master recipe.

# CREAM TAFFY KISSES

Candy kisses are of two types—the familiar teardrop shape we see in divinities and chocolate chips and the scissors-cut shapes we see in the original saltwater taffies. The formula presented here is one of the latter—and one of the best. Oh, it's unmistakably taffy, all right, but more flavorful and richer than most.

So call them kisses, cut'm dainty, wrap'm pretty, and give'm to your valentine.

1. Prepare the marble slab. It should be cold and wiped with mineral oil.

2. Measure and reserve.

**2 tablespoons butter**

3. Measure into a 3-quart saucepan. Blend. Boil. Wash down. Insert thermometer.

**3 cups granulated sugar**
**1⅔ cups light corn syrup**
**½ cup water**

4. When the batch is boiling freely again, slowly stir in the cream. Don't stop the boil. Don't stop stirring. Cook, stirring constantly, to *250* degrees.

**1½ cups whipping cream**

5. Stir in the reserved butter. Cook, still stirring, to *254* degrees.

6. Stir in the salt. Remove from heat.

**⅛ teaspoon salt**

7. Pour the batch out onto the prepared slab.

8. Proceed as in the master recipe, adding the vanilla or other flavoring during the pulling.

**1 teaspoon vanilla extract**

# AFTER DINNER MINTS

A superb peppermint candy. A delightful palate freshener. A nonalcoholic *digestif*. And a family favorite that has benefited from extensive experimentation.

1. Prepare the marble slab. It should be cold and wiped with mineral oil.

**4 cups granulated sugar**
**¼ teaspoon cream of tartar**
**1 cup water**

2. Measure into a 3-quart saucepan. Blend thoroughly. Bring to a boil. Wash down the sides of the pan with a pastry brush dipped in water. Insert thermometer. Cook to *260* degrees in winter, *265* degrees in summer.

3. Pour out onto the prepared slab.

**10 drops oil of peppermint**
**(available in pharmacies)**

4. Handle like taffy, adding 10 drops of peppermint oil while pulling. For detail, see the master recipe, Grandpa's Taffy, page 104, steps 5 through 9.

Acids are elements that act to "doctor" a batch of candy. That is, they inhibit graining. In the old days, vinegar was often used in taffy-making to provide the acid needed for that purpose.

5. After the pulled batch has become quite firm, pull it out into uniform narrow (½-inch) strips. Dispose these on a flat work surface. Cut into small pieces with scissors. Cover generously with powdered sugar.

6. Hold at room temperature—the warmer, the better—for 4 hours. Then sieve the surplus sugar off. (The creme of the mint starts from the outside. It needs air and warmth for another 20 hours to creme up entirely.)

7. After 24 hours put them in a jar with a tight lid to finish mellowing without drying out.

8. When this mint is first cut, it has all the characteristics of taffy. But because the formula is different (it does not contain any corn syrup), the mint will magically change texture completely within the 24 hours it needs for ripening. It develops a very fine smooth grain and becomes firm to the tooth rather than chewy. When you bite on it, the mint disintegrates at once and melts instantaneously in the mouth. Magic!

**VARIATION**

AFTER DINNER BUTTER MINTS

Simply follow the above recipe, stirring in 4 tablespoons butter just before the end of the cook.

# Divinities and Nougats

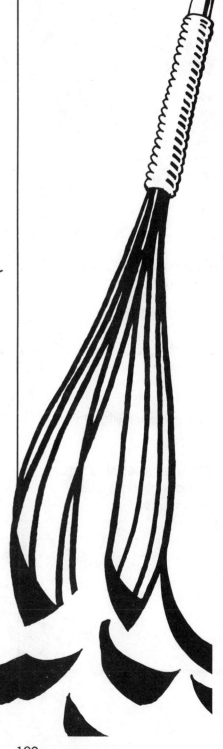

**W**e pair these two because procedurally nougat is a divinity with a higher cook. Both use the same techniques, but because of the differences in cooking temperatures, and in proportion of ingredients, *divinity* is a grained candy and *nougat* is not.

We present to you first the definitive professional divinity. And following it some chewy nougats. We prefer our nougats chewy, and these are our favorites. For a nougat that is hard and brittle, the sugar syrup must be cooked to a higher temperature.

As in all aerated confections using egg white, the essential element of technique is to incorporate—and retain—as much air as possible in the egg whites. In the recipes that follow, and in their variations, this is accomplished by a creative approach to double-cook. Just follow this simple two-step method, and you'll find youself tripping the light fantastic right along with the pros.

And incidentally, if you've ever been told that divinity won't set up properly on a humid day, forget it. Use our recipe. It's guaranteed to turn out the same every time, whatever the weather. Trust us.

NOTE: In order to get maximum volume from egg whites, you must make sure that both they and the bowl in which they're whipped are at room temperature. Also, the bowl and beaters should be very clean and grease-free.

**1 teaspoon vanilla extract**
**½ teaspoon salt**

**1 cup English walnuts**

**OPTIONAL: 2 ounces cocoa butter**

**2 large eggs, whites only**

**2 ½ cups granulated sugar**
**⅝ cup light corn syrup**
**⅔ cup water**

# GRANDPA'S DIVINITY

The main thing that makes this divinity different from others is the addition of cocoa butter at the end of the cook. The cocoa butter gives the divinity a very professional stand-up quality. It points up all the flavors. And because it has a low melting point, it gives the illusion of greater smoothness and tenderness in the mouth. Now with all that going for it, we still list it in this recipe as an optional ingredient because of the problems involved in finding a dependable supply of cocoa butter.

Without cocoa butter, this formula will give you a very good candy indeed. But with the cocoa butter, the divinity's simply . . . divine!

1. Butter a cookie sheet or lay out a length of waxed paper to receive the finished candy.

2. Mix together and reserve.

3. Measure, chop and reserve.

4. Prepare the optional cocoa butter for use. It should be melted to flowing, then cooled so that no heat remains when you're ready to fold it into the batch.

5. Separate the whites into the large bowl of an electric mixer. Whip with a rotary beater until they are stiff, but not dry.

6. Measure into a 3-quart saucepan. Blend thoroughly. Bring to a boil. Wash down the sides of the pan with a pastry brush dipped in water. Insert the thermometer. Cook, without stirring, to *240* degrees. Remove from heat.

7. Slowly add one-third of the syrup (1 cup) to the beaten egg whites, pouring in a thin stream and beating steadily at moderate speed, just until the syrup is incorporated.

One-third of the sugar syrup

8. Leaving the beater running on low, put the rest of the syrup back on heat and cook to **256** degrees. Remove from heat.

9. Beat the remaining two-thirds of the syrup into the egg whites, as in step 7, until it is incorporated.

The remaining two-thirds of the sugar syrup

10. Then continue to beat the batch at a slower tempo until it begins to set. (The batch already has all the air it can hold, so the object now is to form a grain in the candy. This is done by agitation, and may take a little time.)

11. When the batch starts to set, dribble in vanilla/salt solution.

12. When the mass will pile up in the bowl, stop beating and fold in the walnuts and optional cocoa butter.

13. Immediately scrape the batch out onto the prepared cookie sheet or length of waxed paper. Smooth out with a spatula. Or if you prefer to make "kisses," drop by spoonfuls directly from the bowl.

14. When thoroughly cooled, cut like fudge and store in an airtight container.

## VARIATIONS:

1. For a divinity with a slightly richer flavor, substitute ½ cup dark brown sugar for ½ cup of the white sugar.

2. Fold in ½ cup to 1 cup dried or glazed fruit along with the walnuts—or instead of them. The fruit should be chopped. And of course you can use other nuts of your choice.

# NOUGAT CHEW

Unlike Divinity, Nougat Chew has no grain to assist the egg white in achieving a stand-up quality. So we cook the syrup on its second round to 266 degrees instead of 256 degrees. This results in the firmer texture we're looking for.

1. Prepare the marble slab and ½-inch perimeter bars. They should be cold and oiled.

**1 cup English walnuts**

2. Measure, chop and reserve.

**2 ounces (weight) cocoa but- ter, coconut butter, or dairy butter—in that order of preference**

3. Melt to liquid. Reserve. Cool so that no heat remains when you're ready to fold it into the batch.

**3 large eggs, whites only**

4. Separate the whites into the large bowl of an electric mixer. Whip with a rotary beater until they are stiff, but not dry.

**2 cups granulated sugar**
**2 ½ cups light corn syrup**
**½ cup water**

5. Measure into a 3-quart saucepan. Blend thoroughly. Bring to a boil. Wash down the sides of the pan with a pastry brush dipped in water. Insert thermometer. Cook without stirring to *240* degrees. Remove from heat.

6. Slowly add one-third of the syrup (1½ cups) to the beaten egg whites, pouring in a thin stream and beating steadily at moderate speed, just until the syrup is incorporated.

7. Leaving the beater running on low, put the rest of the syrup back on heat and cook to *266* degrees. Remove from heat.

8. Beat the remaining two-thirds of the syrup into the egg whites, as in step 6 above, until it is incorporated.

**2 teaspoons vanilla extract**

9. Continue beating until the batch starts to stiffen. Dribble in the vanilla and beat until very stiff.

10. Stop beating and fold in walnuts.

11. Then add half the melted cocoa butter. Sprinkle one tea-spoon flour over it. Fold into batch. Add the other half of the cocoa butter, and another teaspoon of flour. Fold in.

**2 teaspoons general purpose flour, divided**

12. Scrape out on the prepared slab between the ½-inch bars. Spread smooth with a spatula.

13. When thoroughly cooled, cut pieces ½ inch by 1 inch.

14. Wrap in waxed paper and store in an airtight container. Or dip in chocolate.

## VARIATIONS:

1. Fold in ½ to 1 cup chopped glazed fruit or dried fruit along with the walnuts—or instead of them. Or use other varieties of nuts. This recipe has its roots in Mediterranean cookery, so pistachios or almonds or pine nuts would be appropriate.

2. CHOCOLATE NOUGAT CHEW
Follow the Nougat Chew recipe exactly, but at the end instead of adding the cocoa butter, coconut butter or dairy butter, sub-stitute 2 ounces (weight) of unsweetened baking chocolate, melted and cooled beforehand.

Because you should avoid stirring the mixture as much as possible, you may want to simply swirl in the chocolate. This results in a marbled pattern that is very attractive when cut.

# HONEY NOUGAT CHEW

This is essentially the same recipe as the Nougat Chew, but the addition of honey to the formula requires some changes in proportion of ingredients and considerable change in the battle order.

Since the Mediterranean rim is celebrated for honeyed confections, a honey nougat is particularly Old World in concept. But don't let that limit your choice of nuts to the Mediterranean varieties.

**1 cup nuts of your choice, chopped. (Double the quantity if you wish.)**

1. Prepare slab and bars as in Nougat Chew.

2. Measure, chop and reserve.

**½ cup honey**

3. Warm to a thin liquid over hot water. Keep warm enough to remain melted until ready for use.

**2 ounces (weight) cocoa butter, coconut butter, or dairy butter—in that order of preference**

4. Melt to flowing. Reserve. Cool before using.

**3 large eggs, whites only**

5. Separate the whites into the large bowl of an electric mixer. Whip with a rotary beater until they are stiff, but not dry.

**2 cups granulated sugar**
**1 ⅞ cups light corn syrup**
**½ cup water**

6. Measure into a 3-quart saucepan. Blend thoroughly. Boil. Wash down. Insert thermometer. Cook, without stirring, to **240** degrees. Remove from heat.

7. Slowly add one-third of the syrup (1 ¼ cups) to the beaten egg whites, pouring in a thin stream and beating steadily at moderate speed, just until the syrup is incorporated.

8. Put the rest of the syrup back on heat and cook to **290** degrees. Stir in the melted honey. If the honey has slacked back the batch to below 266 degrees, cook gently to **266** degrees now, stirring constantly. Remove from heat. Ignore steps 9 and 10. Proceed immediately to step 11.

9. If the temperature has not come down as far as 266 degrees, test the batch, off heat, for firmness of the texture: drop a few drops into a cup of cool water. Pop the candy into your mouth and chew. The texture will be exactly the same as that of the finished nougat. If it's too firm, proceed to step 10. But if you're happy with the texture, ignore step 10 and proceed directly to step 11.

10. Lower the heat. Put the syrup back on the burner. Stirring constantly, bring it back to the boil. Still stirring, start adding water one tablespoon at a time, until the temperature comes back down to **266** degrees. (If the temperature inadvertently drops below that, don't worry. Just cook, still stirring, back to 266.) Remove from heat.

11. Beat the remaining two-thirds of the syrup into the egg whites, as in step 7 above.

12. Continue beating until the batch starts to stiffen. Dribble in the vanilla and beat until very stiff.

13. Stop beating and fold in the nuts.

14. Then add half the melted cocoa butter. Sprinkle one teaspoon flour over it. Fold into the batch. Add the other half of the cocoa butter, and another teaspoon of flour. Fold in.

15. Scrape out onto the prepared slab between the ½-inch bars. Spread smooth with a spatula.

16. When thoroughly cooled, cut pieces ½ by 1 inch.

17. Wrap in waxed paper and store in an airtight container. Or dip in chocolate.

NOTE: We don't like to cook honey any longer than necessary. It changes—or even destroys—the flavor. This is why we cook the syrup so high. When the honey is added, the cook is slacked back enough so that the temperature is close to what we want. Any change necessary can be accomplished without very much additional cooking.

**2 teaspoons vanilla extract**

**2 teaspoons general purpose flour, divided**

Thank goodness Julius and Earl kept their master notebook. We refer to it all the time.

Caramel, Sars.

27 Corn Syrup.
10# Golden "C" } crack
1/2 gal H₂O

add
30# 40% Milk
6# 90° grease
3/4 oz Letin
2#3 flour
4. oz salt
3 oz Nan & Coum.

# Marzipan

If you have never tasted freshly-made marzipan, you cannot imagine what a difference there is between it and the hard, dried-out version you often find at holiday time in the little traditional shapes of highly-colored fruits, vegetables and small beasties.

Herewith we present to you the opportunity to acquire a new taste. These are three of the marzipans my Grandfather Davenport offered his clientele. They are "cooked" formulas. The "uncooked" ones use quantities of powdered sugar and dry out very quickly. They are used because they're easy to color and mold, but they must be eaten right away.

Whenever using ground almonds in a recipe, we add a small amount of almond extract to the batch to bring out the flavor of the almonds. In Europe, one or two bitter almonds are added to the grind for this purpose. In this country, oil of bitter almonds can be bought only on a doctor's prescription because in large quantities it is toxic. Incidentally, we use the extract sparingly, and taste as we go, because it's very concentrated.

For those of you interested in food history, the origin of the Marzipan formula has been documented as early as 1671. As the story goes, at the request of his lord, a young German master chef, Franz Marzip from Lübeck, cooked ground blanched almonds in sugar to create an almond dessert that would be compatible with Sauternes wine. Marzipan—known as marzapane in Italy, massepain in France and marchpane in England—has become a classic of confectionary cuisine.

# MARZIPAN MADE FROM SCRATCH

Or almost from scratch. We're not going to tell you how to blanch your almonds. We presume that you would prefer to buy them already blanched—as we do. If you have your own almond tree, of course, go ahead and do your thing.

**1 pound blanched almonds, ground**
**3 large eggs, whites only**

**2 ⅔ cups granulated sugar**
**1 cup water**

1. Prepare a marble slab or other smooth, dry, cold work surface to receive the batch while it cools.

2. Measure. Grind. Reserve.

3. Beat lightly with a fork just until they are well blended.

4. Measure into a 3-quart saucepan. Blend thoroughly. Bring to a boil. Wash down the sides of the pan with a pastry brush dipped in water. Insert the thermometer. Cook, without stirring, to *240* degrees. Remove from heat.

5. Stir with a spoon to start a little grain—just until you see a slightly cloudy surface.

6. Immediately stir in the ground almonds until they are well incorporated in the batch.

7. Put the whole mixture back on low heat. Stir for about 3 minutes or until the mass becomes slightly cohesive. (It should be light, not dense or plastic.) Remove from heat.

**¼ teaspoon almond extract, or to taste**

8. Off heat, stir in the flavoring.

9. Scrape out onto the prepared surface to cool.

10. When the batch is cool, knead it lightly until smooth. A little powdered sugar (3 to 5 tablespoons) can be added to take up the slack moisture and make it easier to handle without sticking.

11. Roll out the batch like thick pie crust. Cut into small squares and dip in dark chocolate. You may add some ground, roasted, blanched almonds to the chocolate coating if you wish. This is a refinement my grandfather initiated.

12. If you're not going to use the marzipan immediately, wrap it tightly in plastic wrap and put it in an airtight container in the refrigerator, where it will keep very well for three or four weeks.

## VARIATIONS:

1. First add the almond extract to establish the basic almond nature of the marzipan. Then you may add other flavorings, and even colorings, as well, always remembering to taste carefully after each addition. Do this as in step 8 above, just before scraping the mixture out of the pan. Try 2 teaspoons of orange flower water, lemon juice or roseflower water. Or maybe coffee, apricot, or pistachio.

2. We sometimes split the batch and add separate compatible flavorings and colors. Then we sandwich the layers: Paint the bottom layer with a thin coating of egg white applied with a pastry brush (break up the egg white with a fork before using); top with the other layer; let rest briefly, then cut into small diamond-shaped pieces; dip in dark chocolate; or crystallize. (See "Crystal Syrup," page 88, for details on crystallizing.)

3. You may use half almonds and half hazelnuts in this recipe, if you wish. Grind them together before starting to cook. The hazelnuts will taste better if they are lightly toasted before grinding: Spread whole blanched hazelnuts in a shallow roasting pan and put into a 350 degree oven for 5 to 10 minutes. Watch them closely and stir them up several times. Take them out when they are very lightly browned. Let cool before grinding.

4. This is a good recipe to use for coloring and molding. Simply add enough more powdered sugar to achieve the texture you need. It will not affect the flavor, and this formula is vastly superior to recipes calling for *all* powdered sugar.

NOTE: When purchasing almond extract, read the label carefully. You can find some that have no chemical additives in them. Make sure there is nothing more than alcohol and water in the solution. The commonly-used propylene glycol, even in small quantities of extract, leaves an unpleasant aftertaste that lingers in the mouth for a long time. This same caveat applies to all flavoring aids. If the one you have in mind isn't made without chemicals (probably because it can't be), forgo it!

*Almonds* **are widely grown for use in pastries and candies. Since biblical times the almond has been popular for the making of sweets. They are grown in the Mediterranean countries and are one of California's largest crops. They are actually the seed of a tree with a plumlike fruit. They are used both raw, as in Marzipan, and roasted for many types of confections. We use the Californian "Non Pareil" almonds. There are many varieties and sizes.**

119

# MARZIPAN CREMES

This is an excellent French-style marzipan that stays moist and tender, making it ideal for dipping in chocolate.

In essence, the formula is a fondant with a bought pre-made almond paste added at the end of the cook. The paste, which is readily available in grocery stores, already has the flavor of bitter almond in it, so we don't call for any additional almond extract. But as always, taste. If you want a little more almond flavor, add the extract in drops until you're satisfied. Do this while you're cremeing the batch.

1. Prepare the marble slab. It should be cold and slightly damp. Dimensions ought to be at least 16x24 inches. (See "Utensils" section, page 16, for discussion of slabs.)

**2 ½ cups almond paste, well packed**

2. Chop very fine and reserve.

**3 cups granulated sugar**
**1 ⅓ cups light corn syrup**
**¾ cup water**

3. Measure into a 3-quart saucepan. Blend thoroughly. Boil. Wash down. Insert thermometer. Cook to **240** degrees.

4. Immediately stir in the chopped almond paste. Mix thoroughly (see note), but don't try to get all the lumps of paste smoothed out.

5. Remove from heat and pour out on the prepared slab.

**CREME THE BATCH**

6. CREME the batch, allowing it to cool during the cremeing process. Mash the lumps of almond paste against the slab with the scraper and blend them through the batch during the cremeing. (See Cremed Fondant, steps 3 through 5, page 84, for detailed instruction on cremeing a batch.)

7. When the cremed batch has cooled, hand roll into small balls. Dip in dark chocolate. If you wish, follow my grandfather's suggestion: Add roasted blanched almonds, finely ground, to the dipping chocolate. The proportions should be 2 cups ground almonds to 3 pounds of chocolate.

NOTE: Normally a fondant should not be agitated until it is poured out on the slab and allowed to cool to lukewarm. In this case, however, the almond paste cools the mass down very quickly. And the oil from the paste acts as a colloid which prevents graining.

# MALLEABLE MARZIPAN

This marzipan rolls out or presses out very nicely for layered candies—or cakes. Because the formula calls for a far smaller proportion of corn syrup, and is cooked to 250 degrees instead of 240, the finished marzipan is more firm and not as sticky as the others.

1. Chop very fine and reserve.

**2 cups almond paste, well packed**

2. Measure into a 3-quart saucepan. Blend thoroughly. Boil. Wash down. Insert thermometer. Cook to *250* degrees.

**1 cup granulated sugar**
**2 tablespoons light corn syrup**
**⅓ cup water**

3. Immediately stir in the chopped almond paste. Mix thoroughly, but don't try to get all the lumps of paste smoothed out. Remove from heat.

4. Put the batch into the large bowl of an electric mixer.

5. MIX at medium speed for 5 minutes or so, until completely blended and smooth. (You may want to use your dough hook.)

**MIX THE BATCH**

6. Lightly dust a flat work surface with cornstarch and scrape the batch out onto it.

7. Knead the marzipan mixture, adding coloring paste or flavors as desired. Don't use any more cornstarch than necessary.

8. When rolling out in thin sheets for layered candies, use a little cornstarch to prevent sticking.

# Glazed Nuts

**W**e're offering you three methods of coating nuts—plus one variation. All are delicious. All are different from each other. The one thing they all have in common is that each will accept virtually any kind, or combination, of nutmeats within their basic formula. The first recipe is the simplest.

## GLAZED ASSORTED NUTS

1. Prepare the marble slab. It should be cold. Make sure it is entirely moisture-free, then wipe it with mineral oil.

**2 tablespoons butter**

2. Measure and reserve.

**2 cups assorted nutmeats, unblanched (walnuts, almonds, filberts, etc.)**

3. Measure and put into a 150-degree oven to warm (but not roast), for addition to the batch at the end of the cook.

**3 cups granulated sugar**
**1 ¼ cups light corn syrup**
**1 cup water**

4. Measure into a 3-quart saucepan. Blend thoroughly. Bring to a boil. Wash down the sides of the pan with a pastry brush dipped in water. Insert the thermometer. Cook to *310* degrees.

5. Immediately stir in the butter and the nutmeats. Allow the nuts to heat through for a moment or two. Remove from heat.

**1 teaspoon vanilla extract**

6. Stir in the vanilla. Pour out on the prepared slab. Spread the nuts apart so that they'll be separate, or in very small clusters, when they've cooled.

7. When thoroughly cooled, store in an airtight container.

# SUGAR-COATED PEANUTS

The cooking process in this formula is completely different from that of the preceding one. This is a good example of double-cook. The result is engaging, engaging.

1. Prepare the slab. It should be cold and dry.

2. Measure and reserve.

**1 cup raw Spanish peanuts, unblanched**

3. Measure 1 cup sugar and ½ cup water into a 3-quart sauce-pan. Blend thoroughly. Bring to a boil. Wash down the sides of the pan.

**1 ½ cups granulated sugar, divided**
**1 cup water, divided**

4. Stir into the batch. Cook and stir over low heat until the batch grains. (It will turn to sugar and begin to form a crust around the peanuts.) Remove from heat.

5. Pour into a coarse sieve. Sieve off the loose sugar and put the peanuts where they will keep warm.

6. Put the sugar that has been sieved off the peanuts back into the saucepan. Blend in an additional ½ cup sugar and ½ cup water. Bring to a boil. Again wash down the sides of the pan. Insert thermometer. Cook, without stirring, to **245** degrees.

**The sieved-off sugar**
**The remaining ½ cup sugar**
**The remaining ½ cup water**

7. Stir in the peanuts and remove from heat.

8. Add the vanilla. Stir the batch until it grains.

**1 teaspoon vanilla extract**

9. Scrape out onto the dry slab and separate.

10. When thoroughly cooled, store in an airtight container.

# BURNT PEANUTS

In case you need reassuring, "burnt" sugar is an old-time term for "caramelized" sugar. Accordingly, what we're going to prepare here is a peanut with a special caramelized-sugar coating that looks as good as it tastes.

And we're going to use the larger Virginia peanuts for this one, rather than the Spanish type.

The first four steps of this recipe are executed very much like the first four steps of Sugar-coated Peanuts, just preceding. But from there the steps become more sophisticated.

Be sure you have provided yourself with a wooden spoon that will slip into every hard-to-reach cranny of your saucepan. For you're about to give a stirring performance, never slacking off from start to finish. And when it's over, you'll take your bow to enthusiastic applause for the best burnt offering any critic has ever acclaimed.

Curtain going up!

1. Prepare the slab. It should be cold. Make sure it is thoroughly dry, then wipe with mineral oil.

**2 ¼ pounds fancy Virginia peanuts, raw, unblanched**

2. Measure and reserve.

**2 cups granulated sugar**
**½ cup water**

3. Measure into a 3-quart saucepan. Blend thoroughly. Bring to a boil. Wash down the sides of the saucepan.

**The reserved peanuts**

4. Stir into the batch. Cook and stir over low heat until the batch grains. (It will turn to sugar and begin to form a crust around the peanuts.) Remove from heat.

**1 tablespoon butter**
**1 teaspoon vanilla extract**

5. Off heat, continue stirring until all the liquid sugar is cooked dry. Then stir in the butter and the vanilla.

6. Immediately put the pan back on low heat. Stir until the peanuts absorb all the rest of the sugar in the pan. Continue stirring until the outer layer of the sugar now coating the peanuts begins to melt (caramelize). Keep on stirring zealously. (You don't want literally *burnt* peanuts.)

7. When the coatings have turned uniformly glossy, pour the now resplendent peanuts out onto the lightly oiled marble slab. Stir them occasionally while they are cooling, so that they won't stick together.

8. When thoroughly cooled, store in an airtight container.

BURNT CINNAMON ALMONDS

Prepare exactly like the above formula, *except*:

1. Use unblanched large almonds.

2. At the same time that you add the butter and vanilla (step 5), also add ¼ cup granulated sugar which has been stirred with 2 teaspoons ground cinnamon.

These almonds are appealing to look at because a portion of the sugar which was added so late in the cook will not get dissolved smoothly into the coating. Instead it will form a rough and translucent surface. Very attractive.

**VARIATION**

**Cinnamon and cassia have virtually the same flavor, although cassia is stronger. Both come from the dried inner bark of evergreen trees native to Asia. And both, according to Exodus, are in great favor with God.**

# Beverage Bar and Soda Fountain

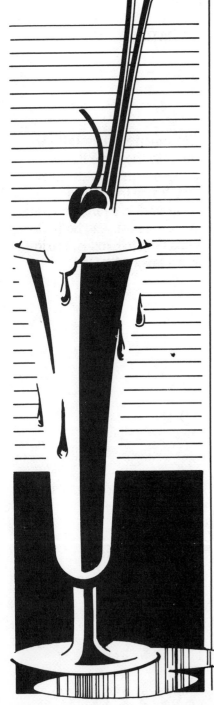

This section comprises chocolate formulas in several forms. The contrast between bar chocolate and cocoa in these applications will be readily apparent, so a word concerning this contrast seems in order. Most bar chocolate such as baking chocolate (bitter) contains all the cocoa butter of the original bean, around 50 percent. Cocoa, on the other hand, comes from processing the original bean to extract most of the cocoa butter, then grinding this residue. Whether we use powdered cocoa or bar chocolate in a beverage is determined by whether we just want chocolate flavor or the added richness provided by cocoa butter. For a detailed discussion of types of chocolate and cocoa, see "Chocolate, the Inimitable" section.

As to the recipes in *this* section, some are basic to our retail chocolate shop operations. Others are from Grandpa Davenport's notebooks. Two of the formulas are very nearly family secrets that we're sworn not to divulge.

As a matter of fact, we have given you many secret formulas throughout this book—without signaling their significance. We've done this deliberately, because we've wanted to guard our heritage. But we also want you to have the capability of producing in your own kitchen everything for a well-rounded home confectioner's establishment. Thus, if you follow our instructions exactly, you'll be incorporating in your own production virtually all the sweets-oriented knowledge—some of it secret, admittedly—of four generations of the Franzen-Davenport clan. This knowledge, born of experience, scientific study, and, in some cases, years of experimentation, is very condensed. But you may be assured that we have ignored none of the basics. We've touched all the bases.

# CARAMEL TOPPING

No, this is not exactly the same formula as our Dilettante Carameled Cream. That is one of the recipes we're sworn not to reveal—as mentioned in the introduction to this section. The product is available in specialty food shops nationwide.

But the caramel topping for ice cream that we offer you here is exquisite, yet relatively simple to make, and a true caramel. Most of the caramel toppings on the grocers' shelves today are simply glucose syrups with caramel coloring added, as well as caramel flavoring. They taste very artificial to us.

This caramel formula, incidentally, comes directly from Grandpa Davenport's notebooks. Toppings were called dressings in his day.

NOTE: The sugar syrup is cooked to such a high reading because this temperature caramelizes the sugar, giving the finished syrup its true caramel flavor. More importantly, the high cook inverts the sugar, making it impossible for it to go back to a crystal state.

We "slack back" the batch with water so that the finished product will be fluid. Otherwise we'd have a hard candy instead of a syrup.

1. Have a kettle of simmering water on the stove ready for sudden use when dictated by the thermometer. Keep a 1-cup measure at the ready, as well.

**1 ⅔ cups light corn syrup**

2. Measure into a small saucepan. Bring to the boil and remove from direct heat, but keep hot until ready to use.

**2 cups granulated sugar**
**¼ teaspoon cream of tartar**
**½ cup water**

3. Measure into a 3-quart saucepan. Blend thoroughly. Bring to a boil. Wash down the sides of the pan with a pastry brush dipped in water. Insert the thermometer. Cook to *320* degrees. The syrup will be a nice golden brown.

**1 cup very hot water**

4. Immediately add the simmering water to the batch. Do this slowly and carefully. It will sputter and splash.

**1 pint whipping cream**

5. Bring the batch back to the boil, and start stirring in the hot corn syrup very slowly, then the cream, maintaining the boil through both additions and stirring constantly. Cook to *224* degrees. Remove from heat.

**1 teaspoon vanilla extract**

6. Immediately stir in the vanilla.

7. When thoroughly cool, pour into an airtight bottle or other container. This syrup will keep almost indefinitely and doesn't need refrigeration.

# MARSHMALLOW TOPPING

Another treasure from Grandpa Davenport's notebook.

1. Measure, warm over hot water and keep warm until ready to use.

**½ cup Simple Syrup (See recipe, page 88)**

2. Separate into the large bowl of an electric mixer. Whip with a rotary beater until stiff but not dry. Reserve.

**2 large eggs, whites only**

3. Measure into a 3-quart saucepan. Blend thoroughly. Bring to a boil. Wash down the sides of the pan. Insert thermometer. Cook to *236* degrees. Remove from heat.

**2 cups granulated sugar**
**1 ⅔ cups light corn syrup**
**½ cup water**

4. Add the corn syrup mixture to the beaten egg whites slowly, in a fine stream, beating steadily the while. When the mixture is incorporated, raise the tempo and beat until stiff.

5. Slack back by whipping the warm Simple Syrup into the batch until it is the desired consistency. The finished topping should be thinned enough to remain fluid when poured over ice cream.

6. Dribble in just before turning off the beater.

**1 teaspoon vanilla extract**

SUGGESTION: For slacking back the batch (Step 5), use warmed honey or warmed maple syrup as a variation.

# VERY NEARLY DILETTANTE EPHEMERE SAUCE
## *(BUT NOT QUITE)*

A superb chocolate sauce worthy of poached pears (Poires Hélène) or to serve with dessert soufflés. And for ice cream sundaes, magnificent! After it's melted slightly, you can pour it over ice cream and depend on it to flow—and to remain thick at the same time. All these pluses in a formula that contains not even a whisper of corn syrup—the sticky, gummy base ingredient of most of the thick commercial toppings.

| | |
|---|---|
| **¾ pound bittersweet chocolate (couverture)** | 1. Chop very fine. Or grate in a food processor. Reserve. |
| **3 cups whipping cream** | 2. Measure into a 3-quart saucepan. Bring to a slow boil and reduce, stirring constantly, to 2¼ cups. This should take about 15 minutes. |
| **⅛ pound unsalted butter** | 3. Stir into the cream at the end of the boil. Simmer just one minute longer. Remove from heat. |
| **¾ cup dark brown sugar** | 4. Immediately stir into the mixture until thoroughly dissolved. |
| | 5. While the batch is still very warm, whisk in the chocolate. Make sure it is thoroughly melted. Beat until the sauce is smooth and glossy. |
| **2 teaspoons vanilla extract, *OR* 3 tablespoons liqueur or other distillate of your choice—white Crème de Menthe, Crème de Cacao, Grand Marnier, brandy, rum, etc.** | 6. Whisk into the mixture until well incorporated, and sauce is smooth. |
| | 7. Stores nicely for several weeks in the refrigerator. Heat lightly before serving. |

**VARIATIONS:**

1. Instead of the brown sugar, substitute ¾ cup almond or hazelnut praline powder (brittle ground to a powder).

2. Depending on your taste, use semisweet or milk chocolate couverture instead of bittersweet.

3. If you want to use *bittersweet* couverture and can't find it, the rule of thumb is to substitute *semisweet* couverture combined with *unsweetened* baking chocolate in the proportions of 3 parts *semisweet* to 1 part *unsweetened*. In this formula, that works out to 9 ounces *semisweet* couverture plus 3 ounces *unsweetened* baking chocolate.

# QUICK AND REWARDING CHOCOLATE TOPPING

Here's a new one for your food processor. When I'm out shopping and run across a new European chocolate bar, I always pick up two or three—to try the new flavor. This sauce is the result of my wanting to use up one of the extras. You can use any 3-ounce chocolate bar to make it. I think you'll find it good enough to grace your most elegant ice creams.

1. Chop fine in the food processor.

**3-ounce chocolate bar**

2. Bring to a boil. Then with the blade running, pour quickly down the feeder tube over the chocolate.

**⅛ cup water**

3. Cut into pieces and drop into the mixture by tube. Process just until thoroughly blended and mixture is smooth.

**4 tablespoons unsalted butter**

4. Add just at the end of processing.

**1 to 2 tablespoons liqueur or other distillate of your choice.**

# BASIC CHOCOLATE SYRUP

This syrup is made with bar chocolate. It doesn't work well in ice cream sodas because the cocoa butter naturally occurring in the chocolate congeals at low temperatures and inhibits carbonation. But this syrup is wonderfully rich and full-flavored for hot drinks. And it makes a superior, velvety milk shake.

**9 ounces baking chocolate (unsweetened)**

**1 ¼ cups water**

**1 ½ cups granulated sugar**

**2 large eggs, yolks only**
**⅛ teaspoon salt**

**1 teaspoon vanilla extract**

1. Carefully melt the chocolate in a double boiler.

2. Boil the water in a 2-quart saucepan.

3. Completely dissolve the sugar in the water.

4. Slowly add the chocolate to the water; blend thoroughly.

5. Using a whisk, slightly beat the egg yolks with the salt. Whisk a little of the hot mixture into the yolks. Add the yolks to the remaining chocolate mixture. Blend well, whisking lightly. Over heat, simmer for I minute, still whisking. Do not boil. Remove from heat. Stir in the vanilla.

6. Cool thoroughly and refrigerate.
(This sauce will keep in the refrigerator for a couple of weeks.)

7. Add to milk for making hot chocolate to the strength you like.

# BASIC COCOA SYRUP

This syrup is a good base for chocolate sodas because it's made with cocoa powder instead of bar chocolate. The cocoa butter in bar chocolate inhibits carbonation in the glass, whereas the low percentage of cocoa butter in cocoa allows maximum carbonation.

    The cocoa syrup also blends very well with milk, hot or cold. And it will keep in the refrigerator for up to two weeks.

**1 ½ cups powdered cocoa**
**2 cups granulated sugar**
**⅛ teaspoon salt**

1. Mix together the cocoa, sugar and salt.

2. Bring the water to a boil in a 3-quart saucepan. Gradually whisk in the cocoa mixture. Return to the boil, still whisking, and boil for I minute. Off heat stir in the vanilla.

3. Pour through a strainer and cool. Store in the refrigerator for up to two weeks.

**2 cups water**

**1 teaspoon vanilla extract**

# CHOCOLATE ICE CREAM SODA

Just as in the olden days, we at the Dilettante train our soda jerks to do it right. They learn to use the Basic Cocoa Syrup (recipe this section) because it mates so perfectly with carbonation. They learn the procedural steps, always exactly the same. And they get very efficient with a little practice. As you will.

If the fountain businesses in your town use "industrial" syrups, it's well worthwhile to buy your own seltzer bottle, a good supply of cartridges, and makings for your own syrups.

What we offer you here is the classic soda fountain special. You may use other syrups than chocolate for variety, if you wish. And any flavor of ice cream you like. But the basic procedure hasn't changed for generations. It's time your kids found out what the real thing tastes like.

1. Into a 12-ounce glass, put the syrup. Add a squirt of soda water from a seltzer bottle. Drop in a very small scoop of ice cream or whipped cream to lighten the mixture.

**4 tablespoons Basic Cocoa Syrup (recipe above)**
**Seltzer bottle, charged**
**1 small scoop vanilla ice cream, or flavor of your choice**
***OR* a spoonful or two of whipped cream**

2. Thoroughly mix with a long-handled spoon.

3. Fill nearly to the top of the glass with seltzer water.

4. The force of the carbonated stream will probably stir the mixture sufficiently. If not, stir lightly.

5. Immediately add one small scoop of ice cream to the glass, and top with whipped cream.

**1 scoop ice cream**
**A good dollop of whipped cream**

6. Serve with a straw and a long-handled spoon.

# CAFÉ LIÉGEOIS DILETTANTE

Traditionally, this is either a beverage or a classic *coupe*, depending on who's telling it. The one thing that seems to be essential to all versions is that they must comprise either chocolate or coffee, or both, in their basic flavors—topped by slathers of whipped cream.

Because of this general confusion surrounding the origin of the delicacy, we didn't hesitate to develop our own version of Café Liégeois. And we didn't ask the city fathers of Liège for their reaction to our audacity. We had the feeling that they, being Belgians and good businessmen, would respond with a Gallic shrug and something noncommittal that would translate, "Fine. Whatever makes you happy. Just spell our name right, please."

Herewith our version, a *coupe*. Try it. Savor the unexpected bonanza of textures. And be happy.

NOTE: It is important to pack the ice cream very tightly—so that the coffee does not readily dissolve it. What actually happens is that the coffee quickly crystallizes the ice cream wherever it touches it, forming a nice crunch. For that reason our staff is instructed to suggest to customers that they eat this dish from the outside in, spooning bites all around the outside. Thus the cold coffee constantly crystallizes the newly exposed layers of ice cream. Sound interesting?

1. Chill a large champagne *coupe*, or one of the currently popular French jelly glasses, the large heavy-bottomed ones.

**Italian coffee gelato**

2. Make two or three very tightly rolled scoops of rich coffee gelato. Stack them in the glass.

**Rich black coffee, chilled**

3. Pour chilled strong coffee around them. Don't pour the liquid completely over the ice cream.

**Stiffly-whipped cream (enough for seconds)**

4. Top with stiffly whipped cream, unsweetened.

# CHOCOLATE EGGNOG

Also called Boston Chocolate Cream, this is simply made—and simply g-o-o-o-d. Nutritious, too.

**1 cup milk**
**2 large eggs**
**½ teaspoon vanilla extract**
**3 tablespoons of your favorite chocolate or cocoa syrup**

1. Measure all ingredients into a blender jar.

2. Process and pour into two chilled glasses.

# COCOA COLD BUT SPIRITED

Some sherries and ports, as well as a number of spirits such as brandies and fruit liqueurs, marry very well with chocolate.

This formula, being a liquid, is particularly hospitable to experimentation. Add a jigger or two of some aromatic liquid to the ingredients you're about to put into the blender jar. Buzz and taste. Get a couple of critical buddies to help in the tasting department.

1. Chill stemmed glasses in the freezer, so that they will be rimed with frost at serving time.

2. Measure all the ingredients into the blender jar. Process thoroughly until frothy.

¼ cup powdered cocoa
¼ cup whole milk
2 cups rich vanilla ice cream
1 cup dry sherry, Madeira, Oporto, Marsala, or other fortified wine of your choice
OR 3 to 6 ounces distilled spirits of your choice, depending on alcoholic content

3. Serves three guinea pigs...uh...experimenters.

# COCOA HOT OR COLD

For a lean drink, low in calories, low in cholesterol, low in effort, low in cost.

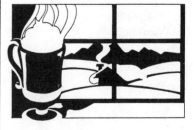

1. In a porcelain bowl, stir together the cocoa and the sugar. Use more or less cocoa, to taste.

¼ cup powdered cocoa
¼ cup granulated sugar

2. Slowly add the water, working the ingredients until you have a smooth, thick paste.

1 cup water

3. Stir in either scalded or cold milk, along with the vanilla and whatever spices you may desire. Serves 4 to 6.

3 cups milk
1 teaspoon vanilla extract

# HOT CHOCOLATE I

We're going to offer you five recipes for hot chocolate made with bar chocolate. Obviously, the cocoa butter in the bar chocolate makes a richer drink—with more profound chocolate flavor—than cocoa would. In fact, there is a saying among old-time confectioners, "Nothing conducts the flavor of chocolate as well as cocoa butter." We agree. And think you will.

A word about the whipped cream we use in our shops. We serve it unsweetened. It startles some of our customers, but once they really taste the cream, they tend to become sudden enthusiasts. Try it.

**⅔ cup water**
**4 ounces bitter (baking) chocolate, broken into small pieces**
**½ cup granulated sugar, or to taste**

1. Measure into a 3-quart saucepan: the water, the sugar, the chocolate. (With this ratio of liquid to chocolate, it's not necessary to melt the chocolate first.)

**⅛ teaspoon salt**

2. Bring to a boil, stirring constantly, Add the salt, and simmer gently for 3 to 4 minutes, still stirring.

**4 cups milk**

3. Add the milk and slowly bring it almost to boiling (scald), stirring constantly. Remove from heat.

**1 teaspoon vanilla extract**

4. Stir in the vanilla.

**Whipped cream**

5. Serve in your most festive cups, and pass the whipped cream. Yields 4 to 6 cups.

**VARIATIONS**

**Hot Chocolate II**. Same as Hot Chocolate I, but substitute rich coffee for the water.

**Hot Chocolate III**. Same as Hot Chocolate I, but substitute:
(a) Cream for all or half of the milk.
(b) Semisweet chocolate for the bittersweet.

If you feel you'd like less chocolate flavor, cut the quantity of chocolate by as much as one-half.

Also, you might like to add a little cinnamon or cardamom when you put in the milk.

**Hot Chocolate IV**. Same as Hot Chocolate I except:
(a) Before starting the recipe, separate the yolks from 4 large eggs into a bowl. Whisk lightly just until blended.
(b) Substitute milk for the water.
(c) When the hot chocolate is ready to serve, take it off heat and pour about ¼ cup of it into the prepared egg yolks, whisking all the while. Then pour the yolk mixture back into the batch. Whisk until frothy and pour into cups. Top with a sprinkling of nutmeg. And pass the whipped cream—unsweetened, of course.

# HOT CHOCOLATE V

This will give you another approach to using bar chocolate for making your hot beverage.

1. Melt the chocolate either in a double boiler or in a microwave oven.

2. When the chocolate is melted, add the scalded milk and cinnamon. Mix thoroughly.

3. Reheat briefly, stirring constantly. Take care not to let the mixture boil.

4. Serve in mugs with a cinnamon stick in each for garnish. Yields 4 mugs.

**MELTING CHOCOLATE:**
Chop chocolate small. Pour water into the bottom pot of a double boiler to within 1 inch of the top pot. Bring barely to a simmer and no more. Then put the chocolate in the top part of the double boiler and place it over the warm water. Stirring constantly, slowly melt the chocolate.

CAUTION: Melted chocolate, by itself (not buffered by other ingredients), must never be allowed to reach a temperature higher than *120* degrees. This rule will allow you to melt—and remelt—chocolate without harming it. A rapid-rise thermometer is helpful for monitoring chocolate temperatures.

ALSO: Make very sure that no steam or condensation from the spoon comes in contact with the chocolate—at any point. If the natural starch in chocolate combines with water, the mass will thicken, making it lumpy and unusable.

4 ounces semisweet chocolate
2 ounces bitter (baking) chocolate

3 cups scalded milk
2 teaspoons ground cinnamon

Cinnamon sticks for garnish

# Dipping

In this section, we'll be dealing with simple dipping and then with professional-style dipping, among other things.

But first, a word about tempering. When we melt, cool and agitate chocolate in preparation for dipping or molding, we say we are *tempering* chocolate. Because of the way chocolate is formulated, it is necessary to use the finest grade to get the best results. The highest quality chocolate coatings are referred to as *couverture*. They have large percentages of that incomparable, unduplicatable, and almost mystical ingredient: cocoa butter.

For us candymakers, cocoa butter is one of Mother Nature's greatest gifts. Its unusual chemical complexity provides the confectioner with an ideal enrobement for candy centers. When "pure" couverture is tempered precisely, the cocoa butter

forms an extremely tight network of molecules (called fat crystals) that retards moisture transference and creates a highly reflective surface, giving the chocolate its shiny eye appeal.

But alas, handling chocolate properly requires time and understanding. Without exact temperature controls, chocolate coatings can become gray, a condition we call "fat bloom" and/or gritty, a condition we call "sugar bloom." Although the flavor is still good, the texture or appearance—or both—are spoiled.

So in this section we provide several techniques for controlling "bloom," the easiest of which is how to make "bloom resistant" chocolate for Simple Dipping. It sets to a satin finish.

Then we'll give you instructions for tempering "pure" chocolate—that's couverture just as it comes from the manufacturer. This method gives a shiny finish. And you'll be ready for Professional-Style Dipping.

We also provide The Troubleshooter, a list of often-asked questions related to dipping—with answers provided.

Next comes a Technical Summary—for those of you with a scientific itch to scratch.

And finally, divers suggestions, advice, discussions of coatings other than chocolate, etc.

# SIMPLE DIPPING (SATIN FINISH)

First we have to make a "bloom resistant" chocolate coating, and temper it properly. Then we can consider simple dipping. We confectioners have found that by adding just a little clarified butter to pure couverture, we can make a sort of foolproof coating that the trade calls "bloom resistant" chocolate. The added oils lubricate the cocoa butter molecules, making it unecessary to control every slight variation of temperature that could otherwise cause graying. Using this tempering process, you will sacrifice none of the flavor, and only a little of the characteristic snap and shine of "pure" chocolate. You will find the resulting satin sheen pleasing, and be amazed at the relative ease of this technique.

### *Ingredients*
Bittersweet, semisweet, or milk chocolate couverture, and clarified butter. Ratio: 4 tablespoons clarified butter to 1 pound of chocolate. Note: How to clarify butter, page 89.

### *Amount of Chocolate to Melt*
We calculate the coating to be about ⅓ of the total weight of the finished product. Example: 1 pound of centers will take about ½ pound of coating chocolate. In order to totally immerse the centers, you will need some depth of chocolate in the melting pot. For this reason, no matter how many—or few—centers you are dipping, melt at least 3 pounds of couverture.

### *Yield*
1 pound of finished chocolate dipped centers of "continental" size (¾ inch in diameter) yields about 32 individual pieces.

### *Utensils*
1. A double boiler
2. *Flat bottomed* wooden spoon
3. Spatula
4. Waxed paper or bakers' parchment paper
5. Various flat cookie sheets or baking trays
6. Table fork or specialized dipping fork(s)
7. Yogurt thermometer, or any rapid rise thermometer that registers in the 80 degrees to 120 degrees range.

### *Preparing Centers for "Bloom Resistant" Chocolate*
1. When using this type of bloom resistant chocolate, the centers can either be at normal room temperature or come from refrigeration with similarly consistent results.

**Pure chocolate keeps indefinitely without spoiling. But "bloom resistant" chocolate with clarified butter should be kept in an absolutely airtight container and used within several months. If you use it for anything else besides dipping, remember that you have altered its melting point.**

**A regular double boiler, depending on the size, is often too narrow to permit the use of the long professional dipping forks. If this is the case, simply transfer the chocolate to a bowl with a wider rim and replace it over the double boiler bottom pot.**

2. Centers should always be absolutely surface dry.

*Melting "Bloom Resistant" Chocolate*
1. Chop chocolate into small pieces.
2. Pour water into the bottom of a double boiler to within 1 inch of the top pot. Heat to just under the simmer. *No more.*
3. Put the chocolate and the cooled clarified butter in the top part of the double boiler and place it over the warm water.
4. *Stirring constantly*, slowly melt the chocolate. Using a thermometer to monitor the temperature, NEVER ALLOW THE DIPPING CHOCOLATE TO EXCEED 120 DEGREES, AND BE ABSOLUTELY SURE NO MOISTURE INVADES IT.
5. Thoroughly incorporate the clarified butter into the chocolate.

*Cooling "Bloom Resistant" Chocolate*
1. Remove the double boiler from the stove and replace the water underneath with tepid water.
2. Gently stirring, cool the chocolate to just *below* 88 degrees. Use your thermometer for accuracy. You are now ready to begin *fork* dipping. (If during the dipping process, the chocolate becomes too cold, heat it again. But this time do not let it go above 90 degrees.)

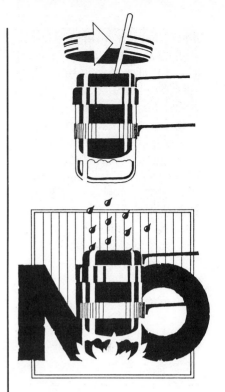

*Fork Dipping with "Bloom Resistant" Chocolate*
1. When the proper temperature is achieved, drop a center into the chocolate and, with the fork, gently but completely immerse it.
2. Slide the fork underneath and lift the center out.
3. Gently shake it up and down so that the chocolate slides over all the sufraces, forming a uniform coating.
4. Carry the center to your waxed-paper-lined tray, scraping the bottom of the fork against the side of the bowl.
5. When close to the paper, turn the fork upside down, allowing the dipped piece to drop off the fork onto the waxed paper.
   Alternatively, you may set a corner edge down and slip the fork out from underneath the chocolate, or gently nudge it off with a knife which also has a little melted chocolate on it.
6. When using "bloom resistant" chocolate, it is important, after a dozen or so pieces are dipped, to *place them in a refrigerator for up to 30 minutes to set.* Otherwise, the coating will develop gray streaks.
7. Stir the chocolate thoroughly after every few times you dip.

*Serving and Storing Finished*
*"Bloom Resistant" Dipped Chocolates*
1. Always serve at room temperature.
2. Store in a dry, cool place (65 to 68 degrees) or in a refrigerator.

**When using "bloom resistant" chocolate, we always use a fork and dip from the double boiler, rather than hand dip, because the added oils create a thinner couverture that is difficult to handle any other way.**

**"Bloom resistant" chocolate is rather thin when cool and will not be viscous enough to hold a decorative impression. We seek simply to achieve smooth, evenly coated surfaces, and for this reason a regular table fork is adequate.**

Mama became a very skillful chocolate dipper. She was good with her hands—needlework, handwriting, etc., so when Papa began making chocolates at home, she naturally became his candy dipper. She was extremely fast. And she didn't "dribble" chocolate around. Her pieces didn't have "feet" and her designs were very legible. Her dipping was truly professional and looked nice when packed.

—*Aunt Pat*

Idaho Falls
Feb 25 1958
1# sugar
1# glucose
12 oz Evaporated milk
28 oz Ice Cream Mix
5 oz Paramount Crystals
2# butter.
2 teasp Van. (Pure)
1/2 butter flavors -

My uncle Irving (my dad's oldest brother) was the first to teach me dipping when I was quite young. He had worked in grandpa's factory as a young man, but later chose carpentry as his own craft. I'll never forget how amazed I was when I saw this big husky man tie an apron around his middle, sit down at a table, and start dipping centers. With his enormous forearms and thick, muscular fingers, he nimbly dropped little chocolate-covered morsels—each with a delicate inscription on top—in neat clean rows before him. All with a sort of deliberate rhythm and grace that were beautiful to observe. If you've ever watched Issac Stern deftly fit his wide fingers onto the closely set strings of his violin, you know what I'm talking about.

# PROFESSIONAL-STYLE DIPPING (Shiny Finish)

### TEMPERING

Again, before we can talk about dipping, we must deal in detail with the question of tempering the chocolate.

To achieve the highly lustrous shine and characteristic "snap" of well tempered couverture, we cannot add to it any fats with a lower melting point (like butter). The chocolate must remain "pure" just as it comes from the manufacturer with nothing added. Then it must be properly melted and allowed to cool *undisturbed*. When it comes down to the appropriate temperature it is agitated so that the glycerides start clinging together, a process we call fat crystallization. If this is accomplished at the right temperature, the cocoa butter and cocoa solids all stabilize at the same moment, giving the chocolate a hard shiny surface.

Three temperature zones must be controlled. First, the warmth of the candy centers, second, the coolness of the room, and third, the temperature levels of the couverture itself. The entire control process is so simple to accomplish that the slight variations in climate will strike you as inconsequential, perhaps. However, to obtain consistently attractive chocolates without bloom, following the rules is absolutely necessary.

### *Ingredients*
Bittersweet, semisweet, or milk chocolate couverture (just as it comes from the manufacturer—with nothing added)

### *Amounts of Chocolate to Melt*
You should begin with considerably more chocolate than you'll actually use just for coating the centers. A pound of couverture will cover approximately 2 pounds of undipped centers, but begin with at least 3 pounds of couverture. When using "pure" chocolate it's easier to sustain the proper temperatures when you're working with larger amounts. Also, when you're hand dipping, a crust of chocolate often solidifies under the dipping puddle.

### *Yield*
A pound of continental sized candies (about ¾ inch in diameter) yields about 32 pieces.

**If you're using *bittersweet* couverture for professional-style dipping, treat it as if it were *semisweet* when you follow the instructions for tempering and dipping.**

**Semisweet chocolate or liquors (bitter baking chocolate) keep almost indefinitely. (They contain no milk solids.) In fact, they improve with age.**

**Pure dipping chocolate can be melted over and over again after it hardens as long as it is never heated beyond 120 degrees. It keeps *indefinitely*.**

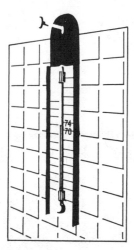

ZONE I    Centers

ZONE II    Dipping Room

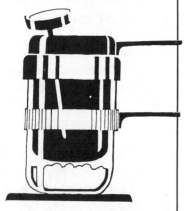

ZONE III    Chocolate

*Utensils*
1. A double boiler
2. *Flat bottomed* wooden spoon
3. Spatula
4. Waxed paper or bakers' parchment paper
5. Various flat cookie sheets or baking trays
6. Table fork, specialized dipping forks or a pair of meticulously scrubbed hands
7. Yogurt thermometer, or any rapid rise thermometer that registers in the 80 to 120 degree range
8. Wall thermometer
9. Formica countertop or marble slab (take the chill off the slab by running it under warm water, and then wipe it *absolutely* dry)

*Preparing Centers for Pure Chocolate* (Temperature Zone I)
Keep the centers in a room (other than the dipping room) with the temperature at 70 to 74 degrees. If the centers are colder, they cause fat bloom to develop when they come in contact with the warmer chocolate. Also, there is danger the centers will expand later at normal room temperatures, which are usually above 65 degrees, and burst through the chocolate, forming a leak. When centers are between 70 and 74 degrees, they are at their maximum expansion. (Truffles require special handling, including a double dipping technique. See instructions on truffle dipping at the end of the "Truffles" section, page 197.)

*Preparing the Dipping Room* (Temperature Zone II)
Lower the room temperature to between 65 and 70 degrees (68 degrees is ideal). This is easily accomplished by opening a window or turning on the air conditioning.

*Melting "Pure" Chocolate* (Temperature Zone III)
1. Chop chocolate into small pieces.
2. Pour water into the bottom of a double boiler to within 1 inch of the top pot. Heat to just under a simmer. (NO MORE THAN 140 to 160 DEGREES. DON'T ALLOW STEAM TO FORM.)
3. Put the pure chocolate in the top part of the double boiler and place it over the warm water.
4. *Stirring constantly*, slowly melt the chocolate.
Using a thermometer to monitor the temperature of the chocolate, BRING IT TO A FULL 120 DEGREES, BUT NEVER ALLOW IT TO *EXCEED* 120 DEGREES. BE ABSOLUTELY SURE NO MOISTURE INVADES THE CHOCOLATE.

### Cooling "Pure" Chocolate

1. Remove the double boiler from heat, and replace the water underneath with tepid water. (Not below 75 degrees, nor above 82 degrees.)
2. Let the chocolate sit, *without stirring*, until it comes down to a temperature of 84 to 86 degrees for semisweet chocolate, or 82 to 84 degrees for milk chocolate.
3. Now stir the chocolate with a spoon rather quickly and steadily until it becomes thick.
4. Replace (and maintain) the water in the double boiler with slightly warmer water (88 to 90 degrees). And while stirring, slowly raise the temperature of the couverture to 88 degrees for semisweet chocolate and to 86 degrees for milk chocolate. But do not let it go above 90 degrees, in either case.
5. You are now ready to fork-dip, or hand-dip, directly from the top pot of the double boiler.

**Make very sure that no steam or condensation from the spoon comes in contact with the chocolate—at any point. If the natural starch in chocolate combines with water, the mass will thicken, making it lumpy and unusable.**

## DIPPING

### Fork Dipping with "Pure" Chocolate

1. Drop a center into the tempered chocolate and, with the fork, gently but completely immerse it.
2. Slide the fork underneath and lift the center out.
3. Gently shake it up and down so that the chocolate slides over all surfaces, forming a uniform coating.
4. Carry the center to your waxed-paper-lined tray, scraping the bottom of the fork against the side of the bowl as you go.
5. When the fork is close to the waxed paper, turn it upside down, allowing the dipped piece to drop off it onto the paper. *Alternatively*, you may set a corner edge down and slip the fork out from underneath the piece, or gently nudge it off with a knife which also has a little melted chocolate on it.
6. Stir the chocolate thoroughly after every few times you dip.
7. When using "pure" chocolate, let dipped pieces sit and solidify at the proper room temperature. *Do not refrigerate them!*

**Note: Keep the fork itself slightly warmer than the chocolate or a crust of solid chocolate will form around the tines of the fork and it will be messy to use. This can be easily done by keeping the fork under the light globe of a portable reading lamp.**

### Making Decorative Markings With Dipping Forks

1. Dipping forks come with two, three or four straight tines—or a hoop which is either round or pear-shaped.
2. Pure tempered chocolate can be indented slightly by touching the prongs to the coating after the piece has been deposited on the tray. It is thick enough to hold the shape of the mark until it sets up thoroughly. The various different forks leave a variety of different marks.

**Feet. A candymaker's term which describes an irregular-shaped base of a dipped chocolate.**

*Slab Dipping Professional Style (In Pure Chocolate)*
In slab dipping, we speed up the tempering process by partially cooling the chocolate on a marble or Formica surface. We pour a portion of the melted chocolate (while it is still slightly too warm to dip) onto the work surface. Then we stir this puddle of chocolate until it comes down to dipping temperature. This gives us the opportunity to replenish the melting pot with new melted couverture without disrupting the temperature of the actual dipping chocolate. We call this method "continuous melting." It has the great advantage of accommodating a larger volume of centers to be dipped. And, of course, it's faster as well.

*Cooling Pure Chocolate for Slab Dipping*
1. Melt the chocolate in the double boiler as previously outlined in "Melting Pure Chocolate." Cool as outlined EXCEPT:
2. STOP THE COOLING AT 93 TO 95 DEGREES, AND HOLD THE CHOCOLATE AT THAT TEMPERATURE BY REPLACING THE TEPID WATER UNDERNEATH WITH SLIGHTLY WARMER WATER (94 DEGREES).
3. With your right hand lift some of the chocolate onto the work surface, a smooth Formica top or marble slab that has had the chill taken off it.
4. With a side-to-side hand motion (not up and down which would trap unwanted air bubbles) slowly agitate the chocolate until it reaches the desired 84 to 86 degrees for semisweet chocolate or 82 to 84 degrees for milk chocolate.
5. When it reaches this temperature, agitate more quickly. It will become quite thick—which is what you want.
6. Again, with your right hand carry a small amount of the warmer chocolate from the double boiler and deposit it into the cool chocolate in your dipping puddle. Ideally, this will raise the temperature to 88 degrees for semisweet chocolate and 86 degrees for milk chocolate couverture. (Be careful that the overall temperature of the dipping puddle never rises above 90 degrees.)
7. During the dipping process the chocolate inevitably will cool too far and once again become too thick to handle.
8. Continue the pattern of adding warmer chocolate from the 93 to 95 degree reservoir—to warm up the puddle to dipping temperature. (Never exceed 90 degrees in your puddle.) Then proceed with your dipping. You will soon find yourself falling into the soothing rhythm of slab dipping. The pattern, the cycle, of this process which at first glance appeared complex, will quickly become automatic.

When dipping by hand, depending on how much chocolate you are using, it becomes a little tricky to continually hold the water jacket temperature at the proper level of 93 to 94 degrees. In the beginning, for accuracy rely on a thermometer. However, as you become familiar with these temperature ranges, a touch with the finger will tell you what you need to know.

As for the chocolate in the dipping puddle, it will be the right temperature if it feels cool (not neutral) when lightly touched to the lower lip. (Remember the average body temperature is 98.6 degrees. At 95 degrees, the chocolate will feel neither hot nor cold but neutral. The lips are one of our most accurate thermometers because they always remain constant, even if the body temperature fluctuates.) When the chocolate is *too* cold, it simply becomes too viscous to give a smooth-flowing uniform coating around the center.

9. If you run out of warm (93 to 95 degrees) chocolate, you can remelt—and cool—more chocolate in the same, or in a different, double boiler.

### Hand Dipping Technique (Slab Dipping)

1. Place the tray of undipped centers to your left (if you are right-handed) and keep the left hand chocolate-free.
2. Position your dipping puddle directly in front of you, and put the waxed- or parchment-paper-lined tray on your right.
3. Pick up a center in the left hand. Make a slight dent in it with the thumb.
4. Fill the right hand with chocolate and lay the center in the middle of your palm. Gently close your hand so that the chocolate comes up over the entire center, filling the dent with chocolate.
5. Open your hand. With your thumb, slide the chocolate down to the end of the first two fingers. Shake your hand gently up and down until the coating is evenly distributed on all surfaces of the center. Carry the piece over to the paper-lined tray, wiping the excess chocolate off the back of your fingers on the side of the slab or counter.
6. Turn the hand over until the dipped piece is within ¼ inch of the waxed-paper-lined tray. Then release it by spreading the fingers apart, allowing the candy to drop gently to the paper. This is called the split dip and is perhaps the easiest of all dips.

Alternatively, as you turn the fingers over, simply allow the piece to drop off the ends of your fingers. A single string of chocolate will form. (This is called "stringing" the chocolate.) Use the string of chocolate as a writing tool to form the desired inscription on top of the dipped piece.

7. If all the temperatures are correct, the coating chocolate begins to stabilize in 1½ minutes.

## SERVING AND STORING

1. Always serve chocolates dipped in "pure" couverture at room temperature.
2. Store in a cool dry place (65 to 68 degrees). The dipped candies should be allowed to rest, undisturbed, for 48 hours. (Undesirable crystals can develop up until the time the chocolate is fully stabilized.)
3. Direct sunlight must also be avoided during storage. Even when chocolates are kept properly cool, sunlight can cause a bloom to form.
4. Never refrigerate chocolates which have been dipped in "pure" couverture!

Notice that in hand-dipping, the top becomes the bottom as the piece leaves your hand. When you've made a dent in the center before squeezing the chocolate over it, more chocolate fills into that space—which provides an extra cushion of chocolate on the bottom when it is inverted onto the paper. (We call this "bottoming" the centers.) Otherwise, the weight of the center, afloat in its coating, settles it downward, forming too thin a shell on the bottom. Then if the centers expand they burst through the thin coat of chocolate. The result is an unsightly "leaker."

An alternative to forming dents in the centers is to pre-bottom the little rascals: Holding the center gently, simply rub some tempered chocolate onto its little bottom. Let the chocolate set up, then dip the center in normal fashion.

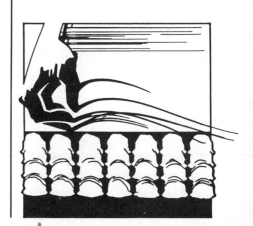

The two major enemies of chocolates dipped in "pure" couverture are "fat bloom" and "sugar bloom." The first has to do primarily with improper control of the three temperature zones already discussed. The second with improper storage.

Even when chocolates are kept properly cool, direct sunlight will also cause a bloom to form.

# FAT BLOOM

What causes this unsightly development? Heat, sunlight, improper storage. How can fat bloom be avoided? By following the rules meticulously—as all professionals are also forced to do. There really aren't any magic shortcuts or techniques.

### The Heat Hazard

Fat bloom occurs when the temperatures are too high in any one of the three zones we've already discussed in the instructions: "Preparing Centers for Pure Chocolate," "Preparing the Dipping Room," "Melting Pure Chocolate," and "Cooling Pure Chocolate," If any one of these zones is allowed to reach too high a temperature, fat bloom will occur.

*Explanation*: Good grade couverture is 33 to 35 percent cocoa butter. The cocoa powder is not dissolved in the cocoa butter but suspended in it. If the chocolate is too slow in solidifying, the cocoa particles settle to the bottom and the cocoa butter floats to the top. The yellow of the cocoa butter superimposed over the brown cocoa particles creates a gray appearance.

*Prevention*: This is prevented if the cocoa butter, which is at a dipping temperature of 88 or 86 degrees, becomes sufficiently solid within *100* seconds. (The temperature of the chocolate must drop to 80 degrees within that time period.) This will happen if the temperature of the dipping room is approximately 20 degrees lower than the dipping temperature of the chocolate. The cooler atmosphere of the dipping room literally pulls the heat from the chocolate.

Hence, to find an ideal dipping room temperature we subtract 20 from 88 (the dipping temperature for *semisweet* chocolate) or from 86 (the dipping temperature for *milk* chocolate), thus arriving at the ideal dipping room temperature of 68 or 66 degrees.

### The Sunlight Hazard

*Prevention*: Direct sunlight on the finished chocolates must be avoided. Even when they're kept properly cool, sunlight can cause a bloom to form.

## Improper Storage Hazard

*Prevention*: This should not be a great problem for the home confectioner. If you do not have an air-conditioned work area and storage area, you will know better than to dip chocolates in the hottest summer weather. And of course, you would seldom have to worry about shelf life even if you decide to take a chance on the weather. If it turns hot before the chocolates are all consumed, you'll just have to put up with some heat bloom—or call the neighbors in and gobble 'em all up before they turn gray. Refrigerating chocolates which have been dipped in "pure" couverture is not the answer, either. See "sugar bloom," below.

### SUGAR BLOOM

This unfortunate development is most likely to occur during the storing process. When condensation is allowed to gather on the surface of a finished piece, it dissolves some of the sugar in the chocolate. When the sugar crystallizes again, it forms larger crystals than before, and this gives a speckled, gritty texture. Because refrigerators have so much moisture inside, finished pieces that have been dipped in "pure" couverture should never be refrigerated.

However, sometimes (especially in the summer months), chocolates which have been dipped in "bloom resistant" coating will become a little soft. They can be kept in the refrigerator, if necessary, with minimal adverse affect.

One other exception to the NO REFRIGERATION rule. If you have some creamy dipped truffles you are afraid will spoil without refrigeration, put them in a paper bag, then into a tightly sealed plastic bag. The seal will keep most of the moisture out and what does get in will be absorbed by the paper bag.

One last caution: Even when kept out of the refrigerator, chocolates are prey to another culprit which causes condensation and its accompanying sugar bloom. That's temperature fluctuation of any kind. Keep the chocolates where the temperature is constant.

**Ideally, finished pieces should be be stored at temperatures between 65 and 68 degrees, and should not be disturbed for 48 hours. (Undesirable crystals can form up until the time that the chocolate is fully stabilized.)**

# THE TROUBLESHOOTER
### Some Dipping Problems and Solutions

1. Dull surface
    • Dipping puddle is getting too many cocoa butter crystals from the natural buildup in the crust
    • Centers are too cold
    • Temperature in the dipping room is too cold
    • Relative humidity is too high

2. Greasy surface
    • You may have a compound coating and don't know it
    • You may not have melted the chocolate high enough (120°)

3. Streaky surface
    • Chocolate not stirred enough just before dipping

4. Fingerprints
    • Handling before the chocolate is completely set up
    • Handling during condensation or when relative humidity is too high (causing condensation)

5. Fat bloom
    • Not melting the chocolate high enough (120 degrees)
    • Excess heat or sunlight

6. Sugar bloom
    • Condensation of accumulated moisture in the storage environment

7. Leaky centers
    • Centers too cold before dipping
    • Coating too thin

8. Feet
    • Dipping chocolate too warm
    • Coating chocolate too thickly applied

**When depositing a freshly dipped center onto a tray, if the couverture is too warm or there is too much, it dribbles down the sides, forming an irregular unsightly base which we candymakers call "feet." But never fear, when the extra chocolate is melting in your mouth, this cosmetic error is easily forgiven.**

## TECHNICAL SUMMARY
For small restaurateurs or specialty food operators we offer a brief technical summary of the laws governing the temperatures and agitation points necessary for achieving consistent results. Keep in mind that these guidelines apply only if the coating chocolate is free of any fats other than cocoa butter—and if the cocoa butter content of the chocolate falls within the 33 to 35 percent range.

*Why Pure Chocolate Responds to Temperature and Agitation*
Cocoa butter contains six glycerides. They are not entirely free and liquid until chocolate is melted to 120 degrees. When chocolate is solid they are linked together in a tight network of molecules we call fat crystals. These crystals are not to be confused with the sharp, granular type that form in sugars. These are simply the molecular colonies that eventually form as chocolate solidifies. Between the glycerides' melted state and solidification, four different types of crystals can form, each within a different temperature range, each with a slightly different textural quality and with varying degrees of stability.

Crystallization is caused by molecular friction. Large contrasts in temperature produce crystallization. But manual agitation is the most potent force. When we want to form a particular type of crystal, we agitate it at its peak crystallization point. When we don't want certain crystals to form we avoid agitation. We anticipate the peak crystallization points by reading the temperature.

The fat crystal formations that we are concerned with are *GAMMA, ALPHA, BETA PRIME AND BETA.*
*Gamma crystals* are undesirable. They form only when the chocolate comes in contact with a surface under 62.5 degrees. Gamma crystals have a life of only a few seconds. Of themselves they are inconsequential. But gamma crystals under the right conditions do become alpha crystals.

*Alpha crystals* are also undesirable. They have a life span of an hour or so at just under 70 to 75 degrees and can at this point pass into the solid chocolate, causing fat bloom. For this reason it is important to prevent gamma crystals from forming. This is accomplished by seeing that no surface or air temperature under 75 degrees comes in contact with the tempering or tempered chocolate.

*Beta prime crystals* are also undesirable. They form of themselves within the range of 62.5 to 72.5 degrees. They can also form from alpha crystals. They have a complete melting point at 82.5 degrees (just below the point to which milk chocolate is best cooled before dipping). It is important to prevent them from forming. This is easily done if the surfaces with which the chocolate comes in contact are never below 75 degrees (the water jacket).

*Beta crystals* are the most stable and desirable. They are the smallest and form a tight bond, causing the surface of the chocolate to be very smooth and therefore highly reflective and shiny. They are the most successful in preventing moisture transference. They crystallize between 72.5 and 92.5 degrees.

When tempering chocolate, always heat it to a full 120 degrees. Many books advise only 110 to 115 degrees. Probably because of a justifiable concern that someone will overheat the chocolate. But chocolate as it comes from the manufacturer is not consistently free from the larger fat-crystal formations that can cause bloom. Only at 120 degrees, is *all* unfavorable fat crystallization destroyed.

Never stir chocolate during the cooling process when its temperature is between 120 and 95 degrees. (Large visible crystals may form after the couverture solidifies.)

If time permits, the ideal way to cool chocolate is to allow it to cool down, without stirring, to 84 to 86 degrees for semisweet and 82 to 84 degrees for milk chocolate, before beginning *any* stirring.

To speed cooling, you may stir (slowly) between 95 and 88 degrees with minimal adverse affect.

Stirring should be done with a side-to-side motion, not up and down. (This latter can form bubbles in the chocolate.)

*Never* stir chocolate below 82 degrees.

Under ideal conditions, chocolate should *never* come in contact with any surface cooler than 75 degrees.

## Melting Tips

1. Cocoa beans contain about 7% starch, which is cooked when they are roasted, before they are ground into chocolate. Cooked starch has a definite affinity for moisture. The condensation that gathers on the back of the stirring spoon is enough to cause even a pound of chocolate to thicken suddenly, making it unusable for dipping.

2. Take the necessary time to chop or grate the chocolate as small as possible (matchstick size pieces) because the heat invades all the surfaces more quickly and evenly, making it less likely that portions of the chocolate will become overheated.

3. Since excess heat of any kind also causes chocolate to thicken, you may want to *guarantee* that the couverture does not exceed 120 degrees. This can be done by taking the double boiler off heat when the water has reached 120 degrees. The chocolate will take longer to melt, but also it will not be necessary to constantly stir it. If you use warmer water (140 to 160 degrees) in the double boiler, the melting is quicker. But you must continuously stir to be sure that no part of the chocolate remains in stationary contact with the sides of the container and becomes too hot. It is inadvisable to heat the water any higher than 160 degrees, because if steam is created there is risk it will get into the chocolate.

# IMAGINATIVE COATING CONCEPTS

*To Practice Dipping Without Wasting Chocolate*

Want to practice dipping? Want to do it without sacrificing any of the centers you've made so lovingly? Try this. Temper a weighed-out quantity of couverture, following all the rules. When it's cooled and thickened, spread it about ½ inch thick on a sheet of waxed paper. Just before it completely sets, cut it into ¾-inch squares.

Allow it to rest for 48 hours. Then treat it just like a candy center. Bring it to room temperature for dipping.

Using the right proportion of coating to centers, weigh out a fresh quantity of couverture. Temper it properly, and dip the prepared cubes of chocolate. If bloom appears, start over. Practice until you've mastered all the variables. Then simply remelt all the chocolate again. No waste. And you haven't spoiled any centers.

Remember, each time you remelt chocolate, bring it again to 120 degrees—to be sure to break temper.

*Working With Molds*

1. All the same principles of tempering that apply to dipping with chocolate apply to molding with chocolate. When using plastic or tin-lined molds, be sure the temperature of the mold itself is uniformly warmed to 75 degrees to 80 degrees if doing thin molds, and 86 degrees to 88 degrees if making solid molds. Then allow to set at room temperature.

2. Do not prematurely unseal the mold.

3. An ounce (weight) of cocoa butter may be added to 5 pounds of couverture to aid the separation of the chocolate and mold but it should be added during the melting process.

4. If you want to use antique chocolate molds for molding, be sure that the tin lining is absolutely smooth. Cracks and creases will not release the chocolate well.

5. Almost anything with a smooth shiny surface can act as a a mold for chocolate. Leaves, washed with water only so as not to strip away the natural oils, are wonderful molds for making chocolate shapes. Just be sure the leaves are not of a toxic variety.

6. Aluminum foil is good material for making molds.

7. Many European confectioners mold their chocolates instead of hand dipping them. So their chocolate is formulated with a

higher cocoa butter content—to make unmolding easier. Sometimes they also add hard fats other than cocoa butter, which their government standards allow them to do. Our government is more stringent in its definition of chocolate. See "Compound Coatings," this section.

### Microwave Melting
This is not a bad way to melt chocolate. But since every microwave oven is slightly different from others, and the rays are random, it is important that if you have no carousel, you turn the plate frequently. Also the chocolate will retain its shape even when melted and this is deceptive. Make sure you zap it only for a short time, then stir it and repeat this until it is uniformly melted. Insert your thermometer between takes to make sure the chocolate does not become too warm. Experiment with small amounts first.

### Melting "Pure" Chocolate with Liquids or Fats for Recipes
For dipping or molding we keep all moisture away from chocolate since even a small amount of moisture will make the chocolate thicken and seize. But when you make mousse, souffles or cakes often you want to mix liquids or melt fats with the chocolate. This can work very well, oddly enough. The chocolate's response to a large amount of liquid is entirely acceptable.

*The rule of thumb is that if you're using half as much liquid as chocolate, you can add it to the unmelted chocolate (chopped small) and heat the mixture directly on heat until the chocolate begins to melt.* Then take the saucepan off heat and let the choclate slowly finish melting.

Or, of course, you can melt the chocolate separately and then add it to the butter, cream, or other liquid, which must be at nearly the same temperature as the chocolate in that case (120 degrees). Use a whisk or spatula and add it rather quickly. The chocolate to the cream, not the cream to the chocolate.

### Decorating with Chocolate.
1. For an easy garnish, use a vegetable peeler or similar tool, to scrape shavings from a bar or large brick of chocolate.
2. Another way is to temper some chocolate to the higher dipping temperature and spread it thinly and evenly on a slab. Just before it sets, using a trowel or putty knife, scrape underneath the chocolate crust and form "cigarets," or strips, and set aside on another tray to set up fully. There are many decorations to be made with chocolate and many wonderfully illustrated books to demonstrate the use. Whatever the method, remember to temper the chocolate properly before starting to work it.

**Cocoa butter is highly resistant to rancidity. The high cocoa butter content of chocolate couverture makes a perfect enrobement for buttercremes or truffles which contain a great deal of dairy butter.**

**Parchment paper, available at specialty shops, is slightly heavier than waxed paper, and its Teflon coating releases solidified chocolate perfectly. It is reusable.**

Why would anyone use compound coatings? Well as far as I'm concerned, nobody should. But I suppose you could justify using them for molding some types of decorations that are not intended to be eaten. However, anything that looks like chocolate is likely to *get* eaten. So I think if it *looks like* chocolate, it ought to *be* chocolate.

A rapid-rise thermometer is helpful for monitoring chocolate temperatures.

## COMPOUND COATINGS

### Chocolate-Flavored "Compound Coatings"

The government in this country, more so than in any other country, defines certain food products. If a label says chocolate, that food can have no added types of fats other than dairy fats. Coconut oil, soybean or palm kernel oils are often added to chocolate, singly or collectively, in a hydrogenated form, to substitute for cocoa butter. If such are used, the product can't be called chocolate. It becomes a "compound coating." With the advent of plastic molds, the hobbyist, often interested in cosmetics more than in taste, will often choose compound coatings rather than real chocolate. This is because the compounds pull away from the mold very nicely and are shinier. They obviously look like chocolate. But the compounds have very different handling qualities from chocolate. Be sure to ascertain from your retailer whether you're buying chocolate or a compound coating. (The compounds are much less expensive to produce than chocolate because of the lack of cocoa butter content).

### Tempering Compound Coatings

1. Compounds are much easier to handle than pure chocolate because the hard fats in them melt at higher temperatures, and the glycerides are not nearly as complex.
2. Melt compounds to 120 degrees the same as chocolate.
3. Temper the same way basically EXCEPT: because each type of compound is different, it is imposssible to list all the various melting and setting points. You will have to experiment. They can usually be refrigerated with less adverse affect than real chocolate.

### Pastels

These are compound coatings. Colored pink, green, yellow, and so on, they're usually made entirely with high-melting fats, not cocoa butter. These include hydrogenated coconut oils, soybean oil, palm kernel oils. Pastels are very widely distributed, and come in white, as well as colors, to simulate the appearance of "white chocolate" made with cocoa butter. Like all compound coatings, they usually have a higher melting point and a less complex glyceride structure than chocolate, making them much easier to handle than cocoa butter products. This is why they are used by many *chocolatiers* in the summer months when temperatures are higher, making heat problems for chocolate. In fact, pastels are often referred to as "summer coatings."

Pastels as well as "white chocolate" are highly sensitive to overheating because of their higher milk solids content. They should never be heated beyond 95 degrees. (You risk denaturing the milk solids.) Compounds made with hydrogenated fats stabilize, however, at slightly higher temperatures than cocoa butter coatings. They can be dipped at slightly higher temperatures, and can be refrigerated without adverse effect.

## OTHER COATINGS

### "White Chocolate"

By government standards there is no such thing as "white chocolate." Why? Because in order to be called chocolate a product must contain cocoa solids. So-called "white chocolate" does not. So what is it called? Manufacturers make up fantasy names for it. Retailers usually just call it white chocolate. It is made with cocoa butter, sugar, and milk solids. It is difficult to find. It looks the same as many compound coatings made with fats other than cocoa butter, which we generally refer to as pastels. How can you tell the difference? By the smell for one thing. (Pure refined cocoa butter has virtually no flavor, but it does retain a slight aroma of chocolate.) "White chocolate" is usually more ivory-colored than white pastel coatings and it definitely melts like chocolate. It must be tempered like chocolate. EXCEPT: *Never* exceed 95 degrees during the initial melt-down, because the increased milk solids will denature.

### Coating with Fondant

For Coating Fondant recipe, see page 87. For complete instructions on fondant dipping, see Cherry Cordials Part III page 170. If almond extract isn't compatible with the centers you want to dip, use some other flavoring of your choice. Don't add Convertit to your coating fondant unless you're making Cherry—or other fruit—Cordials. Convertit is a commercial invertase whose sole function in the Cherry Cordials recipe is to convert fondant to liquid after a fondant-dipped center has been dipped a second time in chocolate.

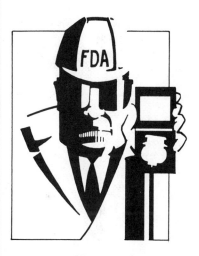

The federally approved, commercial "confectioners glaze" used by some to shine panned goods, such as coated nuts or jelly beans, is shellac. Honestly!

The formula that we use is one that my Great-uncle Julius brought from Europe. It calls for gum arabic and glucose. It has a wonderful shine, but allows the chocolate to "breathe" and give off the aroma of chocolate.

# Combining Forms

The recipes in this section are in two or more parts, combining various formulae. This first one combines a caramel jacket and a fudge center, two elements which are used in many other combinations.

# LOG ROLL CREMES

## I

### LOG ROLL CARAMEL

Caramel jackets are for pouring over bars and wrapping around cream centers or pouring onto nougats—a lot of what we all love about candy bars. What is the difference between this formula and Grandpa's "stand-up" Cremed Caramels? Less cream and lower cook, primarily.

1. Prepare the marble slab. It should be cold and completely dry. Then wipe it with mineral oil. Oil half-inch bars as well.

2. Measure each and reserve.

**2 ounces (weight) cocoa butter**
**4 tablespoons dairy butter**

3. Bring to a boil. Remove from heat and keep warm.

**1 ⅔ cups light corn syrup**

4. Measure into a 3-quart saucepan. Blend thoroughly. Bring to a boil, stirring. Wash down the sides of the pan with a pastry brush dipped in water. Insert the thermometer.

**2 cups granulated sugar**
**1 cup whipping cream**

5. As soon as the batch is boiling freely again, slowly stir in the hot corn syrup. Do not stop the boil. Then add the cocoa butter and the dairy butter. Still stirring steadily, cook to *238* degrees. Remove from heat.

6. Stir in the vanilla. Then pour out onto the prepared slab between the half-inch bars. Allow to cool.

**1 teaspoon vanilla extract**

7. Now you'll need to use the slab for the fudge center, so if you have only one slab, do this: When the caramel is cool, slide the batch, using two spatulas, onto a smooth oiled work surface. Then prepare the slab again and make the following fudge.

2 tablespoons butter

1 ¼ cups light corn syrup

3 cups granulated sugar
1 cup whipping cream

**CREME THE BATCH**
1 teaspoon vanilla extract
½ teaspoon salt

NOTE: The Log Roll Caramel by itself (without the fudge), when cut into squares after the batch is cold, makes an excellent caramel to dip in chocolate, either dark or light. If you do plan to make dipped caramels, you might like to add 1 cup chopped nuts of your choice at the end of the cook. Then cool on an oiled slab between half-inch bars, as directed, before cutting.

## II
## LOG ROLL FUDGE

1. Prepare the slab. It should be cold and perfectly dry, then wiped with mineral oil.

2. Measure and reserve.

3. Bring to a boil. Remove from heat. Keep warm.

4. Measure into a 3-quart saucepan. Bring to a boil, stirring. Wash down the sides of the pan with a pastry brush dipped in water. Insert the thermometer.

5. As soon as the batch is boiling freely again, slowly stir in the hot corn syrup. Do not stop the boil. Cook, stirring constantly, to *238* degrees. Remove from heat.

6. Add the butter, and start to CREME the batch immediately, right in the pan. Keep stirring until the batch starts to thicken. Add the vanilla and the salt. Keep stirring until it starts to set.

7. Scrape out onto the oiled slab and knead until it is cool enough to form into a roll.

## III
## FUDGE AND CARAMEL COMBINED

1. Place the roll of fudge in the middle of the cooled caramel jacket. Bring one side of the caramel up over the fudge and wipe the oil off the edge. Dampen this edge slightly and bring the other edge up and let it lap over the first about 1 inch. Press together.

2. Close the ends and using both hands in a rolling motion, spin the mass out to about 1 inch in diameter. Cut in strips 1 foot long and roll tightly in waxed paper to keep them round while they are cooling.

3. When completely cold, cut with a sharp knife, in a quick sawing motion, into pieces ¾ inch long.

4. Wrap in waxed paper so that they will keep their shape. Twist the ends.

5. Store in an airtight container.

# SCOTCH KISSES

1. Make a batch of Marshmallow I. When cold, cut into half-inch cubes. Roll the cubes in powdered sugar. Separate out on waxed paper and allow to dry overnight at room temperature.

2. Next day, make a batch of Log Roll Caramel. Spread ¼ inch thick on a cold, oiled slab, between quarter-inch bars, also oiled. Let the bottom set very briefly, without cooling much.

3. While the caramel is still hot, cover half the sheet of caramel with a layer of cut marshmallows. Bring the other half of the caramel up and over the top of the marshmallows. Handle with slightly-oiled canvas gloves, if necessary.

4. When cold, cut in squares and wrap individually in waxed paper, twisting the ends.

5. Store in an airtight container.

**1 batch Marshmallow I (recipe, page 92)**

**1 batch Log Roll Caramel (recipe, page 157)**

# PENUCHE CARAMELETTES

1. Make a batch of Grandpa Davenport's Penuche. When cold, cut into ¾- inch squares.

2. Spread the pieces out on waxed paper to dry a little.

3. Make a batch of Log Roll Caramel. At the end of the cook, pour the batch into the top pot of a double boiler with boiling water in the bottom pot—to keep the caramel hot.

4. With a bonbon fork, dip the cold penuche squares in the caramel. Then drop them into a bowl of finely chopped walnuts or pecans.

5. Butter your fingers and roll the candies into the shape of a ball. Then roll the balls in waxed paper and twist the ends.

6. When thoroughly cool, store in an airtight container.

**1 batch of Grandpa Daven-port's Penuche (recipe, page 71)**

**1 batch of Log Roll Caramel (recipe, page 157)**

# ROCKY ROAD

And here we have the hands-down, all-time favorite chocolate confection of the All-American high schooler. And indeed a very alluring combination of flavors and textures for any chocoholic.

**1 batch Marshmallow I (recipe, page 92)**

1. Make a batch of Marshmallow I. When cold, cut into half-inch cubes, roll the cubes in powdered sugar, and separate out on waxed paper.

ATTENTION: Allow the marshmallows to dry at room temperature overnight. (If any surface moisture remains, it will bind the chocolate.)

**1 pound couverture milk chocolate**
**2 ounces cocoa butter**

2. Next day, melt the chocolate along with the cocoa butter in a double boiler.

3. As soon as the chocolate mixture is melted, exchange the hot water (in the bottom pot) for cold water—to cool the mixture. Stir until it begins to thicken.

4. Lift out the top pot of the the double boiler and carefully wipe the entire outside surface, bottom and sides, to make sure there is no moisture left to drip into the bowl, then scrape the contents into the large bowl of an electric mixer.

5. Whip with a rotary beater. As you beat, the chocolate will thicken up like whipped cream, and become wonderfully aerated.

**2 cups English walnuts, coarsely chopped**

*Walnuts* are probably the most popular nuts used in candy-making. English walnuts are grown in California, and many varieties grow in France, Turkey and Italy. Under the umbrella term, "English Walnuts," are sheltered many other varieties: French Chaberts, Mayettes, California baby toppers, French Bordeaux.

6. When the chocolate is airy and light, stop beating and gently fold in the chopped walnuts, then the marshmallows. (The marshmallows should be at room temperature. If they are too cold they will harden the batch before you can spread it out.)

7. Scrape out the batch onto waxed paper. Lightly spread and smooth with a spatula.

8. When thoroughly cold, cut into squares and store in an air-tight container.

# BLACK-WALNUT TANGO

This is a very accommodating basic formula. If you don't want to use black walnuts, try any number of other kinds of nut instead—and add any compatible flavoring to go with.

And of course this is a natural for Rice Krispies. Try about a cupful. If that seems a little skimpy to you, add as much as one cupful more. And use vanilla extract, to taste, for flavoring.

1. Chop the black walnuts.

2. Melt the chocolate, with the cocoa butter, in a double boiler. Stir in a few drops of black walnut flavoring, to taste. Then stir in the walnuts.

3. Allow the mixture to cool until it feels cool to the lips.

4. Pour out on waxed paper between quarter-inch bars.

5. When the chocolate is starting to set, score in squares or rectangles. Or wait until thoroughly cold and break in chunks like peanut brittle.

*Black walnuts* have thick, very hard shells from which the kernels cannot be removed in one piece. Most of them are prepared for sale by the farmer and his family. The use of black walnuts in confectionery is somewhat limited, because they have a very strong flavor.

3 ounces (weight) black
    walnuts, chopped

1 pound milk chocolate,
    couverture grade
1 ounce (weight) cocoa butter
A few drops, to taste, black
    walnut flavoring

MELTING CHOCOLATE: Chop chocolate small. Pour water into the bottom pot of a double boiler to within 1 inch of the top pot. Bring barely to a simmer and no more. Then put the chocolate in the top part of the double boiler and place it over the warm water Stirring constantly, slowly melt the chocolate.

CAUTION: Melted chocolate, by itself (not buffered by other ingredients), must never be allowed to reach a temperature higher than *120* degrees. This rule will allow you to melt—and remelt—chocolate without harming it.

ALSO: Make very sure that no steam or condensation from the spoon comes in contact with the chocolate—at any point. If the natural starch in chocolate combines with water, the mass will thicken, making it lumpy and unusable.

# PEANUT ROLL

**1 pound roasted blanched Spanish peanuts**

1. Prepare the peanuts. Spread the raw nuts in a roasting pan. Set in a 350-degree oven for 7 to 10 minutes. Stir up frequently to keep them from burning. As soon as the husk comes off easily and the nut underneath is a light golden brown, remove from the oven. Chop the peanuts in a food processor. Or put them between two sheets of waxed paper and crush them with a rolling pin. Blow the husks off. (A hair dryer does the job handily.)

**1 batch Log Roll Fudge (recipe, page 158)**

2. Make a batch of Log Roll Fudge. When it's cool enough to form into a roll, use both hands in a rolling motion to spin it out into a long roll about ¾ inch in diameter. Roll it up in waxed paper to keep it round until it cools.

3. When cold, cut into pieces 2 ½ inches long.

**1 batch Log Roll Caramel (recipe, page 157)**

4. Now make a batch of Log Roll Caramel. At the end of the cook, pour it into the top pot of a double boiler. Allow to cool a little, then set over hot but not boiling water to hold an even temperature.

5. Dip the cold fudge in the hot caramel, using a bonbon fork.

6. Roll the bars in the prepared peanuts and lay out on waxed paper until set.

7. Dip in milk chocolate at room temperature.

You say you don't care all that much for peanuts. Well then, use some other kind of nut. Same drill. Just blanch 'em, dry roast 'em, and chop 'em fairly small. If you decide on pecans or walnuts, they don't have to be blanched. Just toasted and chopped.

*Peanuts* are grown in pods underground. The United States grows most of the world's supply. The two most common varieties are Spanish (used primarily in brittles and peanut clusters) and Virginia peanuts (used for salted or sugar-coated confections).

# PEANUT CARAMEL BAR

Wholesome, old-fashioned, and perfectly delicious!

1. Measure and reserve.

**3 cups raw Spanish peanuts**

2. Prepare the marble slab. It should be cold, thoroughly dried, then wiped with mineral oil. And you'll need half-inch bars, also oiled.

3. Melt the cocoa butter and stir in the cornstarch. Then blend in the flour. Reserve.

**2 ounces (weight) cocoa butter**
**3 tablespoons cornstarch**
**¼ cup general purpose flour**

4. Measure into a 3-quart saucepan. Blend thoroughly. Bring to a boil. Wash down the sides of the saucepan with a pastry brush dipped in water. Insert the thermometer. Cook to *240* degrees.

**2 cups granulated sugar**
**1 ⅔ cups light corn syrup**
**½ cup water**

5. Add the peanuts. As soon as the batch starts to boil again, stir it in a figure-8 pattern to keep the peanuts from burning. Do not let the spoon touch the sides of the pan above the surface of the batch. Cook to *320* degrees.

6. Stir into the batch. Cook to *225* degrees.

**1 cup whipping cream**
**½ cup milk**

7. Stir into the batch. Cook to *238* degrees. Remove from heat.

**The cocoa butter/cornstarch/ flour mixture**

8. Stir in immediately.

**1 teaspoon butter**
**1 teaspoon vanilla**
**¾ teaspoon salt**

9. Pour out onto the prepared slab between the half-inch bars.

10. When cool, cut into rectangles 1 inch by 3 inches.

11. Dip in milk chocolate. (See "Dipping" section, page 138, for instruction.)

**NOTES: Like all caramels, these need a few days to mellow and soften. For VARIATIONS, see the note at the end of Peanut Roll, opposite.**

# COCONUT BAR

Grated fresh coconut, not mixed with any of the dried kinds, can be used in any coconut confection. But in the formula here, we have chosen to use both fresh and dried. The reason? Dried coconut has a more concentrated flavor—and it is useful for soaking up surplus liquid in the batch. If you want to use fresh coconut in a recipe that calls for dried, you'll have to put in a little more of the fresh, but there isn't a rule of thumb for how much. You'll just have to experiment. If you can't find dried coconut without preservatives, try one of the specialty food shops—or a health food store.

**4 ounces fresh coconut, shredded**

1. Weigh. Shred. Reserve.

**½ pound macaroon coconut**

2. Weigh and reserve.

**1 cup granulated sugar**
**1 ¼ cups light corn syrup**

**½ cup water**

3. Measure into a 3-quart saucepan. Blend thoroughly. Bring to a boil. Wash down the sides of the pan with a pastry brush dipped in water. Insert thermometer. Cook to *230* degrees. Remove from heat.

**1 tablespoon all-purpose flour**
**1 teaspoon vanilla**

4. Off heat, stir in the flour. Mix well. Stir in the vanilla.

5. Stir in the coconut, both the fresh and the dried.

6. When the batch is cool, roll into bars and dip in dark chocolate. Or you can roll it into balls, place a roasted almond on top of each, then dip.

# CARAMEL NOUGAT CHEW

1. Make a batch of Nougat Chew. Scrape it out onto a cold, oiled slab equipped with oiled half-inch bars. Spread the nougat only ¼ inch thick. (A layer of caramel will top it, and we need the bars to contain both batches. So you may not be able to use the whole batch.) Smooth the top as well as possible with a spatula. Allow the nougat to cool thoroughly.

**1 batch Nougat Chew (recipe, page 112)**

2. At the end of the cook, pour the batch of Grandpa's Cream Caramels or Peanut Caramel Bar over the layer of nougat to fill the space up to the top of the bars. Smooth with a spatula.

**1 batch Grandpa's Cream Caramels (recipe, page 98)**

**or 1 batch Peanut Caramel Bar (recipe page 163)**

3. When cold, turn the batch over so the caramel is down. Cut in squares. Separate on waxed paper so the cut edges can dry.

4. When all surfaces are dry, dip in chocolate. Or wrap in waxed paper, twist the ends, and store in an airtight container.

# Cherry Cordials

"How do you get the liquid cordial inside the chocolate coating?" The question came for the thousandth time, followed by the guesses. "Hypodermic needle? Molds that can be covered with melted chocolate after they're filled with liquid? Magic? What?"

Well then, how indeed do we get the liquid cordial inside the chocolate coating? The answer is, of course, "We don't." What we do is what this section is going to explain to you—in detail. There are two main methods of creating this cherry cordial magic, and the key to both is our old friend fondant.

Properly approached, fondant can be persuaded to break suspension and become permanently liquid—and magnificent—within a few days after it has received its chocolate enrobement. It's magic, all right. The magic of natural physical laws at work.

You'll see.

We plan to take you step by step into the inner sanctum of the cherry cordial stronghold. First we'll preserve the cherries in as good brandy as we can afford. It will take from a week to several months to get the job done.

When the cherries are ready, we'll use a fondant recipe from "The Support Group" section to get on with our candymaking, having armed ourselves in advance with a good supply of fine couverture chocolate.

Now a word of reassurance for those concerned with the alcohol content of a completed chocolate-dipped cherry cordial. After laboratory testing, we've discovered that the alcohol ranges only from .04 to .07 percent of the total weight.

If you like cherry cordials, but want them totally nonalcoholic, you can always make substitutions. You'll find we've suggested a few.

# BRANDIED CHERRIES

This recipe calls for fresh cherries. The tart ones we call pie cherries are very good. But the big black Bings are wonderful, too. They're meatier, hold their flavor well, and are beautiful to look at. And their natural sweetness can be offset by the addition of a little lemon juice to the fondant at dipping time.

If you're using fresh cherries, plan on using about 1 pound of fruit to make 1 quart of brandied cherries. And incidentally, you should use jars with glass tops and the wire flip-up latches—for convenience in adjusting the sugar level when it's time to do that.

A quick variation using commercial maraschino cherries follows this recipe.

**1 pound fresh cherries**

1. Remove bruised or damaged fruit. Rinse cherries in cold water. Pit them, unless you're leaving the stems on. In that case, don't pit. (If you leave the stems on, they'll be easier to handle when you're dipping.)

2. Carefully place the fruit in the jar; do not pack down. Fill right to the top so that none of the cherries will float when the liquid is added.

**⅓ to ½ cup granulated sugar (depending on the sweetness of the cherries)**
**A good brandy—or other distillate of choice as long as it's 80 proof or more. The higher the proof, the better.**

3. Combine the sugar with some of the brandy you'll be using. Pour the mixture over the cherries. Fill the jar with brandy.

4. Cover closely, using a rubber sealing ring. Tip the jar over and back a couple of times to blend the sugar and brandy well.

5. Store in a dark place. Turn the jar over occasionally during the long hibernation to follow.

6. Let the cherries rest for 2 to 4 months. Then taste to decide whether you want to add more sugar. Add up to 1 cup more, if desired. Cover tightly again and let rest for another week.

7. Your brandied cherries are now ready to use for Cherry Cordials. Or for Cherries Jubilee. Or for garnish with game dishes or duckling. (If you can see that you'll have some of the syrup left over, leave a few cherries in the jar for garnish.
Serve the brandy as an after-dinner libation, garnished with a brandied cherry, of course.)

## VARIATION:

Open a jar of commercial maraschino cherries (with or without stems). Drain off the sugar syrup. Replace with brandy. Let macerate for a week before using for Cherry Cordials.

REMARKS: Maraschino cherries may be used, just as they come from the jar, for making Cherry Cordials. Drain for 20 minutes before proceeding with the recipe—as if they were brandied cherries.
In this country, *maraschino cherries* is something of a misnomer. The preparation is without alcohol, and therefore obviously contains no maraschino. This last is a liqueur made from the *marasca*, a bitter wild cherry. Incidentally, the Italians pronounce the *ch* in maras*ch*ino as if it were *k*, not *sh*.

# CHERRY CORDIALS

All right. After several months of waiting, we've just this morning tasted our Brandied Cherries for the last time from the jar. No more waiting. They're perfect! The next time we taste them they'll be enrobed in glossy rich chocolate. We'll be able to pop the finished nuggets into our mouths. The chocolate coating will yield to slight pressure, and release a myth-evoking nectar. Immediately following that, we'll bite into the firm central morsel and chew it, along with the velvety chocolate coating, experiencing a sensory blend of textures and fluids not often combined so felicitously.

But not so fast! Stop dreaming and go make a batch of Fondant for Cherry Cordials, page 85. The fondant has to ripen for 24 hours, remember? So tomorrow will be the big day.

**Cherry Cordials, continued**

Now this is tomorrow. (And you thought tomorrow never came!) First thing we'll do this morning is to gather, in one place, all the elements we'll need for putting together our "chocolate covered cherries." These essentials are listed at your left. Go fetch them all. Then at last you can start combining them. Countdown!

*Part I: Prepare the Chocolate*

1. See "Dipping" section, page 138, for detail.

**2 pounds high-quality couverture chocolate, bittersweet (if you can find it), OR semisweet, OR milk chocolate—in that order of preference**

2. Make sure the chocolate is all ready to use before beginning. After dipping the fruit in the fondant, you must be prepared to proceed almost immediately to dip it in chocolate (just as soon as a light crust is formed on the outside). Because the fondant may begin to convert at once, depending on how much juice is left in the cherries.

*Part II: Prepare the cherries for dipping*

**1 quart Brandied Cherries**

1. Drain the cherries in a sieve. Pat them dry with a towel, making sure not to squeeze or damage them. Let them drain for about ½ hour. Their surface should be dry so that the fondant will cling. A little powdered sugar dusted over them wouldn't hurt.

*Part III: Dip the fruit in fondant*

**8 ounces prepared Fondant for Cherry Cordials almond extract OPTIONAL: ¼ teaspoon Convertit (Invertase)**

1. Melt the fondant in a small double boiler, making sure it reaches at least **145** degrees. Stir in a little almond extract, to taste. Add the optional Convertit (commercial invertase) at the same time.

2. Don't try to dip the whole batch at once. Melt about half the fondant at the outset. (If too much is melted, it may get too hot before you can use it up, and some of the moisture will evaporate.)

**Sometimes, depending on how much moisture is in the cherries—or how long you have drained them—the fondant will start to liquefy too quickly. For this reason do not dip too many cherries in fondant before dipping them in chocolate.**

3. At 145 degrees, the fondant should have just about the consistency of dipping chocolate. Drop a cherry into the fondant and cover it by passing the bonbon fork underneath it and bringing the melted fondant up over the top. Then slip the fork under the cherry again and lift it out. (This will become one rolling motion with a little practice.) Lay it on waxed paper. If stems are on, just dip the fruit into the fondant, holding it by the stem, and pull it out again.

4. Allow it to stand for a few seconds. If it can be removed from the paper intact, dip the rest of the cherries in the same way. If it is too soft to remove from the paper, heat the fondant a few degrees higher than 145 and try again.

*Part IV: Dip the fondant-coated fruit in chocolate*

1. Now prepare the fruit for dipping in chocolate: Just as soon as the fondant-dipped cherries have cooled completely (this won't take long, perhaps 10 minutes), dip a forefinger in the tempered chocolate. Rub a coating of chocolate on the bottom of each piece and stand it back on the paper. This is called "bottoming."

2. As soon as the chocolate solidifies on the bottom of the cherry, dip the whole thing in chocolate. Stand each piece again on waxed paper until the chocolate is set. (Fruit Cordials need a thick, even coating of chocolate to withstand the pressure of interior expansion. They can crack and leak if the chocolate is too thin.)

3. Store for four days in a cool room. Overwarm storage adds to the twin risks of expansion—and consequent leakage. After about four days, the fondant will have drawn the juice out of the cherry, and the juice will have melted the fondant (which at the outset already had all the moisture in it that it could hold in suspension). And there you have it, a brandied cherry afloat in cordial, all enclosed neatly in a protective shell of chocolate.

Sometimes the chocolate-covered cherries have not converted, or have only partially converted. There could be any one of several reasons for this. Perhaps the cherries were drained too long so that not enough moisture remained in them to liquefy the fondant. Perhaps the fondant was applied too thick—the fondant layer should be quite thin. Or perhaps the fondant was allowed to get too hot and lost so much moisture by evaporation that a normal amount of moisture in the cherries was not enough to entirely liquefy the fondant.

Whatever the problem, it might have been avoided if you had added the optional invertase to the fondant while you were making it. Invertase is a powerful little ally in the cordial magicking business. Remember, the commercial product is called Convertit.

So if you have a problem, better luck next time around. Meanwhile you have a batch of delicious chocolate-cremes-with-a-cherry-in-the-center! Anything wrong with that?

**NOTE: The fondant in any of these fruit cordials needn't be fully liquefied. But if you want to ensure more liquefaction, use a little invertase. (Always use invertase sparingly. You can't see its liquefying effect at the time you add it. It takes about four days for its chemical reaction to occur within the chocolate-enclosed center.)**

***Invertase* is derived from yeast. It helps convert crystalline sugar into invert sugar.**

**VARIATIONS**

Pineapple chunks or tidbits, packed in heavy syrup, can also be used for making cordials. Either as they are, right out of the can—just drain and dip—or drained and macerated in brandy or high-proof rum for about a week.

STUFFED CHERRY CORDIALS
(a) When you have become skillful in handling cherries, try this. Using a small sharp knife, cut a slit in a brandied cherry and pull out the pit.
(b) Thin some marzipan with a little kirsch and pipe it into the cherry where the pit was. Proceed with the double-dipping as if it were a normal brandied cherry. How's that for gilding the lily?

# CHOCOLATE CHERRY CUPS

True to our word, we now offer you an alternative to dipped cherry cordials. These are made in little cuplets, or in plastic candy molds. Both cuplets and molds are available in specialty shops. The approach may not be traditional, but it's easier—and probably faster—than dipping. And the resultant candies taste just as good as the others.

This molded style, incidentally, is adaptable to virtually any kind of center.

1. Gather together all the ingredients and marshal your utensils.

**1 quart Brandied Cherries**

2. Drain the cherries in a sieve for about a half-hour. Pat them dry, taking care not to squeeze or damage them.

**Cuplets or candy mold**

3. Separate the paper cuplets, leaving them about 4 thick, so that they will maintain their shape. Or use the rigid foil cups—singly. Or use a candy mold.

**2 pounds high-quality couverture chocolate, bittersweet (if you can find it), *OR* semisweet, *OR* milk chocolate—in that order of preference.**

4. Temper the chocolate in a double boiler. (See "Dipping" section, page 138, for detail.)

172

5. With a teaspoon pour some tempered chocolate into each cuplet. (Fill halfway.) Rotate the cup. Drain out the excess. Turn the cuplets over (the candy mold likewise), and set them on a waxed-paper-lined tray. Let them set up.

6. When they are fully set, peel the paper back (if you're using paper cuplets), and put the chocolate shells in a fresh paper.

7. Mix the fondant with a liqueur of your choice until it is quite fluid. Add the optional Convertit (commercial invertase) at the same time.

**8 ounces Fondant For Cherry Cordials (page 85)**
**Flavorings**
**OPTIONAL: ¼ teaspoon Convertit (invertase)**

8. Pour a little fondant into each cup, then put in a cherry or a half cherry. Add a little fondant, leaving enough space to fill the cup with a layer of tempered chocolate.

9. As soon as the fondant has crusted over slightly, using a teaspoon, gently pour more tempered chocolate on the top of each cup. Make sure to spread the chocolate to all the edges— to create a complete seal.

10. When the chocolate is just starting to set up, but before it is completely set, garnish with some glazed orange peel, grated, or with a glazed violet, perhaps.

*Once you feel comfortable making chocolate cuplets, the variations are endless. Just put your imagination to work. We'll suggest a few to get you started.*

1. Use other fruits instead of cherries:
• Pineapple, just out of the can, or brandied like cherries. (See variations at the end of Brandied Cherries, this section.)
• Raisins. Use the biggest, plumpest raisins you can find. They'll probably be California goldens. Brandy them as if they were cherries. But soak them for only 2 weeks to a month. Use several in each cup, depending on their size.
• Use smallish morsels of candied ginger instead of fruit.

2. Thin a truffle paste of your choice with a little Simple Syrup (page 88). Use this instead of fondant, to surround the fruit in the chocolate-coated cup. Top with a final layer of tempered chocolate, of course. See recipes in "Truffles" section, page 185.

3. Use truffle paste alone (without thinning) to fill the chocolate -coated cups. Top with the usual layer of tempered chocolate.

## VARIATIONS

**In Austria, my uncle Julius made cordials with Morello cherries. When he came with his family to our West Coast, he found that he preferred Bing cherries for his cordials. The Bings have a sugar content balanced with a high acid level resulting in the distinctive tangy quality for which they have become famous. The stone is small and the flesh is thick, crisp and juicy.**

**To guarantee tree-ripened fruit for our cordials, each year we reserve the quantity we'll need from orchards in the Yakima Valley.**

# Dipped Nuts, Fruits and Exotica

For the novice, this is the place to start your dipping career. Nuts are firm and need no special handling for successful dipping, especially when dipped singly. But Peanut Clusters need a few explanations so we'll start our instruction with them. Following them, the same rules will apply to all the rest of the items for dipping that we list.

*Revolving pans (dragée pans)* are what we use to coat nuts and dried fruits in. They are shaped a little like cement mixers or stone polishers. They are usually of copper to conduct hot and cold temperatures. Revolving pans are used in the drug industry for coating pills. These pans were constructed crudely as early as 1840, but were not successfully developed until 1858 by the famous French dragée-maker Peysson, a colleague of the famous confectioner of the same period, Jacquin.

Great-uncle Julius introduced the use of the revolving pan to our west coast where he set up a dragée operation for the Wilson company—who named the dragée line, Wilsonettes. For a time Julius received a royalty of 1 cent for each pound of dragée produced in this country.

PEANUT CLUSTERS should be made with roasted Spanish peanuts. To roast the peanuts, spread 1 pound of raw nuts in a roasting pan. Set in a 350-degree oven for 7 to 10 minutes. Stir up frequently to keep them from burning. As soon as the husk comes off easily and the nut underneath is a light golden brown, remove from the oven. Blow the loose husks off. (A hair dryer does the job nicely.) Don't worry if some of the husks are still sticking to the nut. They'll give added flavor to the dipped clusters. Allow to cool completely (overnight wouldn't hurt), to allow the oil on the surface to be reabsorbed into the peanuts, lest the delicate balance of the dipping chocolate be adversely affected.

To dip the peanuts, and form them into clusters, melt an equal quantity (by weight) of couverture chocolate—milk chocolate, semisweet, or bittersweet. See "Dipping" section for how to melt chocolate and for detailed instruction on dipping.

Pour a little tempered chocolate on the slab and cool to dipping temperature. Add a like quantity of peanuts and mix well. Then with your hand, pick up some of the batch and lay it on waxed paper in a cluster. (Do not mix too much at a time. If the chocolate gets too hard, you'll not be able to form clusters.)

Now you're ready to take on any other variety of nut for dipping. We list a few here to get you started:

FILBERTS are nice dipped in clusters of three. They may be roasted just a little or dipped raw. Husks on, in either case.

ALMONDS should be roasted like peanuts. Dip them singly in chocolate and lay them on waxed paper to set. Don't blanch the almonds.

BRAZIL NUTS (midgets are the best for dipping). Don't roast them or blanch them. They may be dipped plain. OR dip them first in fondant, as in Cherry Cordials, page 170. Allow the fondant to set, and cool thoroughly. Then dip in chocolate.

MACADAMIA NUTS should be dipped singly.

CASHEWS are sold ready to eat. Get very large jumbo ones, prime grade, and coat them singly, like almonds or Brazil nuts.

# NUTS

**Filberts** and *hazelnuts* are almost indistinguishable, horticulturally speaking. The strains have been exceedingly crossbred. A full 80 percent of the United States filbert production is in Oregon. For chocolate or confectionery the domestic nuts are very good. For eating out of hand, salted, imported hazelnuts from the Mediterranean are a little smaller and more flavorful. They are always slightly roasted.

*Brazil* nuts are not nuts but seeds of a tropical fruit tree that grows to enormous heights in the jungles of Brazil.

*Cashew* nuts are the seeds of a fruit and should be dry roasted when they're to be used in candies. They're native to South America, and were taken to India where they have become a food staple.

*Pistachio* nuts grow on small trees in the Mediterranean regions and in California. Because of their wonderfully distinctive flavor, confectioners like to use them in the blander centers, such as vanilla creams.

# FRUIT

Maybe you'd like to try your hand at dipping fruits? Here are some suggestions. Remember, all fruits, whether glazed or fresh, must be surface dry before dipping. And dipped fresh fruits should be eaten within a day or two.

*GLAZED PINEAPPLE* should be cut into bite-size chunks before dipping. *OR* cut small, and made into clusters. Let all sticky surfaces dry before dipping, of course.

The same advice goes for all glazed and dehydrated fruits. The little seedless *RAISINS* are especially well suited to the cluster treatment. And *DATES* taste like honey when coated with chocolate. (We pit and stuff them first with fondant or marzipan.)

As for fresh fruits, try:
*BANANAS* cut in bite-size rounds.
*STRAWBERRIES*
*GRAPES*
*ORANGE SLICES.* After you've peeled the oranges, separate them into sections. It will be impossible not to make small tears in the membranes, so let the slices air-dry for half a day, or up to a full day, before dipping. The surface dries and the membrane pulls tight, giving a little crunch when you bite into them.

By now you've turned into a dipping fool, and who knows where it will stop. As a matter of fact, several years ago I attended a convention of the National Confectioners Association where I met a family who were finding enough followers to support a business founded on chocolate-coated pickles!

So:
*PICKLES*
*ESPRESSO BEANS*
*CANDIED GINGER* (cut into bite size and dipped singly)
*PRETZELS* (yes, salt and all)
*COOKIES* (we dip Fudge Brownies in *white* chocolate)

We draw the line at grasshoppers and ants, but each to his own taste. Somebody must have bought them a few years ago when they were on grocers' shelves everywhere.
Go!

*Dates* My grandpa loved them. Just stuff'm and dip'm, they're great! The mejouls and honey dates from California are wonderful. If you believe in "Love thy neighbor," present him/her/them with a beautiful box of mejouls you've dipped in milk chocolate yourself.

*Figs* dipped in chocolate! Need I say more.

# Chocolate Cremes

What do you mean when you say chocolate creme? Most of our customers mean a creamy center—of any flavor—coated with chocolate. So do we, really, but we refer to these creamy centers as handrolls.

A handroll is, as a matter of fact, none other than our old buddy, fondant, made light and fluffy—and truly elegant—by the magic properties of egg white. This egg white is in the form of Mazetta, another old friend, and is added to the batch of fondant during the cremeing process—along with the basic flavoring agent. These fondant-based centers can be given any number of flavorings for tremendous variety. Obviously, except for their texture, handrolls are relatively uninteresting by themselves. They must be dipped in rich high quality chocolate. Not only does this enhance the flavor, but prevents your creamy center from drying out. (If we dip them in a white or pastel coating we call them bon bons—this is often done to dress up the visual appeal of a gift box.)

It is an important distinction that chocolate cremes are a significantly different eating experience than truffles. Commercially they are most often made too large (an economic advantage). A creme center should be small enough to graciously pop into the mouth all at once. Immediately the chocolate mingles with the fondant—which dissolves quicker than the coating—creating an illusion that the chocolate is not so sweet. It is also very important that the handrolls be flavored subtly. If the flavor of the center is too strong, it satiates the taste buds and you will not want to reach for another. In addition to our master handroll formula, we offer you a beguiling coconut center along with its variations.

# Master Recipe
# VANILLA CREMES *(Handrolls)*

The first recipe we've chosen for this section—the vanilla cremes—will show you how we make something extraordinary out of that pedestrian helper, our old friend fondant. In each of these new guises, the unprepossessing duckling becomes an elegant swan. Once dipped, the transformed creme is truly a fit companion for the lordly truffles and cordials, and well able to take its place beside them in the confectioner's magic realm.

      Here then is a basic vanilla creme center (handroll). Dip it in chocolate, and you have a chocolate creme, right?

**1 batch Mazetta**
    **(recipe, page 86)**

1. Make a batch of Mazetta. Reserve.

**1 batch Cremed Fondant**
    **(recipe, page 84)**

2. Make a batch of Cremed Fondant, following the recipe exactly, steps 1 through 3.

3. When the white creme shows on the back edge of the scraper, fold in half the batch of Mazetta. When that is incorporated, blend in the other half.

**1 teaspoon vanilla extract**
**Other flavorings as desired**

4. Add the vanilla and continue cremeing until the fondant begins to lose its translucent quality and starts to hold its shape. It will become increasingly opaque.

5. Just before the batch "sets" (it won't take long at this stage), scrape the mass into a corner of the slab and allow it to rest for a few minutes.

6. Give yourself a brief sit-down break.

7. Now the fondant is ready to work. Dust a part of the slab with powdered sugar.

8. Pull off a piece of fondant the size of an egg and roll it out on the sugared slab to about an inch thick. Cut it with a knife into pieces half an inch long, or as large as you wish.

9. Dust your hands with powdered sugar, and roll the pieces of fondant between the palms of your hands until they are round.

10. Place them on waxed paper to cool thoroughly.

11. When they are room temperature, about **70** degrees, dip them in chocolate (see Dipping, page 138.)

## VARIATIONS

1. Use some other extract for flavoring. (Remember, the oils are much stronger than the extracts. Add oils by drops.)
    If you're using fruit flavorings, always add an equal quantity of fruit acid. For the above batch, use ¾ teaspoon fruit acid (powdered citric acid blended with an equal quantity of water). Powdered citric acid is available in pharmacies.

2. Use ½ teaspoon finely grated orange or lemon rind.

3. If you wish to make three flavor groups out of one batch of fondant, this is the way to proceed:
    (a) Prepare the above vanilla creme center exactly as the recipe is written, steps 1 through 7.
    (b) Now divide the batch into 3 equal parts. Leave one part unchanged (plain vanilla). To a second part, add—and knead in—a few drops of oil of peppermint, to taste. To the third part, add ¼ teaspoon lemon extract, and ¼ teaspoon fruit acid, to taste. Knead it in.
    (c) Finish as in the master recipe, steps 8 through 11.

4. Another variation that's a natural for this creme is the addition of 6 ounces (weight) of shredded coconut at the end of step 4 of the master recipe. Finish as in the master.

5. Add 1 cup chopped walnuts or other nuts of your choice. Same drill as for the coconut.

REMARKS: If you roll the batch while it is too warm, the centers will become hard and crack when a dent is made in them preparatory to dipping.
Do not use too much powdered sugar or the chocolate will not stick to the centers.

**Citric acid is the candymaker's "salt" used to offset the sweetness of simple fondant cremes and for enhancing the fruit flavored candies. It is made from the rinds of limes, lemons or oranges.**

# PINEAPPLE CREMES

1 small can crushed pineapple
    and its juice (approx-
    imately 10 ounces)
1 cup granulated sugar

1 batch Vanilla Cremes
    (master recipe page 178)

½ teaspoon pineapple
    flavoring
1 teaspoon fruit acid (equal
    parts powdered citric acid
    and water combined)

1. Put the pineapple and the sugar into a small saucepan. Blend thoroughly. Bring to a boil. Wash down the sides of the pan with a pastry brush dipped in water. Insert a thermometer and cook to **236** degrees. Reserve.

2. Make a batch of Vanilla Cremes, steps 1 through 3.

3. After you've blended in the Mazetta, add the pineapple, along with the pineapple flavoring and the fruit acid, to the batch (step 4). Continue cremeing until the fondant starts to pile up on the slab.

4. Finish the batch and dip, as in Vanilla Cremes.

# COCONUT CREMES

Attention, coconut lovers! This recipe uses entirely fresh coconut. And most of it gets cooked right in the batch. The result is an unequaled richness of texture and an unparalleled density of flavor. The coconut we add after the cook not only firms up the batch for handling, it also gives us a crunchier texture—and adds an additional nuance to the flavor.

6 ounces fresh coconut,
    shredded (page 89)

5 cups granulated sugar
⅔ cup light corn syrup
1 cup water
⅛ teaspoon salt

1. Weigh. Shred. On two separate sheets of waxed paper, make two separate mounds of shredded coconut, one weighing 4 ounces the other weighing 2 ounces. Reserve.

2. Measure into a 5-quart saucepan. Blend thoroughly. Bring to a boil. Add 4 ounces shredded coconut. Wash down the sides of the pan with a pastry brush dipped in water. Insert thermometer. Cook, without stirring, to **236** degrees.

3. Remove from heat. Cool to lukewarm in the pan.

4. Stir in the vanilla. Then gradually work in all that remains of the reserved coconut.

5. Butter your hands and shape the batch into balls of the desired size. Allow to cool thoroughly.

6. Dip in dark chocolate. Before the chocolate has completely set up, top each piece with a roasted almond.

1. COCONUT MOLASSES CREMES
   In procedure, this formula is almost identical to the one above. But the addition of molasses to the ingredients requires changes in the quantity of sugar and corn syrup. These three changes are made when measuring the ingredients into the saucepan (step 2) before starting the cook:

Change corn syrup to ⅓ cup
Add ⅓ cup light molasses
After this mixture (plus the 1 cup water and ⅛ teaspoon salt in the original) has come to a boil, and you've added the coconut, washed down the sides of the pan, and inserted the thermometer, you'll have to stir the batch constantly right to the end of the cook. (Molasses scorches readily.) Otherwise, proceed exactly as in the original, first to last.

2. CRYSTALLIZED COCONUT CREMES
   For an attractive presentation, use either of the above formulas. Color the batch by kneading in paste coloring just before shaping into balls. Cool thoroughly. Then instead of dipping, crystallize them. See Crystal Syrup, page 88, for crystallizing procedure.

**CREME THE BATCH**

**1 teaspoon vanilla**
**The remaining grated coconut**

**VARIATIONS**

**There are some wonderful creamed coconut spreads available—mostly in oriental grocery stores. These are nice in fondant or buttercream candies. (And not bad on toast in the morning either.)**

# BUTTERCREMES

We have explained how to make creme centers or handrolls by making fondant and adding mazetta. With another turn of the wrist, you can transform your handrolls into velvety butter-cremes. Actually, buttercremes are much more popular with our clientele because they are richer and less sweet. But with the butter always comes the problem of potential rancidity if they are held for any length of time. This is a problem you home cooks seldom face. However, candymakers often resort to using preservatives (a practice we won't allow). Another effective way to deal with rancidity is to cook the butter right in the batch as we do with fudges. In fact, all of the fudges make wonderful dipped centers just as they are. And if you prefer, you could make a batch of mazetta and fold it into any of the fudges during the cremeing process to make a wonderful cooked buttercreme. The other method is to make a batch of cremes and fold uncooked, softened unsalted butter into the batch during the cremeing process. Then follow the same procedure for dipping as for any of the other cremes. But remember, you can't store these very long outside of refrigeration.

How much butter do we use? The rule of thumb is simple. For every 4 cups of sugar we allow ⅓ cup of butter.

## VARIATIONS

1. Rum Buttercremes. Make a batch of vanilla cremes and at the end of the cremeing process knead or fold into the batch ⅓ cup unsalted butter and add 3 teaspoons of a favorite dark rum.
2. Coffee Buttercremes. Same as above only use some instant espresso and make a very concentrated solution of espresso and add a couple of teaspoons, or to taste.
3. Mint Buttercremes. Same as above only use a few drops of oil of peppermint. Be careful! Easy on the mint.

The only limitations to buttercreme variations are your imagination.

**The colder a batch of fondant or fudge during the cremeing process, the longer it takes to creme it and the smoother the batch. Technically a super-saturated solution, when cooled to below 120 degrees before cremeing (roughly, lukewarm), will form fine crystals undetectable as such by the human tongue.**

J.R. - 6-'28

Hand roll center.
Add. Toffee flavor
as follows =
   Melt 20# gran. sugar
dry - let it get nice
and brown - clear -
all melted. - Bring
it back with fresh
cream to a good
ball. - add 4oz Rum
flavor - add to batch
just as it is -
about to set.
It should be same
temp'ture as batch.
   Good heat.


make hand roll &
just before it comes
up add 10# Hardies
almond paste. which
has been mixed with
5# or more of batch
till nice and smooth
on Hobart.
   color light green
if needed add
a little bitter almond
flavor, but be care
-ful.

Too much intensity of any one flavor element bombards and satiates the taste buds, leaving room for only one bite. If you want your guests to reach for another bite, learn to combine opposing flavors subtly.

# Truffles

It's hard to imagine the French cuisine without chocolate. No *mousse au chocolat* to end the perfect dinner. No *chocolat chaud* to take the chill off a bright cold day in winter under the bare chestnut trees of a sidewalk café. No *truffe au chocolat* to warm the soul when chocolate craving strikes. Ah, no chocolate truffles! That is indeed the most unimaginable catastrophe of all, no chocolate truffles anywhere in this cold cold world.

Now having offered you the unimaginable, it's only a short step further to offer you just the opposite. You will find it easy now to imagine with what joy the French greeted the breach in the wall of chocolate secrecy with which the Spanish had repelled invaders for so long. Behind the chocolate wall, the Spanish had hoarded to themselves a technique which only they in all of Europe knew, a technique they had learned in their Indian conquests of Central America. How to convert the cocoa bean to edible use.

Once the secret became the property of French chefs, the cuisine in that food-loving country was never the same again. It was just at the beginning of the great awakening among the aristocracy to the joys of the table—not to mention the political advantages that could be anticipated as a result of lavish entertaining at table. A great chef was beginning to be considered a jewel beyond price—to any nobleman worthy of his gouty big toe.

A chocolate truffle is a rich chocolate center with a textured coating suggestive of the celebrated black truffle of Périgord.

Well, with cocoa beans to play with, and the knowledge available at last to use them, the chefs in the kitchen of every great house were soon pounding out delicacies that became standards for the world.

And when we say pounding, that's just what we mean. Without our modern machinery for producing the high grade couverture chocolate we take for granted today, the process was unbelievably tedious and laborious. And prohibitive in cost. The raw beans that arrived from the Americas, at who knows what astronomical prices, still had to be fermented, then roasted, then ground by hand, then ground some more, pounded and pounded in mortars to as fine a texture as could be managed, in order for them to be used at all in cooking. And it was out of all this labor that one of the greatest glories of French confectionery was born. It seems very likely that some long-forgotten godfather-chef christened the newborn "Truffle" because of a distinct resemblance to the rare and fabled black truffles of France's Perigord region. (Especially if the confection happened to be a bit rough-textured from insufficient pounding.)

Whatever the case, the chocolate truffle has held its preeminent position ever since, as the undisputed monarch of confections, the most exquisite, elegant and sophisticated sweetmeat in all the western world. And the most loved, if our clientele can be considered an indicator.

No longer the sole property of the great creative chefs of the past, nor exclusively a morsel for kings and queens and dauphins, today's chocolate truffle has become a thing to bring joy to any household where loving cooks gather in kitchens to experiment with the world's great cuisines.

When you read the formulas which fill this section, we can just hear your snort of disbelief. "For heaven's sake, is that all there is to it?" you'll say—and with good reason. Someone else has taken all the work out of it for you. You have only to perform the final steps, and you can serve the finest professional truffles right from your own kitchen.

The recipes we're offering you represent a broad cross section of truffle types. All are based on couverture grade chocolate from the best manufacturers. You'll find several brands available in chocolate shops and in other specialty food shops. Choose them according to your taste. They vary considerably from producer to producer.

Feeling that some of you would not want to have to learn to dip candies just to make some truffles, we have further simplified these recipes by allowing you to finish them without dipping—by rolling the shaped truffle paste in cocoa or grated chocolate.

But we suspect that most of you, after you've become comfortable with making the truffle centers, will find you want to go all the way. So take a look at our truffle dipping instructions at the end of this section—and the general dipping information in the "Dipping" section. Lever up your courage and have a go. But be prepared to find that once you've tried this most professional of all the confectioner's arts, you won't want to rest until you've dipped every morsel of food in the house small enough to enrobe in chocolate. Dipping's fun. And habit-forming. Honest!

# Master Recipe
# THE ROYAL CHOCOLATE TRUFFLE

Rich, dense, dark chocolate. That's this truffle. No other flavor is added to it to challenge the supremacy of King Chocolate. This one's for the purist who doesn't want anything to come between him and his beloved chocolate. (Or her, as the case may be.)

Now to call this truffle a basic is to seem to derogate it. But it truly *is* basic, in that all other truffles are simply elaborations on it, growing directly out of it. This is the founding father, if you will, of a great royal family. The other formulas, which follow this one, have other textures and flavors. But all have a rich chocolate base and are made in essentially the same way.

**⅔ cup whipping cream**

1. Measure into a 3-quart saucepan and bring just to the boil. Remove from heat at once and cool to **120** degrees.

**1 pound semisweet chocolate (couverture)**

2. Chop fine and melt in a double boiler to **120** degrees.

3. Add the chocolate to the cooled cream (not the cream to the chocolate) and stir until the mixture is smooth.

4. Scrape the batch onto a cookie sheet, spreading it evenly.

5. Refrigerate for half an hour or so, or until firm.

6. Remove from the refrigerator and form into small ball shapes with a melon-ball scoop. Put them on a sheet of waxed paper.

**¾ cup cocoa powder (natural process), for coating**

7. Each time you have formed a half-dozen or so, roll them in cocoa powder. Arrange them on a handsome serving plate and put them back into the refrigerator. If the truffle paste gets too warm to hold its shape well, refrigerate it briefly until it is again firm enough to work.

8. When the entire batch is finished and stacked prettily on the serving plate, keep refrigerated until 15 minutes before serving.

## VARIATIONS

1. Add as much as ¼ cup of your favorite liqueur at the end of step 3 to create your own variations. Finish as in the master formula.

2. Use any flavoring extract or oil that appeals to you—even a few drops more of vanilla, if you wish. (But don't forget that the couverture chocolate is probably already flavored with vanilla.) And of course, both almond and peppermint go well with dark chocolate. Add the flavorings a little at a time at the end of step 3, tasting carefully as you go.

3. Divide the batch at the end of step 3, and stir in different flavorings for each portion, then finish as in the master.

4. If you want to give a fluffy texture to our basic Royal Chocolate Truffle, take the mixture out of the refrigerator just before it is set (step 5). Scrape it into the chilled bowl of an electric mixer and whip it with a rotary beater until it is fully aerated. Chill thoroughly. It will retain the air you've whipped into it.

   When you're ready to form it into ball-shape pieces, work it a small portion at a time, keeping the remainder refrigerated. Don't roll in cocoa.

   When the entire batch is finished, freeze until solid. Then dip (in white chocolate, if the flavor contrast appeals to you) to keep the air trapped inside the filling.

   Incidentally, take care not to let the truffle come back to room temperature after it is whipped—not until it has been dipped (and therefore is securely protected by a solid shell of coating). See instructions for dipping truffles, (page 197).

**MELTING CHOCOLATE:** Chop chocolate small. Pour water into the bottom pot of a double boiler to within 1 inch of the top pot. Bring barely to a simmer and no more. Then put the chocolate in the top part of the double boiler and place it over the warm water Stirring constantly, slowly melt the chocolate.

CAUTION: Melted chocolate, by itself (not buffered by other ingre dients), must never be allowed to reach a temperature higher than *120* degrees. This rule will allow you to melt—and remelt—choco late without harming it. A rapid-rise thermometer is helpful for monitoring chocolate tem peratures.

ALSO: Make very sure that no steam or condensation from the spoon comes in contact with the chocolate—at any point. If the natural starch in chocolate com bines with water, the mass will thicken, making it lumpy and unusable.

# WHITE RUSSIAN TRUFFLES

This formula depends as much on milk chocolate for its special quality as on the Kahlúa. So give yourself the pleasure of shopping for the milk chocolate you will use. And parenthetically, you should shop just as assiduously and judiciously for your dark chocolate couvertures, the semisweet and bittersweet types. The following criteria apply equally to them.

Do your tasting seriously, with discriminating care. Judge the chocolate flavor. Is it clear? Is it intense? Judge the sweetness. Is the product too sweet for your taste? Is there enough cocoa butter added to the chocolate to make it melt in the mouth—to a rich and unctuous cream? And what about the aftertaste? Is it clean and pleasure-giving? Without any off-taste at all? Give special attention to texture. Is one product as smooth, as velvety as another? With no hint of graininess?

All of these elements differ widely among the various manufacturers. The original beans are blended and roasted to the taste of each company, so you just have to find the one that appeals most to you.

Go on, sacrifice yourself on the altar of scientific research. You'll never have a better excuse!

| | |
|---|---|
| **1½ pounds milk chocolate (couverture), for coating** | 1. Grate fine. Reserve. |
| **1 cup whipping cream** | 2. Measure into a 3-quart saucepan and bring just to the boil. Remove from heat at once and cool to *120* degrees. |
| **1 pound milk chocolate (couverture), for melting** | 3. Chop fine and melt in a double boiler to *120* degrees. |
| | 4. Add the chocolate to the cooled cream (not the cream to the chocolate) and stir until the mixture is smooth. |
| **¼ cup Kahlúa** | 5. Stir into the batch—until well incorporated. |
| | 6. Finish as in the master recipe (page 188) steps 5 to 8. EXCEPT: Roll the shaped centers in grated chocolate instead of cocoa (step 7), pressing it into the truffle paste to make a dense coating. |

# CHOCOLATE SILK TRUFFLES

The egg yolks in this formula give it a wonderfully silken, smooth texture. We shudder to add that this truffle has sometimes been called Parisian Pudding.

1. Measure into a 3-quart saucepan. Blend thoroughly. Heat slowly, stirring constantly just until the mixture thickens. Do not let it boil. Cool to *120* degrees.

**5 egg yolks, large**
**⅓ cup whipping cream**

2. Chop fine and melt in a double boiler to *120* degrees. Remove from heat.

**1 pound semisweet chocolate (couverture)**

3. Using a wire whisk, beat the chocolate into the egg yolk/cream mixture until the mass is smooth.

4. Whisk into the batch piece by piece until thoroughly blended.

**¼ pound unsalted butter at room temperature**

5. Whisk in the flavoring, making sure it's well incorporated into the batch.

**¼ cup to ½ cup dark rum, or to taste**
***OR* another distillate of your choice**
***OR* extract of choice, to taste**
**1 cup cocoa powder (natural process), for coating**

6. Finish as in the master recipe (page 188) steps 5 through 8.

Salted or unsalted? That is the question. The answer: sometimes yes and sometimes no. Salted butter is not just salty. It is more highly cultured; meaning, it has more of what we associate with the flavor of butter. In chocolate truffles, the butter content being proportionately very high, the flavor of salted butter is too assertive for many tastes. But in buttercremes, which are mostly sugar, it is a different matter. We generally prefer regular table butter in those.

# AMARETTO TRUFFLES

The procedure in this formula gives you still another option or two in your approach to truffle-making.

**1 pound semisweet chocolate (couverture)**

1. Cut very fine, or shave. Reserve.

**1 cup whipping cream**

2. Measure into a 3-quart saucepan and bring just to the boil. Remove from heat.

**6 tablespoons unsalted butter at room temperature**

3. Immediately stir in the butter until it has completely melted.

**The shaved chocolate**

4. Add to the cream/butter mixture, stirring until the chocolate is fully melted and the batch completely smooth.

**½ cup Amaretto liqueur OR almond extract, to taste**

5. Stir in the flavoring, mixing well.

6. If the mixture is too thin for piping with a pastry bag, pour the batch into a bowl and refrigerate until it stiffens slightly but is still soft, 10 minutes—or a little more perhaps. Then take it out and whisk it lightly to ensure a uniform texture and temperature throughout.

7. Spoon the mixture into a pastry bag fitted with a half-inch plain tip. Pipe out little mounds, about ¾ inch in diameter, onto a cookie sheet. You may have to put the pastry bag into the refrigerator briefly from time to time. (The truffle paste will have a tendency to melt around your fingers.)

8. Freeze. This should take 20 to 30 minutes.

**1 cup cocoa powder (natural process), for coating**

9. Put the cocoa powder into a plastic bag. When the truffles are frozen, shake them in the cocoa. Do it in several takes if you wish. As each handful is coated, put the finished ones back in the freezer in a fresh plastic bag. Close it tightly. Keep frozen until serving time is near.

10. Arrange on a serving plate, and allow 15 minutes at room temperature before serving.

11. If you decide you want to dip these truffles, see instructions for double-dipping frozen centers at the end of this section.

# UNTROUBLESOME TRUFFLES

Here's one to do in your food processor—still another procedure for your collection of truffle methods. And one you can adapt for almost any truffle formula. We warn you, though, once you've made truffles this way, you may never melt chocolate again. They're so easy and quick to do in the processor that this formula gives you a wonderful way to get even with your spouse next time he/she arrives home with unexpected dinner guests in tow. Just hand him/her this recipe and point to the machine.

1. Insert the chopper blade in the processor. Chop the chocolate very, very fine.

**½ pound semisweet chocolate (couverture)**

2. Heat to just below the boiling point.

**½ cup whipping cream OR ½ cup strong coffee**

3. Immediately remove the processor cover and add the hot liquid all at once. Cover and process until the mass is fully homogenous and perfectly smooth.

4. Through the feeder tube, add the butter to the processor bowl. Cover and process just a second or two more—enough to blend the whole mass into a creamy mixture.

**2 tablespoons butter**

5. Put the processor bowl into the refrigerator for a few minutes.

6. When the batch is firm enough to be shaped, finish it as in the master recipe (page 188) steps 6 through 8.

**1 cup cocoa powder (natural process), for coating**

## VARIATIONS:

1. If you want very dark chocolate centers, use bittersweet chocolate. If you can't find it, substitute 6 ounces (weight) semisweet chocolate plus 2 ounces (weight) unsweetened baking chocolate.
    2. Use milk chocolate couverture.
    3. After all the other ingredients are blended to a cream, add some chopped ginger, or nuts, or praline powder, to taste.
    4. Add 2 tablespoons liqueur of choice, or 2 teaspoons orange juice concentrate at the end of processing.

# BLACK SATIN CREAM TRUFFLES

Bittersweet chocolate being sometimes hard to find, we're offering a suggestion for a substitute—if you need it. Instead of a full pound of bittersweet chocolate, use ¾ pound of *semi*-sweet couverture and ¼ pound of *un*sweetened baking chocolate.

Incidentally, there is no liquid in this formula. We use only butter to soften the chocolate. Another difference: Instead of rolling the formed truffles in cocoa powder, we coat them with finely grated chocolate to give a little more support. (Because of the quantity of butter, the truffle paste is very soft.)

**1 ½ pounds bittersweet chocolate (couverture), for coating**

**1 pound bittersweet chocolate (couverture), for melting**

**½ pound unsalted butter at room temperature**

**2 teaspoons vanilla extract**

1. Grate and reserve.

2. Chop fine. Melt in a double boiler to **120** degrees. Remove from heat.

3. Gradually whisk the softened butter into the chocolate until it is completely incorporated and mixture is smooth.

4. Whisk into the batch until it is thoroughly incorporated.

5. Finish as in the master recipe (page 188) steps 5 through 8, EXCEPT: roll the shaped centers in the prepared grated chocolate instead of in cocoa (step 7). Gently press it in, so that the grated chocolate really adheres to the truffle paste, making as dense a coating as possible. This will form a more supportive crust for this particular center.

# IRISH COFFEE TRUFFLES

There's much more to recommend this concoction than the noggin of the poteen it contains. And you don't have to be Irish to appreciate it. If you love Irish Coffee, you won't be able to resist trying this formula.

1. In a small saucepan, heat the coffee. Pour it into a mixing bowl and cool to *120* degrees.

½ cup espresso or other strong coffee

2. Chop fine. Melt in a double boiler to *120* degrees.

1 pound semisweet chocolate (couverture)

3. Beat with a wire whisk bit by bit into the chocolate until the mixture is smooth.

½ pound *unsalted* butter at room temperature

4. Gradually whisk the chocolate/butter mixture into the coffee, beating until thoroughly blended and creamy.

5. Add to the mixture. Stir until well incorporated in the batch.

½ cup Irish whiskey

6. Finish as in the master recipe (page 188) steps 5 through 8.

1 cup cocoa powder (natural process), for coating

# PRALINED TRUFFLES

This is a very good example of a simple pralined truffle. It will give you the basis for endless variations, using other liqueurs with other complementary brittles—almond brittle with Amaretto, for example. Or walnut brittle with Liquore di Noce. Or coconut brittle with Piña Colada. Mix or match, it's dealer's choice. And it just happens to be your turn to deal.

1. Grind to powder in a food processor or blender. Don't overdo it. You don't want a paste for this recipe. Reserve.

Enough hazelnut brittle to make ¾ cup when ground

2. Chop fine. Melt in a double boiler to no higher than *120* degrees.

½ pound semisweet or bittersweet chocolate (couverture)

3. Whisk bit by bit into the chocolate until the butter is melted and well blended in.

¼ pound unsalted butter

4. Whisk into the chocolate mixture until well incorporated.

¼ cup Frangelico liqueur

5. Whisk into the batch, whipping until it is all well blended together.

The reserved ¾ cup ground brittle

6. Finish as in the master recipe (page 188) steps 5 through 8.

1 cup cocoa powder (natural process), for coating

# CRÈME FRAÎCHE TRUFFLES

Imported crème fraîche is available in specialty food shops. But if you don't find some readily, try using sour cream, instead. We think it tastes more interesting than one of the alternative homemade substitutes—which never really taste like French crème fraîche, anyway.

This truffle is a little more fragile than most. Dipping it in chocolate will prolong its shelf life a little, but if they are rolled in cocoa, or grated chocolate—or dipped—these should be eaten within a few days to a week. This is true of the sour cream version, as well. Because in neither case is the cream scalded in this formula.

**1½ pounds semisweet chocolate (couverture), for coating**
**OR 1 cup cocoa powder (natural process), for coating**

1. Grate fine and reserve.

**1 pound semisweet chocolate (couverture), for melting**

2. Chop fine. Melt in a double boiler to *120* degrees. Remove from heat.

**4 tablespoons unsalted butter at room temperature**

3. Gradually whisk into the melted chocolate until it is completely incorporated and the mixture is smooth.

**½ cup crème fraîche**
**OR ½ cup sour cream**

4. Whisk this mixture into the crème fraîche, blending thoroughly.

**The grated chocolate**
**OR the cocoa powder**

5. Finish as in the master recipe (page 188) steps 5 through 8. EXCEPT: If you've decided to roll the shaped centers in grated chocolate instead of cocoa (step 7), gently press the chocolate into the truffle paste, so that it really adheres, making a dense coating.

# HOW TO DIP TRUFFLES

Truffles are a special breed of center for dipping. Because truffles are almost always a little soft at room temperature—and some of them are very soft—they must be well chilled, or actually frozen in order to handle them for dipping in chocolate. Since a chilled center will turn pure couverture gray, truffles become the perfect candidate for Simple Dipping, which creates a satin finish. So for the easiest approach, turn to pages 140-141 and follow the instructions for Simple Dipping. If you want your truffles to have the snap and shine of professionally dipped chocolates using only pure couverture, we offer another solution—double dipping. Here is how you do it.

So for the easiest approach, turn to pages 140-141 and follow the instructions for Simple Dipping.

1. Have your ball-shaped truffle centers on trays in the refrigerator or freezer (the truffle recipe has told you which), ready to dip. They have *not* been rolled in cocoa or grated chocolate.

2. Turn to pages 138 ff. Follow carefully the steps for dipping—either simple or professional style—EXCEPT: you will not bring the truffle centers to room temperature before starting. They'll be dipped directly at refrigerator or freezer temperature.

3. Now when the aforementioned gray look appears, not to panic. Simply bring the dipped truffles to room temperature (70 to 74 degrees). The soft centers are now all nicely protected by a chocolate coating—an unbeautiful chocolate coating, but one that retains a handsome round shape, nonetheless.

4. So, when these little frogs have come to room temperature and all surfaces are completely dry, just dip them in chocolate one more time. Now look what you've done. You've magicked them into handsome young princes. My, my.

5. You may use whatever chocolate seems compatible to you for your masterpieces—the milk chocolate couverture through the bittersweet. And no doubt from time to time you'll be in the mood to use "white chocolate." But make sure the sweet vanilla flavor doesn't conflict with the flavor of the center you're coating.
   "White chocolate" involves a slightly different approach to tempering than do the chocolate chocolates. In the initial meltdown, it should never be allowed to exceed 95 degrees or the increased milk solids in "white chocolate" will denature. But otherwise, approach both the tempering and dipping as outlined above for the brown chocolates.

**Simple Dipping. Truffles are perfectly suited for Simple Dipping, which achieves a satin finish because they are chilled.**

**Double Dipping Professional Style is a way to overcome the chilled center problem necessary to handle the soft texture of most truffles.**

**Parchment paper is excellent for receiving freshly dipped chocolates. It has a special coating that releases the solidified chocolate. It is heavy. And washable—for reuse.**

**Excess dipping chocolate can be hardened and remelted many times as long as it is never heated beyond 120 degrees Fahrenheit.**

# TRUFFLE MINT

Confectioners call this truffle a "melt away." Since many folk have as strong a bias in textures as in tastes, this formula satisfies those who want a firm, light texture that melts away quickly in the mouth—rather than the rich, unctuous texture more usually associated with truffles.

With a minor feat of prestidigitation—or perhaps *juggling* is a better word for it—we simply shift around the basic ingredients, putting them together in a different way, to achieve textural differences. In this recipe, chocolate is suspended in a neutral medium other than cocoa butter. (Dairy butter is specifically not used because we don't want any basic flavor other than the chocolate.) This produces a less intense flavor but gives textural variety.

Our original formula calls for hydrogenated coconut oil, because it has no flavor of its own to compete with the chocolate. But because coconut oil is hard to find, we adapted the recipe to margarine. Use the hard type made with corn oil.

This is a fine formula for building chocolate "gingerbread" houses or Christmas castles. The chocolate bricks are strong—and good to eat besides. And by using margarine instead of butter, we have allowed you to create a centerpiece that will keep well throughout the entire holiday season. And fill the dining room with the tantalizing fragrance of festive mint into the bargain.

Happy holidays!

**2½ pounds semisweet chocolate (couverture)**

1. Chop small and melt in a double boiler to **120** degrees.

**1 pound hard (corn oil) margarine**

NOTE: If you can find some coconut oil (hydrogenated), use it instead of margarine. In which case, use 1 pound 5 ounces of coconut oil for every 2 pounds 13 ounces of chocolate.

2. Melt in a 3-quart saucepan. (Temperature not to exceed **120** degrees.)

3. Whisk the chocolate into the margarine (not the margarine into the chocolate). Mix well.

4. Cool to "soft soap" stage (not in a refrigerator). This means that a spoon will stand up in the mixture, but the mass is still soft.

**1 teaspoon oil of peppermint**

5. Add to the mixture. Whip the batch (with a rotary beater) until it is light and fluffy.

6. Scrape out onto a waxed-paper-lined slab between half-inch metal bars to a depth of ½ inch. Or use a waxed-paper-lined cookie sheet. Most of them have sides about ½ inch high.

7. Spread the batch absolutely flat and smooth. It should be of an even thickness throughout.

Find a straight edge that is a little longer than the width of the batch. Rest it on the bars containing the batch—or on the edges of the cookie sheet. Draw it slowly toward you down the length of the batch, "skeeting" it back and forth as if leveling concrete. This will produce the flat surface you're looking for.

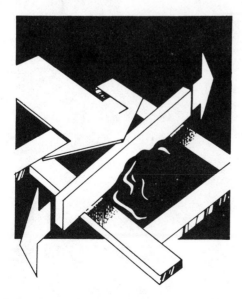

**_Truffle Mint, continued_**

8. As soon as the batch begins to set, cut with a hot knife into rectangles (bricks) ½ inch by ¾ inch.

9. When completely set, dip in milk chocolate. If using for construction, leave undipped.

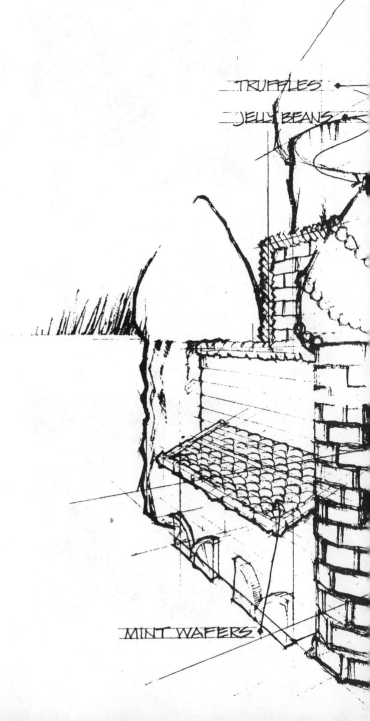

TRUFFLES

JELLY BEANS

MINT WAFERS

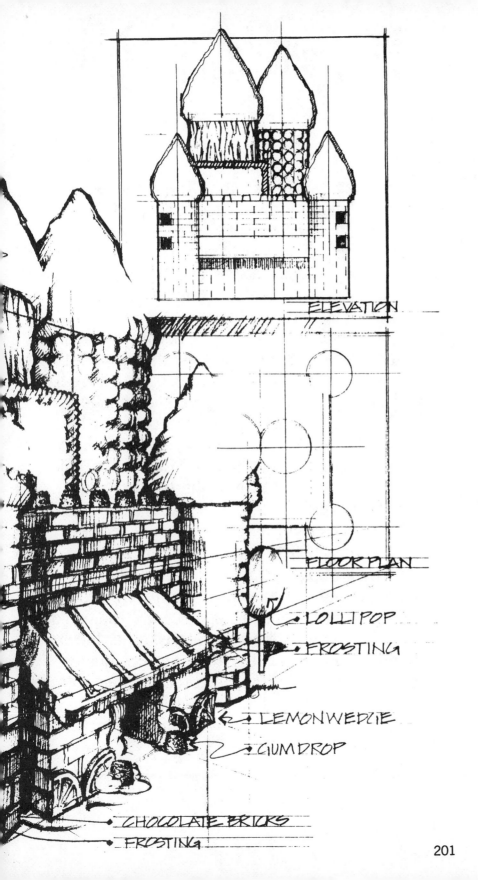

ELEVATION

FLOOR PLAN

LOLLIPOP

FROSTING

LEMON WEDGE

GUMDROP

CHOCOLATE BRICKS

FROSTING

201

# The Generation Bridge

In the beginning was Julius. Then there was Earl. Then Julius and Earl. Then Julius and Earl and Ottilia. And now, because Earl and Ottilia married, there's Dana. That's me. I'm one of Earl's grandsons—the one who decided to carry on the family candymaking tradition. Julius to Earl to Dana. These are the piers that support the bridge that ties our family together. We've been hearing for several decades about the generation gap. But I've refused to endorse the concept, and have deliberately constructed a generation *bridge*.

In this section, you'll find the formulas that, most truly represent the personas of Great-uncle Julius and my grandfather, Earl Davenport. Julius Franzen, as we've said elsewhere, was a highly trained and definitive practitioner of two related arts, pastry making and candymaking, as they were perceived in turn-of-the-century Europe. The first group of recipes—the ones with the fantasy names—come straight from him. They belong to the European dipped-candy tradition of his time. They're still aristocrats, whether they're found in Europe or in the Americas. Fortunately for my family, Julius Franzen brought them with him when he emigrated to the New World.

The next group of recipes comes from Grandpa Davenport (Earl). He and Julius had hit it off from the first day they met. They were exactly the same age, both of them born in 1886. It quickly became apparent that they had great numbers of mutual interests, not the least of which was Julius's beautiful little sister, Ottilia. What more natural than that Earl, the western American, should become the young Hungarian's closest companion, interpreter of his art and eventual keeper of the family candy secrets so painstakingly hand-carried from the Czar's kitchens and the Emperor's kitchens to the New World. Indeed, Grandpa Earl was to become Julius's disciple, chronicler, best friend, and eventually brother-in-law.

Grandpa had a decidedly innovative, creative bent. The chemistry and physics of candymaking fascinated him. The science of candymaking, if you will. In this section, you'll find the crowning successes of his long candymaking life, first as candy factory proprietor, then as food scientist, then as teacher.

As for me, my contributions to the heritage have been primarily variations and modifications of the older formulas that came down to me. As conservator of the museum, I have seen as my first obligation the preservation of the formulas. It has taken me nine years to transform the family formulas into the Dilettante line of confections, pastries and beverages. One of the innovations I have developed is the still-secret formula for

1886–1954
**Julius Rudolf Franzen**
*Master Candy Maker*
to
Czar Nicholas II
and
Emperor Franz Josef I

1886–1971
**Earl Remington Davenport**
*Chocolatier*
Brother-in-law to Julius Franzen

1913–1977
**Irving Franzen Davenport**
*Chocolatier*

1914–
**Jerome Franzen Davenport**
*Le Chef des Pralines aux Arachides*

1949–
**Dana Taylor Davenport**
*Chocolatier*

Dilettante Chocolates
1976

Dilettante Ephemere Sauce, along with numerous recipes for its use. These too are in this section.

I must not finish this colloquy without mentioning the contributions of my father in all this. He is the missing link in the descendancy from Earl to me—and my five brothers, most of whom work with me, each in the special capacity that his educational background prepared him for.

As an adult, Dad elected not to go into the family enterprises. But he grew up in a candy factory, nonetheless, and learned all the facets of the trade, as did his brothers and sisters, and is himself a *confiseur* par excellence. When my brothers and I want to market a new product, whom do we call on to help us work the commercial pitfalls out of it? Why Dad, of course. We call, and he comes a-runnin', ready to do battle with the pots and thermometers and the exigencies of shelf life. After a brainstorming session or two, and with one of Grandpa's—or Julius's—formulas in hand, we all settle down and experiment with batches until one is exactly, precisely right. We did that with Rocky Road just after I started working on this book. In fact, you have the benefit of our labors in the formula you'll find herein. And in many others, as well, that weren't necessarily acknowledged.

So here in this section you have a bridge between the old world of confection and the new. Between the European tradition and the American. As well as the structure that bridges three generations of my family. These formulas represent the family's greatest achievements in our special field, the hard-won secret techniques, the creative combinations of some of the world's most aristocratic and enduring confections. And the labor of years of proud professional dedication to a trade that is also an art.

"We used to spend hours after school shelling walnuts in pop's candy factory. Thank goodness we don't have to do that anymore."
—*Jerome Franzen Davenport*

## Improvisations by Julius

To you experienced candymakers, we offer the following eight formulas taken from Great-uncle Julius's whimsical creations—as examples of what you can do using your own imagination.

One fine day you may say to yourself, "Here I am with a bit of leftover nougat, a dab of truffle paste, some marzipan, now what?" Why, make a marzipan/truffle/nougat sandwich, of course. Beats peanut butter and jelly, any day of the week.

In other words, out of, say, ten formulas from a candymaker's kitchen, you can mix and match and improvise to make a hundred different candies.

Of course, it takes an experienced palate to judge how much marzipan would overpower the more delicate flavors of a nougat. In Julius's improvisations which follow, the proportions represent his judgment, obviously. So, all measurements are approximate and to be used as guidelines—subject, as always, to your own tastes and experience.

The key word here is *improvise.* Be bold. Experiment. Have fun.

And when you do come up with an improvisation all your own, one that really pleases you, give it a flowery, fanciful name in the Belle Epoque style that Julius favored. Just for fun.

# BADINAGE

This combination of chewy nougat and walnut indicates that Julius had an appreciation of one of the basics of food texture dynamics. When chewing something a little more than usual, the flavors of the ingredients are much intensified in the mouth.

1. Thoroughly mix all ingredients. Roll out into a sheet about ¼ inch thick. Use a little cornstarch to keep from sticking.

2. Let rest for 24 hours.

3. Cut into small wafers 1 ½ inches in diameter.

4. After all surfaces are dry, dip in bittersweet couverture. Place half a walnut atop of each just before the chocolate sets.

Great-uncle Julius received royalties on a process he developed for making chocolate "shot". This is a candymaker's term. Consumers know it as decoratifs, jimmies, Sprinx—or by other trade names. It is made by adding water to chocolate which causes the chocolate to sieze and thicken. It can then be kneaded into a paste and sent through a grinder similiar to a spaghetti grinder. This chocolate "spaghetti" is dried and subsequently broken into small uniform pieces. Finally, the shot gets a coating of "shine" applied in a revolving pan.

Julius developed his glazes and shines out of gum acacia, potato dextrine, and glucose.

1 batch Malleable Marzipan
    (page 121)
3 cups Honey Nougat Chew,
    chopped small (page 114)
2 ½ cups English walnuts,
    chopped

# ARABIAN NIGHTS

This is a fine combination of Praline powder and Gianduja—and a little different approach to flavoring. Because both of these ingredients are used in so many formulas, you'll find them in "The Support Group" section, page 82.

1 cup instant espresso coffee powder (2-ounce jar)
4 ounces (weight) cocoa butter, melted and cooled
1 pound 4 ounces dark Praline Powder (page 90)

1 cup Gianduja (page 91)

1. Add just enough water to the espresso to make a thick paste.

2. Melt and cool the cocoa butter.

3. Knead the coffee paste and cocoa butter into the Praline Powder.

4. Roll out half the Praline mixture on your work surface. Spread a layer of Gianduja over it.

5. Roll out the other half of the Praline mix, and cover the Gianduja layer with it. Lightly press the three layers together, and allow to set up very firm.

6. Cut out like dough with a miniature round cookie cutter.

7. When all surfaces are dry, dip in semisweet couverture.

# GABRIELS

This is a classic European confection. I've seen variations of it all over Austria and Switzerland. The layers are usually held together with a little Simple Syrup, but honey is good, too, and even maple syrup.

½ batch Nougat Chew or Honey Nougat Chew (page 112 and page 114)

1. Pour the Nougat out onto a cold oiled slab to a depth of about ¼ inch. When completely cool, using a pastry brush, spread a thin coat of heated honey over the top.

2. Roll out a thin layer of Marzipan. (Use a little cornstarch, as needed, to keep it from sticking.) Cover half the Nougat layer with the Marzipan. Brush it with honey.

1 batch Malleable Marzipan, colored green (page 121)
½ cup heated honey

3. Fold the other half of the Nougat over the Marzipan.

4. Cut into strips ½ inch by 1½ inches. Allow all surfaces to dry.

5. Dip in dark couverture.

Semisweet chocolate couverture for dipping.

# BLACK RUSSIAN TRUFFLES

This is not really a truffle, in that we do not use a truffle paste. But it *is* dark, chocolaty, and a wonderful way to use up a little leftover nougat.

1. Chop the nougat and walnuts together in a food processor.

1 part, by weight, of chocolate-flavored Nougat Chew (page 113, second variation)
1 part, by weight, of English walnuts, chopped

2. Pour in the melted semisweet chocolate. (It has been melted and cooled.)

3. Teaspoon-drop small lumps onto a waxed paper-lined baking sheet. Allow to set, and cool thoroughly.

4. Dip in bittersweet couverture that has been thinned with a little cocoa butter. (About 1 ounce [weight] of cocoa butter to 1 pound of chocolate.)

1 part, by weight, semisweet chocolate (couverture), melted

# FIGAROS

Simple variations of Gianduja, marzipan and flavorings with nougat or other chopped chews are endless. You'll soon be thinking up your own.

½ **batch Nougat Chew (page 112)**

1 **batch Gianduja (page 91)**
1 **batch Malleable Marzipan, colored green (page 121)**

1. Prepare the Nougat Chew. When you've poured it out on the slab, spread to a thickness of about ¼ inch. Let cool thoroughly.

2. Prepare the Gianduja and the Marzipan. All three mixtures should be cool and set.

3. Now you're ready to layer the batches. For the first layer, using your fingers, press the Gianduja out in a thin sheet on a flat waxed-paper-lined work surface.

4. Lay the prepared nougat on the Gianduja, for a second layer.

5. Roll out the Marzipan to ¼-inch thickness, and use it as the top layer.

6. Press the layers lightly together, and let rest to firm up a bit.

7. Cut into small triangles. Let the surfaces dry. Then dip in semisweet chocolate couverture.

# ALMOND PRALINE TRUFFLES

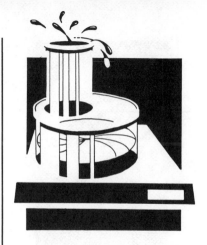

This is a good example of how you can throw together a little of this and a little of that and come up with something very special—if you're a master of your craft. Julius succeeded here in offering us a wonderful truffle while ignoring most of the conventional approaches to formula. It has a fine texture that's not too soft. It has the complex flavor of caramelized sugar, the richness of fresh butter. And besides everything else, it's supremely simple to produce.

1. Melt the chocolate and cool. (See "Dipping", page 138.)

**½ pound semisweet chocolate couverture**

2. In either a food processor or an electric mixer, cream together the fondant and the butter.

**½ batch Cremed Fondant (page 84)**
**½ cup butter at room temperature**

3. Add the Gianduja and process until well blended.

**1 cup Gianduja (page 91)**
**OR 1 cup Almond Brittle ground fine (page 44)**

4. Add the melted chocolate and mix well.

5. Refrigerate the batch for about half an hour.

6. Remove from the refrigerator and form into small ball shapes with a melon-ball scoop. Put them on a sheet of waxed paper. (If you're going to dip them, refrigerate the whole batch, then jump down to step 9 to find out how to dip truffles.) If you're simply rolling them in cocoa, proceed to step 7.

7. Each time you have formed, say, half a dozen centers, roll them in cocoa powder. Arrange them on a serving plate, and put them back into the refrigerator. If the truffle paste gets too warm to hold its shape well, refrigerate it briefly until it is again firm enough to work.

**1 cup cocoa powder (natural process), for coating**

8. When the entire batch is finished, keep it refrigerated until about 15 minutes before serving time.

9. If you decide you'd like to dip these truffles, don't coat them in cocoa powder. In fact, ignore steps 6 through 8, and look up "How to Dip Truffles," at the end of the "Truffles" section, page 197. There's a special technique involved.
    Dip in semisweet chocolate.

**1 cup candied orange peel, or to taste, chopped fine**
**Curaçao for macerating orange peel**

**1 batch Malleable Marzipan (page 121)**

I remember that when a box of candy would come from Uncle Julius in California, we children would always ask Papa if it was to eat or to "test." He would proceed to cut each piece into at least four morsels—and taste each one to see how Julius had made it differently from the usual way. Then he would give his opinion of it. He would make notes on each piece and report to Julius what he thought. (He would send some of his candies to California, too, and I'm sure they would get the same treatment.) When the process was complete (tasting each one) Papa would give the box to us children. And we would have a feast! It tasted divine—even if the chocolates were all in little pieces.

*—Aunt Pat*

# MOON MAIDENS

Once you've developed a taste for marzipan, there's no turning back. You're ready to experiment with every combination of flavors and textures that suggests itself to you. Here's one of the better marriages of oranges and almonds for you to try.

1. Chop the orange peel. Soak overnight in Curaçao to cover.

2. Next day, thoroughly drain the peel. Then mix it into the marzipan until well blended. Start with less than the full cup of orange peel, taste, then add as your taste dictates.

3. When you're satisfied, roll the mixture out on your work surface to a sheet ¼- to ⅜-inch thick. Use a little cornstarch to keep from sticking, if necessary.

4. Cut out into little half-moon shapes. Allow the surfaces to dry. (Miniature cookie and confection cutters are available at specialty kitchen or cake decorating supply houses.)

5. Coat in semisweet chocolate couverture.

# PANTOMIME

When nougat is chopped and added to another center to lend extra texture, a food processor does the job nicely. But nougat *does* tend to get sticky. So sprinkle a little powdered sugar over the mass, and process in short bursts. Don't chop it too fine. You don't want the nougat to turn into a paste.

1. Chop the nougat small in the food processor. Remove to a bowl.

**½ batch Chocolate Nougat Chew, chopped small (page 113)**

2. Scrape the ganache into the bowl and mix together lightly with a spoon.

**1 batch milk chocolate Ganache (made with 1 pound milk chocolate couverture and 1 cup cream) See the recipe, page 90.**

3. Spread the mixture out on a waxed-paper-lined cookie sheet and refrigerate until firm enough to cut, perhaps a half-hour.

4. When firm, cut as desired. Allow the pieces to crust over sightly on the surfaces, and dip in milk chocolate couverture. Drop a piece of candied violet on top of each one before the chocolate sets.

**Small pieces of candied violet for garnish**

"Do the same thing twice, in the same manner, under the same conditions and circumstances, using the same materials, and you will get the same results."

—E. Remington Davenport

*apricott chew Eß%*

*9 cans apricott pulp.*
*(Sun Set brand)*
*60# sugar*
*10# glucose*
*3 g/ Im Rum flavor*
*60# ground W nuts*
*dark cooting*
*shel on 20 y/*

# Grandpa's Remembrance to the Family

We have decided, in solemn family conference, to offer you two of Grandpa Davenport's special recipes. During the last ten years of his life, he and Grandma traveled the country giving master classes in candymaking. At the same time, Grandpa, who was well into his seventies, spent a good deal of his time reducing large commercial batch sizes for home use (not always an easy task—as we've found out). As always, he worked on his unending experiments, too, perfecting old stand-bys and developing new formulas. He loved people, so he shared without stint most of the results of his labors.
But he had a special surprise project in mind during those last years. He produced a group of special recipes just for the family, a sort of memento from him to us, with love. He had these formulas printed in a booklet and presented them to each of his children. This is the first time anyone outside the immediate family has seen any of them. As we've said elsewhere in this book, we can share the recipes, but not the secrets they contain. Simply follow the formulas faithfully, and your results will be exactly the same as ours. The secrets are built in.

Throughout this book and on the following two pages we've also transcribed some of the original formulas from Grandpa's Master notebook so you can see the shorthand style of notation used by early candymakers. Some of these formulas were compiled during the latter part of the Depression when Grandpa owned his own candy factory. Occasionally, unemployed candy-makers drifted through town looking for work. Sometimes these drifters would also sell him a favorite recipe. In this way Grandpa was able to record many original American formulas that might otherwise have been lost. (Most candymakers refused to write down recipes because they were afraid they would be stolen.) And as we mentioned earlier, Grandpa had the fore-sight to record many of the formulas Julius gave him. (Julius's own handwriting appears in the notebook on entries made in the mid-1930s during Grandpa's visits to him in San Francisco.) We're very grateful for Grandpa's remembrance. Considering Julius's roots in Budapest, this legacy of candy formulas is well over 100 years old. And we add this admonition: Use this book as a beginning point for creating your own cooking traditions. We have left you room to record your experiments. We sincerely feel that with just a little care and imagination you can create some of your own candy variations that will be treasured by those who follow.

**The candy classes were started in the 30's (during Depression times), and evolved into the popular demonstrations that were sponsored by the newspapers in the towns where Papa gave classes. The Portland newspaper looked forward to his coming every year. They would hold two classes a day for about ten days.**

*—Aunt Pat*

**Rancidity is due primarily to oxidation of butter and other fats. Most butters are 15 percent water. This also contributes to oxidation.**

"Any person can make good candy if that person is willing to use precision."
—E. Remington Davenport

## A view of my grandfather's Master notebook.

(See pages 4 and 213)

Candymakers' numerical shorthand always designates —in pounds— first the amount of granulated sugar to be used, followed by the inverted sugars. The term "grease," more often simply notated 96° or 88°, is candy-maker's jargon meaning hard coconut oil or cocoa butter.

We've made various adjustments in the formulas when reducing large batches of candy for home use. For example, you will notice the final cooking temperature is often lowered. This is because a batch of molten sugar and butter continues cooking even when it is removed from the burner. And in the uppermost "hard crack" temperatures, a small batch can climb too high too quickly, which results in scorching.

The initials J.R. refer to none other than Julius Rudolf Franzen.

"There is no such thing as luck in candymaking. All that we call good luck comes to us because we obey certain laws; all that we call bad luck comes to us because we break or ignore certain laws."
—*E. Remington Davenport*

# HONEY CHEWS

Grandpa Davenport loved honey, so he used it frequently in his own versions of classic recipes. Or developed his own personal honey confections. This one is very special to our family, and will become so for you, especially if you're a honey lover.

As for the honey to use in your Honey Chew—whatever pleases your palate. We live in bee country, so often when we take a drive in the country we come home with some new type of honey to try—for comparison with others. To honey lovers, it's a rewarding pursuit. Why, at this moment we can whip up a batch that could be called Grandpa's clover chews, or Grandpa's fireweed chews, or Grandpa's Potpourri chews, or Grandpa's Chews à la Inga Jensen's Number 7 (AKA Siwash Huckleberry Blossom Honey).

Exotic tropical honeys? Heck, who needs exotica when we have access to farmers with imaginations like that.

Gathering honey is a wonderful excuse for taking a Saturday drive in the country. Discover your own favorites.

My brother who lives in a mountain town has recently started keeping bees, as have some of his neighbors. Beekeeping was also one of my dad's hobbies when he was a young man. We're all honey-lovers.

**3¾ cups English walnuts**

1. Prepare the marble slab and half-inch bars. They should be cold and thoroughly dried, then wiped with mineral oil.

2. Chop and reserve.

**4 cups granulated sugar**
**1 cup water**
**1 teaspoon cream of tartar**

3. Measure into a 3-quart saucepan. Blend thoroughly. Bring to a boil. Wash down the sides of the pan with a pastry brush dipped in water. Insert the thermometer.

4. Cook without stirring, to **320** degrees. (But when the batch starts to color, stir to the end of the cook, to distribute evenly the browning of the caramelizing sugar.)

**1 pound butter**

5. Stir into the batch immediately. When completely melted, remove from heat.

**1½ to 2 cups honey**

6. Stir in the honey (start with 1½ cups) and test for chewy texture. If the batch is too firm, stir in the other ½ cup honey.

If on the other hand, the texture is too soft, cook the batch just a little more, without adding the rest of the honey. Test again, then take off the heat.

To test for chewiness: drop a few drops of the syrup into a cup of cool water. Pop the candy into your mouth and chew. The texture will be exactly the same as that of the finished candy. In other words, you get to choose how chewy you want your chews.

7. When you're satisfied with the texture, gently stir in the walnuts and the vanilla.

8. Pour out the batch onto the prepared slab, between the half-inch bars, to a depth of ½ inch.

9. When thoroughly cold, cut into ½ inch cubes, using a sharp knife. If you move the knife back and forth quickly, the caramel will hold its shape and will not stick to the blade.

10. Dip in milk chocolate. Allow to mellow for a few days before serving.

**The reserved walnuts
2 teaspoons vanilla extract**

**When preservatives are used to combat rancidity, they are often referred to as antioxidants.**

# APRICOT CHEWS

Grandpa Davenport often used fruit pulp in his chewy confections. This one is made from apricot pulp, but other fruits make very good substitutes. My dad lives in the heart of Washington State's soft-fruit belt, the Yakima Valley, so he uses fresh apricots—or peaches—or pears for his fruit chews, but canned fruit works well too.

The original recipe calls for sieving the fruit pulp, but the food processor does away with all that. No food processor? Cook the fruit first, then put it through a good old-fashioned food mill. Same results as the processor. Just takes a little longer.

1. Prepare the marble slab. It should be cold and thoroughly dried, then wiped with mineral oil. And you'll need half-inch bars. Oil them, too.

2. Prepare and reserve.

3. Chop and reserve.

**1 quart apricot pulp**

**3¾ cups English walnuts**

*Apricot Chews, continued*

The prepared fruit pulp
4 cups granulated sugar
1⅓ cups corn syrup

1 teaspoon vanilla extract
1 teaspoon lemon juice
1 tablespoon brandy
¼ teaspoon citric acid powder
  mixed with ¼ teaspoon water

4. Measure into a 5-quart saucepan. Blend thoroughly. Bring to a boil. Wash down the sides of the pan with a pastry brush dipped in water. Insert the thermometer. Cook, stirring constantly, to *243* degrees. Remove from heat.

5. Stir in the walnuts, then the flavorings.

6. Pour the batch out onto the prepared slab between the half-inch bars to a depth of ½ inch.

7. When thoroughly cold, dust lightly with powdered sugar to make cutting easier. Cut into small rectangles ½ by 1 inch. (If you move the knife back and forth quickly, the chew will hold its shape and will not stick to the blade.)

10. Dip in semisweet chocolate couverture. Allow to mellow for a few days before serving.

"That which we persist in doing becomes easy to do; not that the nature of the thing itself is changed, but that our ability to do, is increased."

(This was in quotes in Grandpa Earl's book, and was one of his favorite sayings. It was attributed to Eldon Tanner.)

# Dana's Dilettante Ephemere Sauce and Truffle Toppings

First off, I want to talk about the Ephemere Truffle. It was Great-uncle Julius's favorite creation, and dates from his sojourn in France, where he continued his studies after the years of apprenticing in his native Budapest. Since that time this truffle formula has been a family secret.

All I'm allowed to tell you at this writing is that Grandpa Davenport spent thirty years experimenting with the Ephemere Truffle until he discovered a procedural method that keeps the butter in the truffle from growing rancid—without using chemical preservatives. This discovery made it possible to develop a sauce that would not turn rancid after it was opened: our celebrated Dilettante Ephemere Sauce. With it, I'm continuing the family tradition, "Shelf life without chemical preservatives."

Fundamentally, Dilettante Ephemere Sauce is a ganache. As are our Dilettante Truffle Toppings. The Toppings are formulated primarily for use over ice cream. But Ephemere Sauce is more concentrated—for making truffles and other desserts. It is, in fact, a truffle paste just as it comes from the jar. Both it and the toppings come in several flavors.

We're offering you recipes using our sauces because they're timesavers. We've already done the hard part. And they're made with the highest quality chocolate, which is not always easy to find. But besides everything else, they can be right there on your emergency shelf when truffle craving strikes. The Ephemere Truffle recipe (page 221), is perhaps the most important one in this section, because in the circumstances, this is the only way you can make our genuine Ephemere Truffle.

The rest of the section is devoted to other suggestions and recipes that use all our Dilettante sauces and toppings. The recipes will give you ideas for adapting the products to your own needs.

For instance, one day a customer came into one of our shops with a big grin on her face. "You know what I did yesterday?" she chortled. "The kids had been pleading all morning for a batch of Rice Krispies cookies. I finally gave in. And when I reached for the package of marshmallows in the cupboard, there was this open jar of Dilettante Ephemere Sauce right on the shelf beside them. I thought, 'Aha, this sauce is so full of butter, I bet I could substitute it for the butter in the recipe—

As a journeyman in Paris very early in this century, my uncle Julius acquired a master formula called "Ephemere." This dark chocolate truffle is made by melting bittersweet chocolate with cream and adding an unusual butter praline.

**Derivation of Ephemere**
**ephemeral** *1a:* **lasting or existing briefly: Fleeting.**
**—Webster's Third New International Dictionary**

equal quantities.' So I did it. And it worked. Boy, talk about the divine to the ridiculous! Just one thing, though. Now the kids won't ever let me go back to the original."

She had brought us a taste of her creation, of course. By golly, it *does* work.

1 cup Dilettante Ephemere Sauce (available in specialty shops or by mail order, see Appendix)

4 large egg whites, at room temperature
¼ cup granulated sugar

# DILETTANTE CHOCOLATE MOUSSE

If you want to make a very fine distinction, this mousse should perhaps be called a mousseline, because there is so much butter in the Ephemere Sauce. But mousse or mousseline, it's quick to make and delicious to eat. So who cares what it's called, really?

1. Soften a jar of Ephemere Sauce by immersing it in hot water for 5 minutes. Measure out 1 cupful into a bowl and reserve. (The sauce should be thinned but still cool.)

2. Beat the egg whites until soft smooth peaks form, while gradually adding the sugar.

3. Fold about ¼ of the beaten egg white into the sauce to lighten the texture. Then fold the entire mixture into the rest of the beaten egg whites. The mousse/mousseline will be rather fluid at this point.

4. Scoop into parfait glasses and chill.

5. Serve garnished with whipped cream and candied violet.

# EPHEMERE TRUFFLES

This formula, using our Dilettante Ephemere Sauce, was designed to give you a means of copying the most exalted truffle we make in our factory—even though we can't reveal to you how to make the paste. You'd have to have the secret formula for that. But the formula *is* embodied in the Ephemere Sauce. And it makes a superb Ephemere Truffle—exactly as if you had been able to make it from scratch. And exactly as we make it for our clientele.

1. Refrigerate for two hours or until firm.

**1 jar Dilettante Ephemere Sauce (16 ounces), flavor of your choice (available in specialty shops or by mail order, see Appendix)**

2. Grate fine. Reserve.

**1 pound semisweet chocolate (couverture), if using grated chocolate for coating**

3. When the Ephemere Sauce is firm, scoop directly from the jar, using a melon ball scoop to form ball shapes. Drop them on waxed paper.

4. Finish as in the master recipe, Truffles section, steps 7 and 8. EXCEPT: If you're rolling the finished centers in grated chocolate instead of in cocoa, gently press it in, so that the chocolate really adheres to the truffle paste, making a dense coating.

**1 cup cocoa powder (natural process), for coating *OR* the grated chocolate**

REMARK: If you're not going to dip the finished centers in chocolate, keep them refrigerated between servings. Like nearly all truffles, they're quite soft at room temperature. In this case, because there is so much butter in the Ephemere Sauce.

   If you *are* going to dip the truffles in chocolate, you'll need a special technique for the job. See "How to Dip Truffles," page 197.

# INSTANT MOUSSE EPHEMERE

This is the quickest, easiest, and showiest recipe imaginable. Prepared in advance in a whipped cream dispenser, it's perfect for informal entertaining. Serve it at the table with a flourish. It's as simple as squeezing the valve.

**For a 1-liter whipped cream dispenser use:**

1 jar Dilettante Truffle Topping or 1 cup Dilettante Ephemere Sauce (both are available in specialty shops or by mail order, see Appendix)

1 pint whipping cream

**For a half-liter dispenser cut the proportions in half, obviously. (It is important that there be extra air space in the dispenser to incorporate the $N_2O$ gas.)**

1. Place a jar of Truffle Topping under running, warm tap water for a few minutes. Just until the sauce is soft and flowing, but not hot. (If you're using Ephemere Sauce measure out 1 cup and gently soften over heat in a saucepan, stirring to avoid scorching.)

2. Combine in a bowl the Topping or Sauce with the whipping cream.

3. Pour into a chilled whipped cream dispenser.

4. Load the $N_2O$ capsule (per manufacturer's instructions).

5. SHAKE WELL.

6. REFRIGERATE UNTIL VERY COLD.

7. SHAKE WELL AGAIN JUST BEFORE DISPENSING.

8. Invert completely and dispense in a circular fashion into crystal serving dishes. Garnish with candied violet or shaved chocolate. (1 liter serves 6 to 8, ½ liter serves 3 or 4)

# TRUFFLED SOUFFLÉ

This elegant soufflé is made in seconds. And why not? After all, we have already amalgamated the chocolate and cream and butter in the sauce base you'll use. The individual soufflés make a handsome presentation. And the sour cream adds its own nuance to the already complex flavor ensemble.

1. Put the eggs, sugar and Topping or Sauce into the blender and mix thoroughly until smooth. Add the milk and sour cream. Blend until absolutely smooth and foamy.

**1 jar Dilettante Truffle Topping or 1 cup Dilettante Ephemere Sauce ( see Appendix)**
**5 large eggs plus 1 egg white**
**½ cup milk**
**¼ cup sugar**
**½ pint sour cream**

2. Pour into six clean, dry ½-cup porcelain ramekins.

3. Bake at **375** degrees for 20 to 25 minutes, or until fully puffed. The liquid in the center should be set.

4. Sprinkle with powdered sugar and serve immediately with softly whipped cream. Or pass a sauceboat of heated chocolate sauce or heated Dilettante Carameled Cream.

# CHOCOLATE ICE

Not a gelato (it's not made with milk or additional cream), this is more like a very refreshing ice—although there *is* cream, and butter as well, in the sauce. This recipe works perfectly in your countertop gelato maker, or any home-style ice cream maker.

As a matter of fact, you can substitute our Truffle Topping or our Ephemere Sauce in any chocolate-flavored version of your favorite ice cream formulas.

Speaking of substitutions, try making this ice with our Mint Truffle Topping. Serve with a mint garnish and iced espresso. Wonderful on the patio on a hot summer afternoon.

NOTE: It is good to allow any ice—or other mixture that is to be frozen—to rest for 10 to 30 minutes before freezing, to let the flavors mingle.

1. Place the jar of either type of sauce under hot running water just long enough to soften it a bit, but not to warm it materially. Measure out the 1 cup Ephemere Sauce, if you're using that.

**1 jar Dilettante Truffle Topping**
**OR 1 cup Dilettante Ephemere Sauce (both are available in specialty shops or by mail order, see Appendix)**

2. Place sugar and liquid and sauce in a blender or in a bowl and mix thoroughly.

**½ cup sugar**
**2 cups water,**
**OR 1 cup water and 1 cup cold strong black coffee**

3. Scrape the mixture into your ice cream maker and proceed as directions for sherbet or gelato (ice) dictate.

# EVER-READY EPHEMERE

Do you have a household that suffers sudden guest syndrome? Often need a spectacular emergency dessert? Or hot chocolate? Or after-theater cappuccino? Here's Ephemere to the rescue. Always at the ready. Always superb in any number of imaginative combinations. We offer you a sampling of applications here to spur on your own imagination to a brisk canter—or maybe even a gallop.

Our Dilettante Ephemere Sauce is available in specialty shops and department stores throughout the United States and Canada or by mail order. (See Appendix.)

**1 jar Ephemere Sauce (serves 6 to 8)**
**Fresh fruit cut in slices or bite-size chunks**
**Small chunks of pound cake, dippable cookies, etc.**

### CHOCOLATE FONDUE

Heat the sauce in a chafing dish. Arrange the dippables on platters. And provide long-handled forks and napkins.

**1 jar Ephemere Sauce**
**Your favorite ice cream**
**Fresh or frozen raspberries**
**Small macaroons**
**4 tablespoons Framboise**
**Whipping cream**
**Shaved chocolate**

### COUPE EPHEMERE

Place the unopened jar of Ephemere sauce under hot running water for ten minutes. Arrange the ice cream, macaroons and raspberries in parfait glasses or wineglasses. Open the jar of warmed sauce, and pour 4 tablespoons of Framboise into it. Stir until well blended. Pour the sauce over the ice cream and berries. Top with whipped cream, and drizzle on a little juice from the berries. Then scatter a few chocolate shavings over all.

**3 tablespoons Ephemere Sauce**
**1 cup milk**

### HOT CHOCOLATE EPHEMERE

Heat the sauce over low heat, stirring to prevent scorching. Heat the milk almost to boiling. Whisk it into the sauce until well blended.

## CAPPUCCINO GRAND MARNIER

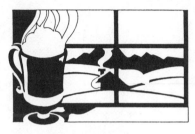

For you who have an espresso machine.
Top off with a little foamed milk and a dollop of whipped cream.

A double espresso
½ cup Hot Chocolate
      Ephemere
1 jigger Grand Marnier
      (optional)
Combine in a heated cup.

## EPHEMERE CHOCOLATE FROSTING

On low speed of an electric mixer, blend the sauce and water together. Slowly add the powdered sugar and beat until light and fluffy.

   This is enough frosting to ice the tops and sides of two round 8-inch layers.

1 jar Ephemere Sauce
3 tablespoons hot water
2 cups sifted powdered sugar

# EPHEMERE MILK SHAKE

In our family, we have a favorite chocolate milkshake, the most velvety of all milkshakes. We'll tell you how to make it. But we won't tell you how to make the Ephemere Sauce that we use for the flavor base. If you can't find Ephemere Sauce, use the Very Nearly Dilettante Ephemere Sauce (page 130) or the Quick and Rewarding Chocolate topping (page 131) and proceed as below. By the way, to make a *double* chocolate milk shake, merely use more sauce or chocolate ice cream instead of vanilla.

1. Measure all ingredients into a blender jar in the order listed. Process until smooth, starting with short bursts if the ice cream is very hard.

2. Yields one tall glassful.

¼ cup whole milk
3 scoops *hard* vanilla ice
      cream, or other flavor of
      your choice
2 tablespoons Ephemere
      Sauce

# Two Celebrated Hungarian Torten

Half of our yearly business at the Dilettante comes from our pastry and ice creams and ices. Most of which are made from recipes I've developed my self. For this book, we've confined ourselves to the other half of our output, the confections—with only two exceptions: the Rigo Jancsi Torte and the Dobosh Torte.

As we've said elsewhere, Great-uncle Julius was a master *patissier*, as well as a master *confiseur*. But he left only a few of his pastry recipes. The Rigo and the Dobosh were not among them. Unfortunately.

These are two Hungarian classics that are not well understood in this country. It required considerable research and experimentation to duplicate them, and we feel that the results of all this labor of love should be shared with kindred cooking spirits. We hope you'll be pleased.

# THE DEFINITIVE DOBOSH TORTE

The Dobosh Torte is probably Hungary's most famous dessert. Traditionally, it is seven-layered with a camamelized sugar glaze on the top. Like the multilayered strudel or the baklava, it has achieved its classic status because it stands alone, a distinctive many-layered entity.

My recipe for the Dobosh was achieved by duplicating the Dobosch Torte served in a little pastry shop in Zurich. The owners were Hungarian, and two of them were master pastry chefs trained in Budapest. Their sterling establishment was located about halfway between Bellevue Platz and the Dolder Hotel. Next time you're in that neighborhood, stop by and try their Dobosch Torte. Let me know how well we've duplicated it.

You'll note that in the paragraph above we've used the "c" in Dobosch, giving it the German spelling—as you'd find it in German Switzerland. Except for these two references, we employ the anglicized spelling more commonly found in English-speaking countries. No "c."

The most important feature of the Dobosh is the texture of the cake. It is not really a cake, nor yet a sugar cookie, but something in between. In this country, most pastry chefs make a génoise (a sponge cake), then simply split the layers and stack them. They call it Dobosh because it's in layers. But the texture of the cake is wrong.

Incidentally, this torte keeps very well. But the caramelized sugar on the top is completely inverted. That means it will liquefy if left uncovered. For this reason, at the Dilettante we make a praline powder we can keep dry in an airtight container until just before serving. Then we simply sprinkle the powder over the whipped cream that we pass with the torte. It gives the crunch and flavor needed to balance the rest of the cake. You may do the same, if you wish, but we've given you the original instructions, nonetheless—as well as our variation.

One last note. The filling, a whipped ganache, is perfumed with arrack, an anise-flavored distillate. If you can't find it readily, anisette does nicely. Or Pernod. Or any other anise-flavored distillate of your choice. And if you're not in the mood for anise, use rum or brandy or any other distillate that appeals to you. (You'll be following a time-honored tradition. Like nearly all

## The Definitive Dobosh Torte, continued

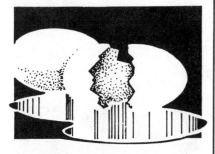

1 ¾ cups plus 1 tablespoon
    butter
2 cups granulated sugar

7 medium eggs

2 teaspoons vanilla extract
2 teaspoons grated lemon rind

2 ½ cups cake flour
½ teaspoon salt

classics, this one has survived very well in spite of a liberty or two taken by other cooks down through the years.)

But, if you don't want to use anise flavoring, don't call your creation a Dobosh Torte. Call it a variation on a Dobosh Torte!

### The Cake

1. Here's the recipe at last. Preheat the oven to **350** degrees. All ingredients should be at room temperature.

2. Butter, then flour the inside of seven 9-inch round cake tins. (In some recipes, the batter is baked on the outside bottom of the pan, but this batter will run over the edges.)

3. Measure into the large bowl of an electic mixer. With rotary beater, cream until very light and fluffy.

4. When the mixture is well creamed, add one by one until all are incorporated.

5. Beat into the mixture.

6. Now sift the flour with the salt. Lower the speed on the mixer and add half the flour until it is just incorporated. Then the other half. *Do not overmix.*

7. Divide the batter into seven equal portions.

8. Spread each portion into a pan (as many as you have). The batter should be about ⅛ inch thick. Make sure it is evenly distributed.

9. Bake as many as you can comfortably fit in the oven at one time for 10 to 12 minutes. *Watch closely.* The layers should be a pale yellow, and not yet brown around the edges. While warm, the cake retains a slight spongy character. When completely cooled, it is almost crisp. If it is brown, it will be far too crisp when cooled.

10. Cool in the pans. When cool, release the sides with a knife, then invert very carefully. This is a rather fragile cake layer, but because of the high butter content it will come out of the pan easily. Reserve.

11. Bake the remaining portions of batter as above.

### The Filling

1. Make sure the Ganache is at room temperature, then whip in an electric mixer until very smooth and fluffy.

2. Add slowly just before the end of whipping.

3. Divide into 12 equal portions, leaving some for the sides of the torte. (It will be about 4 inches high when finished.)

### To Assemble the Torte

Alternate layers of cake and filling, frosting the sides as well. The layers will probably be a little jagged. If you wish, press finely chopped nuts into the sides of the finished cake—for the cosmetic effect.

This torte is best when made in advance and allowed to mellow for a day. So frost the top layer to keep the cake from drying out. It will keep well for up to 2 weeks in the refrigerator.

### The Top Layer à la Praline

1. Turn over a 9-inch cake tin. Wipe the outside bottom with mineral oil. Refrigerate until ready to use.

2. Measure into a 3-quart saucepan. Blend thoroughly. Bring to a boil. Wash down the sides of the pan with a pastry brush dipped in water. Insert the thermometer.

3. Cook without stirring until the batch starts to turn yellow around the edges. Then stir gently until the whole mixture is a beautiful golden brown (*310-320* degrees). Pour out over the bottom of the prepared 9-inch cake tin.

4. While the praline is still slightly warm, just before it sets, score it with a knife into wedge-shaped pieces the size you intend to serve (20 or so). Cool until hard. Keep in an airtight container and just before serving, place one on top of each slice of torte.

Prepare the praline (or just use some brittle you may already have on hand). Break it into small chunks, then grind it in the food processor until it is a powder. Sprinkle it over the top of the torte, or serve it atop the whipped cream you may wish to serve on the side.

**1 batch Ganache, page 90**

**½ cup anisette or Pernod**

**2 cups granulated sugar**
**¼ cup water**
**¼ teaspoon cream of tarter**

**OUR VARIATION**

# RIGO JANCSI TORTE

The Rigo Jancsi is another of those classic recipes whose exact origin is difficult to establish. But the component elements, once understood, are not hard to duplicate. Time-consuming, yes, but not difficult.

One example of the way sources vary is found in *Hungarian Cuisine*, by Jozsef Venesz (Corvina Budapest, 1958), a book written and published in Hungary, and later translated into English by Hungarians. This was the first time I saw Rigo Jancsi made with a jam spread on the top layer, then covered with a glaze of fondant.

While I find the jam a very welcome addition, I prefer a chocolate glaze to fondant as a topping. For our restaurants, we make the cake portion in sheets rather than splitting a taller cake into layers. And we often leave off the jam.

One of the best discussions of the Rigo recipe that I've found is in George Lang's *The Cuisine of Hungary* (Athenum, New York, 1971). But we don't use gelatin in our filling, as described therein. Instead, we use more chocolate. When the torte has set for a while in a very cold refrigerator, the chocolate helps the filling to support the top layer of cake. Then when the finished cake is quite firmly set, it cuts very nicely with a hot, sharp knife.

Rigo Jancsi is a study in chocolate flavors, density, texture and proportion. The filling is like having your whipped cream built in instead of on the side. The glaze has the silky, smooth texture of a truffle, and of course, the chocolate cake delivers a light, chewy cake crumb. All these elements team together to make the *almost* perfect chocolate dessert. (I keep looking for the PERFECT chocolate dessert—and hope I never find it!)

We generally serve the Rigo only on weekends, and people come from miles away just to experience this chocolate classic.

I've included a few of the variations we use—like the jam (which acts as an acidic balance to cut the richness of the chocolate and cream). We sometimes add a hazelnut praline to the filling (we then have a Rigo Polonaise). And sometimes the filling gets an addition of chopped peppermint candy, an innovation created by my sister-in-law, Glenna.

Our cake is more chocolaty than some that you'll see. A signature of our shop is that we substitute cocoa for much of the flour. This makes the cake more flavorful and at the same time more tender, so that when you cut through it with a fork, the filling doesn't ooze out the sides.

Before you start:

• Preheat oven to 350 degrees. Check oven accuracy with a thermometer.

• Set out 11 eggs at room temperature for several hours.

• Prepare a small brew of strong coffee or espresso. You'll need 2 tablespoonfuls.

• Line a jelly roll sheet (11 x 17 inches) with waxed paper.

• If using the Polonaise variation of the Rigo, make a batch of hazelnut brittle. (Use Master Recipe "Brittles" section page 40. But substitute hazelnuts for peanuts.)

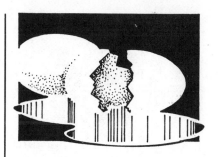

*The Cake*

1. Sift into a measuring cup. Should equal 1¼ cups.

**3 ounces (weight) cocoa, natural process**

2. Sift into a measuring cup. Should equal ½ cup.

**2 ounces (weight) all-purpose flour**

3. Add to the flour.

**¼ teaspoon baking powder**

4. Sift all dry ingredients together twice more. Reserve.

5. Whip, in a chilled bowl, until smooth rounds form. In other words, not too stiff. Refrigerate and reserve.

**½ cup whipping cream**

6. Put 11 eggs in a large mixer bowl and beat, first on low speed, then on high, until full volume is achieved. (Minimum of 15 minutes.)

**11 large eggs at room temperature**

7. Gradually add to the eggs in a slow stream, while continuing to beat.

**1½ cups superfine granulated sugar**

8. Finally, add the coffee. It should be very hot. This helps to set the eggs.

**2 tablespoons reserved strong coffee, hot**

9. When the egg/sugar mixture is whipped to full potential, stop beating. Carefully fold in the flour/cocoa mixture.

## Rigo Jancsi Torte, *continued*

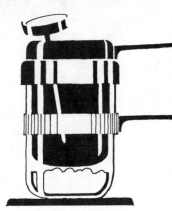

**2 pounds semisweet chocolate (couverture)**

**2 pints whipping cream**

**If Polonaise version, 1 to 2 cups powdered hazelnut brittle**

10. At the last, fold in the whipped cream.

11. Pour the batter into the prepared jelly roll pan, making sure that it remains evenly distributed and level.

12. Place in the preheated oven (middle rack), and bake for 30 minutes or until the cake is firm but slightly underdone. Start checking at 20 minutes.

13. Set the pan on a rack to cool. Do not remove waxed paper.

### The Filling

1. In a double boiler melt 2 pounds of finely chopped semisweet chocolate. Be sure no moisture or steam invades the chocolate.

2. Stir constantly and do not let the temperature exceed *120* degrees.

3. Cool to *95* degrees.

4. Whip until soft smooth peaks form. (Not too stiff.)

5. Gently fold the chocolate into the cream to achieve a light, airy texture. Then whip for a few seconds more, being careful not to cause the cream to separate. The chocolate should incorporate smoothly into the cream. If the cream is too cold, and the chocolate too close to final set point, it will sometimes form little chunks, but that's all right. It makes an interesting texture.

6. At this point, if you're doing the Polonaise version, 1 to 2 cups of powdered hazelnut brittle should be added.

### To Assemble the Torte

1. Cut the cake in two and place one half on a serving plate. Remove the waxed paper. Spread the filling on top of this layer until the filling is smooth and even, and approximately 1½ inches thick.

2. Chill in the refrigerator until the filling is firm.

3. Remove from the refrigerator and carefully put the other half of the cake on top of the filling, peeling off the waxed paper in the process. (The cake is too tender to move without the paper on it.)

4. The cake is now ready to glaze.

### The Glaze

1. Break into small pieces and place in a double boiler. Melt, keeping moisture out. Do not let temperature go above **120** degrees.

**12 ounces chocolate semi-sweet or bittersweet**

2. Add the butter cut into bits and beat the mixture until smooth and shiny.

**5 ounces unsalted butter**

3. Cool slightly and pour over the top of the cake. Refrigerate until the entire finished torte is thoroughly chilled.

4. Cut with a hot knife into pieces 2 to 3 inches square.

5. Serves 10 to 12.

RIGO POLONAISE

**VARIATION**

Add 1 to 2 cups powdered hazelnut brittle to the filling just at the end of the preparation. We have signaled the place for the addition within the Filling recipe, step 6. For the brittle, use our master recipe, "Brittles" section, page 40. But substitute hazelnuts for peanuts.

# Appendix

**Dilettante Chocolates are produced under rabbinical supervision and are strictly kosher, in accordance with the highest standards of Kashruth.**

"They are the best candy in the world."
—*Newsweek*/April 4, 1983

"Another source of superb hand-dipped sweets is the The Dilettante in Seattle."
—*Money Magazine*
February 1982

"Dilettante epitomizes all that is dear to the newly revived tradition of fine chocolates in this country.
—*Chocolatier Magazine*
Premier Issue 1984

"Another source of extraordinary hand-dipped chocolates is The Dilettante."
—*The Book of Bests,* 1981

"The Dilettante's Dana Davenport makes the best chocolates in Seattle—and maybe the world."
—*Seattle Times*/February 6, 1980

"I have eaten Viennese, Parisian, Dutch, Swiss German and New York chocolates of the highest quality, but I have never encountered chocolate like that of Seattle's Dilettante."
—*Seattle Post-Intelligencer*
September 1, 1979

"My idea of a big night out is a couple of hours at the Dilettante."

—Ginny Reilly of
Reilly and Maloney

## DILETTANTE LOCATIONS

Dilettante Chocolates
416 Broadway Ave. East
Seattle, Washington 98102
(206) 329 6463

Dilettante Chocolates
Interstate Center
999 Third Avenue
Seattle, Washington 98111
(206) 467 9593

Dilettante Chocolates #249
Bellevue Square Mall
Bellevue, Washington 98004
(206) 455 4788

Café Dilettante
Pike Place Market
1600 Post Alley
Seattle, Washington 98101
(206) 447-9144

Dilettante Chocolates
Factory and Seconds Counter
2300 East Cherry
Seattle, Washington 98122

The Dilettante Chocolate Shops offer a wide variety of our own pastries, ice creams, espressos, specialty coffees, and hot cocoas. Table service is available at the Broadway and Pike Place Market stores.

# DILETTANTE PRODUCT AND MAIL ORDER LIST

These products are available in specialty shops and department stores throughout the United States and Canada. (As well as in our own shops.)

*Chocolates:*
　　Truffles, Buttercremes, Marzipan, Caramels, and Toffees

*Chocolate Dragées:* (Chocolate coated confections)
　　Hazelnuts, Almonds, Raisins, Espresso Beans, Coffee Nudges, Ginger, and Peanuts

*Ephemere Sauce:* (A ganache for toppings and cooking)
　　Dark Vanilla, Kahlúa, Milk Vanilla, Amaretto
　　(available in 16-ounce jars for home use and in 1-gallon containers for institutional use)

*Truffle Toppings:* (Chocolate ice cream topping)
　　Dark Vanilla, Dark Mint, Dark Amaretto, Milk Kahlúa
　　(available in 10.5-ounce jars for home use and in 1-gallon containers for institutional use)

*Carameled Cream Topping:* (Buttery caramel ice cream topping)
　　(available in 10.5-ounce jars for home use)

*Fondue* (elegant traditional Swiss dessert with kirsch, available in 16-ounce jars for home use and 1-gallon containers for institutional use)

A wide variety of the best couvertures in:
　　milk, semisweet and bittersweet.

*Baking chocolate* ("liquor")
*Unsweetened Cocoas*
*Chocolate Chips*
*Bittersweet Ribbons*
*"Liquor" Wafers*

RHEINGOLD

To honor the international visitors gathered in Seattle to celebrate the performance of Wagner's "Der Ring Des Nibelungen," the Pacific Northwest Wagner Festival of 1981 commissioned Dana Taylor Davenport, *chocolatier,* to create a Festival Confection.

　　"Seeking a sophisticated yet universally appealing candy, I began experimenting with my grandfather's deluxe toffee formula. He spent twenty years perfecting his method of incorporating a high ratio of butter into a sugar solution without the stabilizing influence of corn syrup. This produces an especiallly tender toffee having more flavor than sweetness. I discovered that by adding pecans as the sugar caramelizes, a nutty flavored oil is rendered directly into the butter. To complement these flavors, I selected milk chocolate to coat the Festival confection."

　　In commemoration of that first Seattle Wagner Festival, then, this deluxe toffee was called Rheingold.

**Dana Taylor Davenport was featured making his chocolate truffles for the PBS television production of *Dinner with Julia* in October 1983. Julia and her television crew traveled to Seattle to film the sequence on location in the Dilettante Chocolate Factory on Cherry Street.**

The best part of owning a chocolate factory is the free samples that come from manufacturers all over the world.

The Dilettante Chocolate Assortment won both the Grand Show Award and the Best Domestic Candy Award at the 1982 National Fancy Food and Confection Show held in New York City under sponsorship of the National Association of Specialty Food Trade. Forty nations and thousands of products were represented in the twenty-eighth annual show held at the Coliseum.

The typeface used for the company name and various specialty confections was designed over a period of nine years. It was inspired by a style of calligraphy used at the turn of the century when so many of the family formulas originated. We're proud of this award-winning, graceful style. It is the exclusive typeface of Dilettante Chocolates Inc. We call it Dilefont.

Dana Taylor Davenport has given over thirty television cooking demonstrations since the company began in 1977.

*Dilettante Mail Order Inquiries*

Written requests should be sent in care of:

Dilettante Mail Order
2300 East Cherry
Seattle, Washington 98125.

Mail order phone inquires should be to:
(206) 328-1530

*Mail-Order Sources for Candymaking Equipment*

Bridge Kitchenware Corp.,
    214 East 52nd St.
    New York, New York 10022
(212) 688-4220

Kitchen Bazaar
    4455 Connecticut Avenue N.W.
    Washington, D.C. 20008
(202) 363-4625

Sur La Table
    84 Pine Street
    Seattle, Washington 98101
(206) 622-2459

# Index